Barcode 56890

D1195896

DATE DUE

Understanding
Romeo and Juliet

The Greenwood Press "Literature in Context" Series
Student Casebooks to Issues, Sources, and Historical Documents

UNDERSTANDING
Romeo and Juliet

A STUDENT CASEBOOK TO ISSUES, SOURCES, AND HISTORICAL DOCUMENTS

Alan Hager

The Greenwood Press
"Literature in Context" Series
Claudia Durst Johnson, Series Editor

GREENWOOD PRESS
Westport, Connecticut • London

Library of Congress Cataloging-in-Publication Data

Hager, Alan, 1940–
    Understanding Romeo and Juliet : a student casebook to issues,
sources, and historical documents / Alan Hager.
        p.   cm.—(Greenwood Press "Literature in context" series,
ISSN 1074–598X)
    Includes bibliographical references and index.
    ISBN 0–313–29616–2 (alk. paper)
    1. Shakespeare, William, 1564–1616. Romeo and Juliet.
    2. Shakespeare, William, 1564–1616. Romeo and Juliet—Sources.
    3. Vendetta in literature.   4. Tragedy.   I. Title.   II. Series.
PR2831.H26   1999
    822.3'3—dc21   98–46820

British Library Cataloguing in Publication Data is available.

Library of Congress Catalog Card Number: 98–46820
ISBN: 0–313–29616–2
ISSN: 1074–598X

First published in 1999

Greenwood Press, 88 Post Road West, Westport, CT 06881
An imprint of Greenwood Publishing Group, Inc.
www.greenwood.com

Printed in the United States of America

The paper used in this book complies with the
Permanent Paper Standard issued by the National
Information Standards Organization (Z39.48–1984).

10 9 8 7 6 5 4 3 2 1

Copyright Acknowledgments

The author and publisher gratefully acknowledge permission for the use of the following material:

From *Shakespeare Performance: Romeo and Juliet* by Jill L. Levenson. Manchester; Wolfeboro, NH: Manchester University Press, 1987. Reprinted by permission of Jill L. Levenson.

From Plato's *Symposium*, translated by Michael Joyce, in *Five Dialogues of Plato*. London: J. M. Dent, 1938. Reprinted by permission of David Campbell Publishers.

From *The Essence of Plotinus* by Grace H. Turnbull. Copyright 1948 by Grace H. Turnbull. Used by permission of Oxford University Press, Inc.

Two poems by Arnaut Daniel from *Trobador Poets: Selections from the Poems of Eight Trobadors*, edited by Barbara Smythe. London: Chatto and Windus, 1929. Reprinted by permission of Random House UK Ltd.

From *Love in the Western World* by Denis de Rougemont, translated by Montgomery Belgion. Copyright © 1940, 1956 by Pantheon Books, Inc. Reprinted by permission of Pantheon Books, a division of Random House, Inc., and Princeton University Press.

From *Unto the Sons* by Gay Talese. New York: Alfred A. Knopf, 1992. Reprinted by permission of Gay Talese.

From *Mighty Opposites: Shakespeare and Renaissance Contrariety* by Robert Grudin. Berkeley: University of California Press, 1980. Reprinted by permission of Robert Grudin.

From "Trying to Avoid Romeo and Juliet: In Verona for the Opera, a Visitor Finds There Is No Escaping the City's Most Famous Couple" by Barbara Lazear Ascher. *New York Times*, May 12, 1996. Copyright © 1996 by The New York Times Company. Reprinted by permission.

From "Verona Journal, Dear Juliet: Let Me Tell You About My Problem" by Alan Cowell. *New York Times*, March 15, 1993. Copyright © 1993 by The New York Times Company. Reprinted by permission.

From "Romeo and Juliet in Bosnia" by Bob Herbert. *New York Times*, May 8, 1994. Copyright © 1994 by The New York Times Company. Reprinted by permission.

From "Suddenly Shakespeare: O.K., So He Isn't John Grisham. But More and More Films Are Betting the Bard Can Make Money at the Multiplex" by Richard Corliss. *Time*, November 4, 1996. © 1996 Time Inc. Reprinted by permission.

From "Her So-Called Big-Deal Film Career" by Belinda Luscombe. *Time*, November 4, 1996. © 1996 Time Inc. Reprinted by permission.

From "Shakespeare Rocks" by Lou Carlozo. *Chicago Tribune*, November 11, 1996. © Copyrighted Chicago Tribune Company. All rights reserved. Used with permission.

To Carol, Stephen, and Louisa

in delay
We waste our light in vain, like lamps by day
(3.1.44)

Contents

Preface

This work has two main theses, and so that they may not seem to be smuggled in, let me state them here. The first has to do with teaching. Since the development of personal ideas in original student papers is the most important (and elusive) goal of education from grade school to graduate school and beyond, I espouse nudging students in the direction of high creativity. This can involve all aspects of writing, ranging from (1) titling, (2) tapping their own experience for evidence, to (3) using their dreams in both senses of the word—especially in that period of the life cycle called, with an oddly pejorative ring (see Chapter 7), adolescence. Challenge students when their hormones are in turmoil; avoid putting those boys and girls on hold. My second thesis is that history does not teach half as well as fiction, such as Shakespeare's *Romeo and Juliet*. This play is a joyful and elegiac (conveying a sense of loss) work of collective pure creation whose connection with history is at best tenuous.

I began teaching in the spring of 1963—jazz appreciation in French—at the Lycée D'Ivry in Vitry, then the so-called communist suburb of Paris. Once the rugby players in the back row had hammered my French into some measure of shape (mostly through laughter and abrupt corrections) and once I had forced some of them to realize that certain American musicians have names that are pronounced differently from the French—and we managed to get to know each other—I was astounded to discover how good a public education these sixteen-year-olds had gotten.

In areas of writing about writing, literature (classical and modern), history and philosophy, modern languages, and music and art history, they seemed at a level of achievement near that of American first-year graduate students. I recall interrupting a group trading thoughts on how Cicero slandered Mark Antony in the same way he had slandered others like Catiline before him. This argument was derived from the students' apparent speed reading of some highly difficult passages in Latin prose, and for them—not their instructor in jazz appreciation—this was fun. If education works properly, students learn more from their fellows than from their instructors—but only because those instructors have established the right atmosphere by being good Socratic midwives of feelings and thoughts, by nudging their students toward controlled creativity.

How does one teach creativity? One does not. One nudges, because an instructor will never be there when it happens. As we all know, creativity occurs in non-academic time, in bathtubs or half-conscious moments between sleep and wake. Whether you are a morning person or an evening person, make sure you have a paper and pencil nearby when you are in bed so you will be ready to write down sudden, creative insights in cryptic note form. What if you decide to remember your thought or argument instead of putting a mnemonic device in your notebook? Then you will either forget it or you will rehearse the idea again and again in bed until you are unable to sleep for thirty-six straight hours.

ADVICE TO STUDENTS

All people work the same way. Lethargy followed by deadlinitis. But there are two possible kinds of lethargy before turning in a paper. The good lethargy occurs when you have something written down that you are ignoring or sitting on. The bad lethargy occurs when you do not have a clue about what to write. You are forced to *think up* and *write* and *revise* your paper during the same awful night before the due date. Yet those three processes cannot work

For Better or For Worse®

by Lynn Johnston

© 1996 Lynn Johnston/Dist. by Universal Press Syndicate

This *For Better or For Worse* cartoon by Lynn Johnston tells the story of why one has to be capable of writing about writing. Perhaps so that one gets a full appreciation of language. Perhaps so that one does not become a victim of language, especially the best language. © Lynn Johnston Productions Inc./Dist. by United Feature Syndicate, Inc. Reproduced by permission of United Media.

together unless you have been sitting on them. So you should get the idea in a semi-conscious state. Write when you are confident and tired, say in the afternoon. Revise in the morning after a good sleep and a good breakfast when you are clear-headed. Even if you try it all at once, if you have begun something early you will be writing it and rewriting it while you are asleep. Remember what the jurist Oliver Wendell Holmes once said: "There are no good writers, only good revisers." Also, you must give yourself time to hear good writing read out loud.

The critic and author C. S. Lewis apparently once delivered a brilliant lecture at Oxford on the medieval romance *Gawain and the Green Knight*. When one of his students in the graduate English department, Paul Piehler (now a professor of medieval literature at McGill University in Montreal), afterwards asked why he had never published those fine thoughts, Lewis said, "But Paul, if I did, what would I teach?" Not all teachers are that good. This volume spills forth many of my own classroom thoughts on—and student responses to—Shakespeare's *Romeo and Juliet*, a perpetually popular play in a perpetually popular course. And I use techniques that began to take form when I faced those laughing French teenagers over thirty years ago.

My second thesis—that Shakespeare's *Romeo and Juliet* is high fiction, not history—helps explain the folkloric or ritualistic structure of the play, from its reflection of the Elizabethan sonnet form to its self-deflating plot (see Chapter 4). In his second "Ode to Myself," Shakespeare's close friend and fellow playwright in the same acting company, Ben Jonson, berated his senior fellow for his attraction to "mouldy" stories or fantastic fairy tales. But without the presence of the supernatural in various guises and the narrative mechanics of folktale (ranging from coincidence to sublime graveyard imagery to potion plots to paired characters), Shakespeare is simply not Shakespeare. His plots are not realistic, nor are his symbolic places. Only his psychology is. (Lest modern inhabitants of Verona be offended by my thesis, let me offer that over time, Verona may have slowly become what the great playwright Shakespeare first imagined.)

The job of an editor is slightly different from that of a critic. As an editor, my job is to preserve. This is difficult. The American critic Leslie Fiedler once said, reflecting on a passage in *The Ra-*

mayana, that Americans have a creator god, a destroyer god, but unlike East Indian culture, no preserver god, no Vishnu, no Rama. In this book I have tried to save the wonderful stories and ideas of (1) many forgotten or nearly forgotten authors such as Xenophon of Ephesus, Masuccio Salernitano, or even some of the first efforts of Denis de Rougemont, as well as (2) many well-known authors in new or old forms such as Ovid, Chaucer, and Castiglione. I have also tried to reinforce modern confidence in commentators on Renaissance contrariety (the tendency of authors to "yoke opposites"), the history of vendetta (war among families in city streets) in Italian history, and critics of the play and its many transformations on the stage and screen. And I have reproduced sociological and journalistic reactions to the popularity of this play.

I chose to work on *Romeo and Juliet*, and other plays and poems written around 1595, because I was initially intrigued by Shakespeare's view of melancholy. Romeo and Juliet certainly are melancholy characters; Benvolio, Paris, Friar Laurence, and Rosaline may be too; and Capulet and Lady Capulet are melancholic to some extent—and perhaps for good reason, given their circumstances. However, there is a panicky dwelling on Gothic or horror imagery in the play that I wanted to investigate along with Shakespeare's other chief themes of love, vendetta, contrariety, and mad rush (his notion of excessive hastening). The exposition in *Understanding Romeo and Juliet* is essentially circular because it continually revisits versions of these themes in an effort to avoid leaving out clues and thus imitate the gradual process of learning.

ACKNOWLEDGMENTS

I want to thank Sarah Hilsman of the University of Chicago for proposing aspects—small and large—of the source question that I dwell on for three short chapters; and William S. Anderson of the University of California and Arnold Talentino of the State University of New York at Cortland for their comments on my translations of Ovid and renderings of Chaucer. I would also like to thank Tim Austin, Sister Joan Newhart, and Nick Casati of Loyola University for helping me above and beyond the call of duty with Loyola's many resources during my year's absence from SUNY Cortland. And I would like to thank Frederick Hoxie, Paul Gehl, Richard Brown, and the Newberry Library in Chicago; and Janet O'Hare,

Rose Hawkins, Peter Carroll, and the Wading River/Shoreham Public Library in Long Island, in both of which fine libraries much of this work was written. Last but not least, I would like to thank my recommender, Stephen K. Orgel; my series editor at Greenwood Press, Claudia Durst Johnson; and my senior editor at Greenwood, Barbara Rader.

All citations of Shakespeare are taken from David Bevington, ed., *The Complete Works of Shakespeare*, 4th ed. (New York: Harper Collins, 1992). Parenthetical citations include act, scene, and the number of the first line included in the extract.

1

Analysis of *Romeo and Juliet*

INTRODUCTION

A clock-like machine, William Shakespeare's *Romeo and Juliet* (1595) has four separate movements. First, there is the famous love story of two strong-willed and willful—not simply "star-crossed" (pro. 6)—lovers that ends in two separate suicides in an urban cemetery. Second, there is the continuing vendetta, or violent rivalry, between two families in the relatively unpoliced streets of that same urban center. This civil disturbance in Verona concludes abruptly with an ambiguous peace after only about five days. Third, there is a continual emphasis on paradox, contrariety, or yoked opposites. Fourth, there is terrible and tragic rush in action, speech, and spectacle in the drama; a continual gallop to satisfy sexual desire, bloodlust, and, oddly, delivery of notions of man and existence as paradoxical.

In the prologue, in the form of the dominant poetic structure of the play—the sonnet—we hear that we will only get "two hours' traffic of our stage" (12). This is an improbable fiction because even without breaks, delivering the text would take at least another three-quarters of an hour. Then we are plunged into the dizzying sequence of sad events involving lovers and street warriors, marked at every crossing by chronographia (poetic telling of time)—and thereby sensed rush of time—to an abrupt ending in which the sacrifice on the part of the only children of the two leading families in Verona brings sudden peace and commemoration. Rush reigns throughout. Even the ending leaves us spinning.

All four movements seem to jell and thus are fascinating in the theater, just as if Shakespeare had sat down and produced what his contemporary, Sir Philip Sidney, would have called, in his *Defence of Poesie* (1595), the precious "idea, or foreconceit" of the work, a total plan. This plan in fact includes *Romeo and Juliet*'s comic twin, *A Midsummer Night's Dream* (1595). The hilarious comedy presents in King Theseus' Athens the potential for idealistic lovers' and feuding families' violence and self-violence comically undercut by delay and paradox. The deliberative mirror of the unthinking rush of *Romeo and Juliet, A Midsummer Night's Dream* leads up to happy public marriages and a botched performance of the play of Ovid's original double suicide of Pyramus and Thisbe.

If in *A Midsummer Night's Dream* all is contemplated and nothing really happens, in *Romeo and Juliet* action is all. That is, in mapping out a tragedy of young love and familial gangs at war, a mystical notion of paradox, and an elaborate version of uncontrolled rush, Shakespeare conceptualized a play whose elements triumphantly merge and whose themes echo throughout his later work. These four movements working in concert help explain the enduring popularity of the play in the face of considerable critical disregard. At the turn of the twentieth century, A. C. Bradley argued that Shakespeare wrote only four major tragedies—*Hamlet, Othello, King Lear*, and *Macbeth*—and many critics have followed him. Working on the assumption that Shakespeare matured gradually, many recent critics argue that *Romeo and Juliet* is a young tragedy or a conventional one. But the play, in my opinion, has no such weakness.

As for the lovers, their outcome—double suicide—in good part defines them. At least the suggestion of double suicide bedevils Shakespeare's presentation of passionate love and gives to plays that are seemingly about other themes a compelling (and Ovidian) element of love tragedy. Consider *Julius Caesar* (Portia and Brutus) *Hamlet* (Ophelia and Prince Hamlet), *Othello* (Desdemona and Othello), *Antony and Cleopatra* (Antony and Cleopatra), and even *Macbeth* (Lady Macbeth and Macbeth). One could say that

Hamlet, Desdemona, and Macbeth are murdered, but they seem to maneuver themselves into fatal circumstances. Whether or not these plays present clear-cut double suicides, they all borrow elements from the story of the love of Pyramus and Thisbe in Ovid's *Metamorphoses* (see Chapter 2). From Ovid the story of the children of apparently warring neighbors and their separate double suicides echoes and re-echoes throughout Shakespeare's plays, above all in *Romeo and Juliet* and *A Midsummer Night's Dream*.

In each play Shakespeare carefully removes any hint of suicide pact or even the simultaneity of self-destruction. In all cases, moreover, the actions are separate, rationalized, and obsessive. As in *Othello*, in *Romeo and Juliet* the playwright for a brief time removes the lovers from an overarching civic and political circumstance and allows us, for a moment, to see them only as victims of a shared idealized love—but it is a passion so close to death that as in *Hamlet*, horror or Gothic imagery dominates much of the lovers' poetry. Later romantic and post-romantic interpretations and adaptations of *Romeo and Juliet* in opera and ballet have focused on the lovers' joy and apparently unsolvable problems (see Chapter 5). They also have downplayed the political content. In the uncut version of Shakespeare's play, however, the civic context—the brawls of various sorts and the misrule or ineffectual rule of family, church, and state—is always ominously present.

Vendetta and mob action in city streets constitute a second recurring theme in *Romeo and Juliet*. Shakespeare's works as a whole suggest two likely tyrannies that might make life in society barely livable—the tyranny of the mob of ordinary citizens in the city, and the tyranny of the aristocracy in the open spaces of the country. *Much Ado about Nothing* might have been partially inspired by the brawl in Palermo in 1282 known as the Sicilian Vespers, in which at least 2,000 French soldiers and civilians were killed in riots after a Sicilian woman was insulted by a soldier in front of a church (see Chapter 6). But *Henry VI, Richard III, Sir Thomas More* (if Shakespeare wrote it), *Hamlet, Troilus and Cressida*, and *Coriolanus* all consider in depth the problem of mob action and factional struggle resembling gang warfare. These themes were central to Leonard Bernstein's modern-dress operatic adapatation of *Romeo and Juliet*, *West Side Story* (1956) (see Chapter 5).

Shakespeare's conclusions about vendetta seem to be that rivalry weakens one's humanity and leads to brutal action (of the sort that Juliet's cousin Tybalt revels in). Early in the play Tybalt (whose name, from the Reynard the Fox stories, suggests "cat") says wittily to an armed Benvolio (whose name suggests "good wish"), "What, drawn and talk of peace? I hate the word / As I hate hell" (1.1.70), but he seems to love a hell of his own devising, one that promptly leads from the murder of Mercutio to his own slaughter by an enraged and vengeful Romeo.

Paradox or irony, the play's third movement, has always provided a fertile area in Shakespeare studies. Consider the mystical poem "The Turtle and the Phoenix"; sonnet 94 beginning "They that have the power to hurt and will do none"; or the structure and rhetoric of *Venus and Adonis, Julius Caesar, Hamlet*, and *The Tempest*. Such apparent self-contradiction is evident in Romeo's oxymorons (two-word paradoxes such as "heavy lightness" [1.1.178]) that help define the ineffable nature of love or family feuding. In the first scene, viewing the blood on the stage (probably red dye, because animal blood left an awful smell) the actor playing Romeo must make coherent some of his first and most paradoxical words.

In this introduction to the hero of the play, Romeo creates narrower and narrower self-contradiction for Benvolio:

> O me! What fray was here?
> Yet tell me not, for I have heard it all.
> Here's much to do with hate, but more with love.
> Why, then, O brawling love, O loving hate,
> O anything of nothing first create,
> O heavy lightness, serious vanity,
> Misshapen chaos of well-seeming forms,
> Feather of lead, bright smoke, cold fire, sick health,
> Still-waking sleep, that is not what it is!
> This love feel I, that feel no love in this.   (1.1.173)

Any of these formulas, from "heavy lightness" to "feather of lead," suggests a contradiction that can come near to explaining that violent rivalry is a kind of awful love and that passionate love can lead to a kind of hate or self-hate (as echoed in Juliet's similar tirade [3.2.73 ff.]). Romeo claims to a laughing Benvolio that he is speaking of his own love—still of Rosaline—but his speech is triggered by the sight of blood on the streets of Verona.

This connection between passionate love and bloodlust suggests the central paradox of the play: that in their "satisfaction," acts of love can lead to chaotic sex and self-violence, and rivalry can lead to violent crime. The "satisfaction" of sexual organs and swords can be ultimately murderous, destructive, and self-destructive. As the Franciscan priest, Friar Laurence (whose undisciplined and negligent action "innocently" harms—if not causes the deaths of— all his charges), says in his first speech in the play,

> Virtue itself turns vice, being misapplied,
> And vice sometime's by action dignified.   (2.3.21)

That is, good can lead to bad and bad can lead to good. This is evident throughout the play in marital love's twin, passionate lust, or martial brilliance's twin, murderous rage. But such exchanges may not always be the product of process; they may result from simultaneous opposition—what several Renaissance scholars have called the typical Shakespearean representation of contrariety, or apparent yoked opposites, or contradictions held in dynamic symmetry.

Finally, the play represents unbounded rush throughout. For example, in the first scene of the play Benvolio answers Montague's wife's query about her son Romeo's whereabouts. He says,

> Madam, an hour before the worshiped sun
> Peered forth the golden window of the east,
> A troubled mind drave me to walk abroad.   (1.1.118)

Benvolio speaks of his melancholy and early rising by telling time without numbers (with an assist from Olympian myth) and speaking of his early-morning sighting of his insomniac friend Romeo. This is a typical Ovidian—indeed, Homeric—poetic move. But even in stepping back an hour before the sun, or Phoebus Apollo, "peered forth," he is helping set in motion the rush of the play in the form of chronographia. "What time is it?" "What time is it?" "What time is it?" informs the play throughout. It is late. Everyone is late.

In the recent past, scholars have suggested that Shakespeare creates mythological descriptions of time so often because the outdoor theaters of his time—the Theater, the Rose, and the Globe—had no scenery as such, and audiences had to be told the play time as opposed to the actual time of day when the play was performed. Certainly, one needs to know it is morning in a play in which the time of the action has been reduced from nine months (in Shakespeare's source in Brooke's *Romeus and Juliet*) to about five days. But the purpose of chronographia here is much more complex than the announced time shown on a clock.

Shakespeare uses such poetic descriptions of time in all his plays and many of his poems, but never more intensively than in *Romeo and Juliet*. Indeed, chronographia intensifies throughout the play. And it provides constant reference to the uncontrolled rush or gallop that constitutes one of the play's four central themes. Thus, as we approach the final unraveling of misapplied help and accidental and intentional destruction in the play, we hear Juliet refer to an elementary Olympian myth about time and the action of the sun. This was developed in Book One of Ovid's *Metamorphoses*, in which Phoebus Apollo, who rides in the chariot of the sun to produce day, lends the reins to his beloved son, Phaeton. Juliet says,

> Gallop apace, you fiery-footed steeds,
> Towards Phoebus' lodging! Such a wagoner
> As Phaëton would whip you to the West
> And bring in cloudy night immediately.   (3.2.1)

This is marvelously thrilling poetry inspired by love. But in her extraordinary rush to bring in night—night in bed with Romeo, of course—Juliet refers to a tragedy other than her own impending one.

In Ovid's tragedy Phaeton asked for an incontrovertible promise from his father, Apollo, to help prove to his peers his half-divine origins. In essence, he asked to borrow his father's car. Like any father, with great reservations Apollo allowed him. Driving out of control, Phaeton created havoc in the heavens and earth and helped bring on his own untimely death by a thunderbolt from the king of heaven, Jupiter. Phaeton had been overreaching and in excessive haste, almost by accident. He needed to prove to a friend that he was Apollo's son, and in the process he lost the reins to the chariot of the sun. He memorialized his uncontrolled rush by charring Mother Earth and thereby creating the Sahara Desert.

THE LOVE OF JULIET AND HER ROMEO

To understand what Shakespeare thought of passionate love, one must look through—but also beyond—the lens of the romantic era that gave birth to love's modern glorification. In classical times love was often seen as a lasting madness, as opposed to anger, which was seen as a brief madness. Obviously Shakespeare considered these two familiar definitions from antiquity, so central to the play's mad rush into sex and violence. But he also treats passionate love as a creative force. It generates remarkable poetry in Romeo and Juliet's words (see Chapter 4), much of it witty and comic and even self-ironic, no matter how seriously the words are sometimes spoken in productions.

As a stage construct or stock dramatic character, Romeo is a version of a figure in the Latin comedy of Plautus and Terence, whom Shakespeare loved and often imitated. Usually the character is listed by name and also by type, *adulescens*. Unlike its modern descendent, "adolescent," *adulescens* is a neutral term for "young man or gentleman" in Latin. Owing to to recent psychoanalytic theories of the life cycle, notably by Sigmund Freud and Erik Erikson, "adolescent" may have taken on a largely negative connotation (see Chapter 7), but in Latin *adulescens* suggests both positive and negative characteristics. For example, *adulescens* in Plautus' *Menaechmi* (The Twins), *Mercator* (The Merchant), or *Curcullus* is an idealist, the best poet in the play, yet often a willful young person duped by the attentions of *meretrix* (the prostitute), which he takes for signs of true love. His civic idealism may even tell him that peace comes easy. Consider Romeo's "I thought all for the best" (3.1.103) after Mercutio catches his death blow under Romeo's arm.

A "romeo" today implies a serial lover or seducer, exactly what Shakespeare presents in Theseus, the King of Athens, in *A Midsummer Night's Dream*. In Olympian myth Theseus was the detective hero of Athens, exploding murderous scams, and a serial lover along the lines of James Bond. Romeo is not. He desperately loves Rosaline and then Juliet with idealistic and witty complaining. Although his friend Mercutio intentionally mistakes his words for the

expression of pure sexual desire or heat, there is something far
more psychic in Romeo's loves than simple sexual attraction. There
is much more to Romeo and his loves and to Juliet and her one
love. As in the case of *adulescens*, Romeo and Juliet aim at marriage—as Theseus in his love for the daughter of King Minos of
Crete, Ariadne, tragically does not. Theseus could use the promise
of marriage cynically with Ariadne and others. Romeo does not
have a cynical bone in his body, even though he immediately forgets Rosaline at the Capulet party that he crashes (he does not
even recognize her presence) the instant he sees Juliet—despite
the fact that his accidental discovery of the invitation of Rosaline
to the party was his sole motive for invading the enemy camp's
celebration in the first place.

Shakespeare does not allow us to forget this infidelity, even
though it is not the whole story of this romeo. First, the Chorus
reminds us in a breath-taking deadpan understatement of Romeo's
changeability:

That fair for which love groaned for and would die,
With tender Juliet matched, is now not fair.   (2.Cho.3)

Juliet is tender perhaps because she is younger than Rosaline. As
we know from her nurse—and she still has a nurse—she is two or
three weeks short of her fourteenth birthday. Perhaps Rosaline was
Romeo's age—sixteen to twenty years old; roughly eighteen. Romeo carries a sword in the streets and is fully responsible for his
other "sword" in Shakespearean wordplay (his phallus), whereas
Juliet still has close supervision even though her parents rush into
considering her of marriageable age. Perhaps Romeo chooses Juliet
over Rosaline partly for her youth and lack of self-possession, but
he loves her too.

Romeo's best friend is Mercutio, whose name suggests "mercurial" (changeable) from the name of Mercury. This fast-talking
god is the Olympian counterpart of Woden or Odin, the Norse god
of wild shape-shifting. He is abrupt and charming, a god of thieves
connected with the underworld, magic and messages, and amazing
speed. Mercutio himself reminds us, in one of his diatribes, of
Rosaline's remarkable sexual power over Romeo. Mercutio creates
a bawdy blazon (a body catalogue) of Rosaline in the form of a

mock magical materialization of Romeo, who he hopes can hear him in the distance:

> I conjure thee by Rosaline's bright eyes,
> By her high forehead and her scarlet lip,
> By her fine foot, straight leg, and quivering thigh,
> And the demesnes that there adjacent lie,
> That in thy likeness thou appear to us.   (2.1.18)

But Romeo has transcended transfiguration in desire into what he may have most desired from Rosaline (what "conjures," or raises up, his phallus)—her sexuality. And he has done more than change loves from an uncooperative Rosaline to a highly cooperative Juliet. He has found a soul-mate.

Even though there is tremendous contrast between the Nurse and her charge, Juliet, they have in common a relative rush to sexual experience. The Nurse's first words in the play constitute an oath: "Now, by my maidenhead at twelve year old" (1.3.2). Because she has not sworn on a later version, we can assume the Nurse lost her virginity at age twelve. Rosaline was, however, "in strong proof of chastity well armed" (1.1.210) and had sworn off love of any sort.

The Friar, later still, hearing that Romeo has not slept, fears he has had his way with Rosaline throughout the night:

> God pardon sin! Wast thou with Rosaline?   (2.3.44)

The Friar on the whole seems quite as capable of pardoning sin as is his God. Romeo responds,

> With Rosaline, my ghostly father? No.
> I have forgot that name, and that name's woe.   (2.3.45)

Indeed, he has exchanged Rosaline for Juliet. But Shakespeare does not allow us (or Romeo) to go along with this exchange painlessly. The Franciscan priest now gives Romeo the play's most severe moral lecture, on the abandonment of Rosaline. It parallels Capulet's criticism of Tybalt when he would turn a dance into a bloodbath (1.5). Since it is in rhymed couplets, the priest's speech and Romeo's responses provide a parallel to the central shared sonnet of Romeo and Juliet in the party scene (1.5) that we will look at in a moment (1.5.94ff.):

FRIAR:	Holy Saint Francis, what a change is here!
	Is Rosaline, that thou didst love so dear,
	So soon forsaken? Young men's love then lies
	Not truly in their hearts, but in their eyes.
	Jesu Maria, what a deal of brine
	Hath washed thy sallow cheeks for Rosaline!
	How much salt water thrown away in waste
	To season love, that of it doth not taste!
	The sun not yet thy sighs from heaven clears,
	Thy old groans yet ringing in my ancient ears.
	Lo, here upon thy cheek the stain doth sit
	Of an old tear that is not washed off yet.
	If e'er thou wast thyself and these woes thine,
	Thou and these woes were all for Rosaline.
	And art thou changed? Pronounce this sentence then:
	Women may fall when there's no strength in men.
ROMEO:	Thou chid'st me oft for loving Rosaline.
FRIAR:	For doting, not for loving, pupil mine.
ROMEO:	Thou bad'st me bury love.
FRIAR:	Not in a grave
	To lay one in, another out to have. (2.3.65)

Consider the poetry of this shared passage. It is written in rhymed iambic pentameter couplets (later known as heroic couplets for their use in neoclassical translation of the great epics).[1] The individual line is usually made up of ten or eleven syllables, variably floating with pauses (caesuras) over a rhythm of five feet (metrical units) created by an underlying beat of an unstressed followed by a stressed syllable, as in the word a-gáin. The emphatic beat is continuous, with variations, suggesting the heartbeat.

Shakespeare was educated intensively in rhetoric and Latin grammar at the Tudor New School in Stratford by graduate students from nearby Oxford who were experts in the classics. As a result, his poetry displays certain conventional poetic moves as well as signature ones. For example, Shakespeare uses some fictional imagery that is native to the leading Latin poets in the curriculum of the day: Virgil, Horace, and Ovid. The poetry is both concentrated (packed with meaning) and ambiguous (having multiple meanings), which makes it enjoyable on several levels. The same is true of the best Latin poetry.

Romeo first denies he was with Rosaline, calling the Friar (as he does elsewhere) his "ghostly father."[2] *Ghost* could at the time mean "spiritual" (as in the present German *Geistlich*), as well as "referring to an apparition from beyond the grave." The phrase offers other possibilities as well. If spiritual father is to be distinguished from actual father—though *father* also means "priest"—it may be the Friar is just an advisor, not Romeo's actual supervisor (as his blood-father Montague would be by law). In fact, technically Franciscans were titled "brothers," not "fathers." But Laurence is Romeo's surrogate father in several ways.

Romeo adds paradoxically that he has no memory of the name Rosaline and its "woe." Rosaline had been the subject of his saddest, most tortured and witty poetry, and thus of his emphatic sorrow early in the play, but now she has been forgotten. At this moment the astounded Friar calls on the patron saint of his celibate order, Francis. During the Middle Ages, especially in the times of Shakespeare's beloved Chaucer, a member of the Franciscans—a mendicant (alms-seeking) order of the Catholic Church—was not restricted to one diocese. Begging for his livelihood here and there, the Franciscan sometimes had the reputation of being a less strenuous confessor than his cathedral-based counterpart, and he might even have been somewhat unorthodox theologically, since he was not the official priest of a town in England or Italy.

In this play, however, Friar Laurence apparently has enough status in town to be called on to marry Paris and Juliet in the cathedral of Verona. This well-established Friar now lets loose a true poetic rebuke. However, he forgets his own chiding immediately thereafter when he succumbs to the grips of a sudden and dangerous scheme to end vendetta in Verona by marrying the young scions of the warring houses of Montague and Capulet.

In his diatribe, Friar Laurence accuses Romeo of infidelity and weakness. He adds that all Romeo seems to care about is what he sees in a woman, not what he understands or feels for her in his heart. For Elizabethans, the seat of the emotions was thought to be the liver, not the heart. The heart was reserved symbolically as the seat of intuitive knowledge, fidelity, and courage (from *coeur*, French for "heart"). With yet another oath, "Jesu Maria,"[3] the Friar introduces one of Shakespeare's favorite images (one he shared with the Latin poet Ovid): salt water. The fact that the human body is three-quarters salt water, or that salt water covers three-quarters of the earth's surface, might have been known by Shakespeare. The sea has always been a symbol of change owing to its variable surface. Salt water also appears, however, in various forms as tears, urine, beer, wine, and brine that can pickle and preserve. Brine can also corrode. Salt water may be the essential element of the sublunary world and a central earthly poetic image or symbol as a result.

Shakespeare's Friar first refers to the tears for Rosaline that "wash" (both flood and clean) Romeo's pale cheeks like the ocean washes the shore. Then he speaks of the waste—"vast amount" and "frivolous expenditure"—of salt water that should preserve (one meaning of "season") his love for Rosaline, but all the crying of salt water does not even give his supposed love the taste provided by salt (another meaning of "season"). In other words, his love for Rosaline is now not only unpreserved—dead and decaying (reminding us of the play's Gothic or horror-mode obsession with putrescence)—but also without any salty savor to help him remember it.

After remarking on the time and weather in chronographia—the sun has not yet broken through Romeo's vaporous sighs—the priest remarks on the corrosion of a tear that has metaphorically stained Romeo's cheek. And he might touch Romeo's face at this moment (stage directions are often missing for Shakespeare) as an intimate rebuke. All this witty berating of Romeo seems affable enough, but now the Friar delivers a true lamentation on moral failing in Romeo and, perhaps, in all men.

The Friar sermonizes on Romeo's changeability, infidelity, and weakness using the text of wasted salt water for the forgotten and possibly forlorn Rosaline (as Wife does—to some extent—to Juliet on the subject her daughter's supposed tears over the death of Tybalt [3.5.69ff.]). When the Friar suggests that man's fickleness and promiscuity may lead to similar weakness in women, Romeo finally rebels by reminding the priest that he had scolded Romeo for loving Rosaline in the first place. The Friar counters with priestly hindsight that it was not love but infatuation, or "doting," something merely physical.

Romeo and the Friar then end their trade of lines by sharing parts of a single line that summons the second central image in the play—that of crypts, cemeteries, and the living dead. Romeo says,

Thou bad'st me bury love.

The priest completes the line,

Not in a grave,

and he adds,

To lay one in, another out to have.

Ostensibly the exchange contains a witticism. The priest had requested that Romeo "bury" his unrequited love for Rosaline in his heart. But the image of burial makes him think of the grave. Thus, he seems to be saying, "do not bury Rosaline in a grave only to immediately exhume the living dead, (as it turns out) Juliet."

Why does this horror image of rising from the grave resound so much in the play? Partly because the paradoxical notion of "living death" in phrases like "still-waking sleep" (1.1.181) helps Romeo define his love for Rosaline to Benvolio (see Chapter 4). Rationalized "living death" applied to love really indicates that love makes one feel more alive than ever and more dead than ever because it brings on elation and depression—partly at one's loss of freedom—of various sorts.[4] Being in the land of the living dead, however, seems also to be a product of the idealistic and self-flagellating love that calls for immediate gratification or self-annihilation. Note that Romeo and Juliet's separate suicides occur in the graveyard at the end of the play, but graveyard imagery in both lovers' speeches prepared us much earlier for that ultimate location.

Romeo and Juliet had talked of love as religion when they first met. There they traded parts of a sonnet (somewhat like the Friar and his charge here), creating a witty rendition of love as a religious pilgrimage that is idealistic and fresh. Romeo developed the central conceit (extended metaphor in lyric) out of the notion of himself—especially the parts of his body—as making the quest of a palmer (a religious pilgrim in the Holy Land) for Juliet's body as his shrine. He grasps her hand (palm) and quickly adds in preparation to kiss it,

> If I profane with my unworthiest hand
> This holy shrine, the gentle sin is this:
> My lips, two blushing pilgrims, ready stand
> To smooth that rough touch with a tender kiss.   (1.5.94)

This is not only the typical rhyme scheme (ABAB) of the first quatrain of a Shakespearean sonnet (a fourteen-line poem made up of three quatrains and a couplet), but it is also a brilliant piece of love poetry construing love as a religious pilgrimage. And Juliet has brilliant and witty rejoinders until their shared sonnet ends abruptly with Romeo stealing a kiss on her lips. But as delightful and comic as their poetic repartee here and in the balcony scene remains, there is a dark side to their love that is evident in the lovers' sublime horror or Gothic imagery—especially in their development of an ominous person of Death. This personification is on the lips of both Romeo and Juliet as well as the Friar throughout the play.

Awaiting Juliet, Romeo says to Friar Laurence who is about to marry them,

> Do thou but close our hands with holy words,
> Then love-devouring Death do what he dare;   (2.6.6 [capitals mine])

In this supposedly joyous moment, Romeo's repeated "d" sounds create an alliterative version of melancholy like funeral bells. Why does death—and the grim reaper, Death—occur to Romeo in the same breath as consummation of his marriage? Like so many idealistic young men in Shakespeare (or even middle-aged men like Othello), Romeo wants to die the moment he knows he will get his sexual wish. He wants to live in the thrilling Gothic world of love, being melancholy even when he is sexually happy, especially when he is most happy.

Normally Shakespeare's women counter expression of this suicidal tendency on the part of their men with commonsense claims for pleasure, marital contentment, and the raising of families. Not so with Juliet. When she hears of Romeo's banishment, Juliet takes up the rope ladder as if to use it for a noose and says,

> I'll to my wedding bed,
> And Death, not Romeo, take my maidenhead!   (3.2.136 [capitals mine])

The connection between the grave—and a lover, Death—and her wedding bed with Romeo seems engraved (to risk a Shakespearean pun) on her Gothic imagination, and Romeo seems to answer her even before he sees her again. To Friar Laurence he says,

> more courtship lives
> In carrion flies than Romeo. They may seize
> On the white wonder of dear Juliet's hand. . . .   (3.3.34)

Why would he refer to carrion flies—as if Juliet is already a corpse—as his successful competitors for her hand? Has his horror-filled imagination stained all thoughts of her, including those of his sexual bliss? A personified lover, Death (and its flies), not Paris, slowly emerges in the poetry as Romeo's foil, or erotic rival.

Horror movies may be a popular and profitable form of public entertainment today, creating the illusion of devil-ruled, hellish worlds. All that is needed are red dye, pieces of meat, a fog machine, and scary music to create an image of hell on earth. In Shakespeare's day, however, dwelling on the underbelly of existence and the living dead in various forms was considered an obsessive delusion directly connected with love melancholy. Philip Sidney develops a notion of this peculiar delusion in the last poems of his sonnet sequence *Astrophil and Stella* (1595; see Chapter 4). Moreover, Shakespeare's Hamlet, partly frustrated by his apparent rejection by Ophelia, wants to witness the opening up of the graves at midnight and "drink hot blood" like a vampire (3.2.389). And Ferdinand in John Webster's Shakespearean *Duchess of Malfi* (1613), desperately in love with his murdered sister, Beatrice, concludes that he is a wolfman and digs up graves with his fingers. He begs fellows and doctors assigned to cure his lycanthropia (wolfmanism; in this case, love-induced) to open him up with knives to see that he has actually grown fur—only it is on the inside, like an implanted hair shirt, not on the outside. Perhaps the most famous staging of the horror of love melancholy is *Hamlet*'s scene of Ophelia equating sex and death in her songs.[5] Romeo and Juliet do well enough in equating the living death of love with the living dead of Gothic horror.

The connection between horror and passionate love reverberates in *Romeo and Juliet* and has its logic in homely details of appearance. A lover like Romeo at the beginning of the play cannot eat and probably loses weight. He pines away and looks like he needs more blood. Missing his beloved in his bed, he goes off sleepless in the night, wandering through woods and other lonely, dark landscapes such as graveyards. He goes to sleep like a ghoul during the daylight hours, as Romeo's father (Montague) says to Benvolio, shutting himself in a dark room and making "himself an artificial night" (1.1.140). This is the picture of Romeo at the beginning of the play. It is normal. But it can also betray the effects of a mental disease of the idealistic young lover touched with Gothic or horror obsession. Romeo and Juliet share it well before their separate suicides in the crypt toward the end of the play.

After their wedding night Juliet foreshadows the catastrophe (the fall of the hero and/or heroine) of the play, saying,

> Methinks I see thee, now thou art so low,
> As one dead in the bottom of a tomb.   (3.5.55)

More than mere dramatic irony, these words reflect the diseased and dis-eased imagination of the passionate lover; its full force comes out when she takes the potion that will make her seem to be dead (4.3). Seeing her so lovely in this state, Romeo echoes her words about a very sexual dance of death with the person of Death. He asks,

> Shall I believe
> That insubstantial Death is amorous,
> And that the lean abhorrèd monster keeps
> Thee here in dark to be his paramour?   (5.3.102)

In his sublime yet diseased imagination, Romeo projects his own feelings on the grim reaper as necrophiliac.

VENDETTA IN VERONA

A picture of vendetta in action provides a second prologue to the play in the first scene. Gregory is baiting a reluctant Sampson (both Capulet men, both ordinary citizens) into battle with any Montague men they might encounter. Typically, Shakespeare begins in the middle of a conversation (probably preceded in our minds by Gregory having challenged Sampson's resolve, as in a dare). Their mode of speech is heroic sarcasm, or taunting over-familiarity. They begin with puns on "coal/collier/collar/choler," "ay/aye/I/eye," and "move" (meaning both "emote" and "transport"):

SAMPSON: Gregory, on my word, we'll not carry coals.

GREGORY: No, for then we should be colliers.

SAMPSON: I mean, an we be in choler, we'll draw.

GREGORY: Ay, while you live, draw your neck out of collar.

SAMPSON: I strike quickly, being moved.

GREGORY: But thou art not quickly moved to strike. (1.1.1)

Sampson says he will "not carry coals," a slang expression for "suffer insults," as in submitting to do the dirty work for a boss (here, the Montagues). Gregory replies that they would "then" just be colliers, as if Sampson were literally expressing a desire not to transport coal to people's homes, a lowly trade. Sampson protests this questioning of his bravery and answers that if they are angry, they will draw (i.e., their swords). Gregory then takes "drawing" for pulling back or withdrawing the neck from a hangman's noose. Picking up on his "ay," now meaning "yes," Sampson says he will always strike quickly when moved or angry ("in choler," or choleric). Gregory eggs him on by implying that Sampson always saves himself by rarely getting angry. Only with difficulty would he show so much life (i.e., quickness). Thus, Gregory finds himself baiting Sampson into haste to do battle with the Montagues.

This kind of interplay of short lines of dramatic dialogue has been called stichomythia (short lines in rows). The term was first used in the later fourth century B.C. when Aristotle wrote his praise of tragedy (*The Poetics*) as the highest form of poetry. Stichomythia in a play suggests clipped dramatic speech in the form of call and answer, often reiterating some or all of the previous speaker's words. It also provides the soul of comedy and is there called repartee. But in tragedy it ominously implies a sequence of dares to a potentially violent opponent—as in "I dare you," (answer) "I double dare you," (answer) "I triple dare you"—that leads to escalating reciprocal violence in words, then to actual violence in baiting and egging each other on to dangerous acts, and then to death—as occurs among the ordinary citizens of two factions in the first scene of *Romeo and Juliet*.

Loosened up by rivalrous interplay, Gregory and Sampson discuss the possibility of drawing a symbolic sword in raping the enemies' most prized possession in all-out vendetta: their virgin women. Sampson brags, "When I have fought with the men, I will be civil with the maids—I will cut off their heads" (1.1.23). When Gregory asks in disbelief, "The heads of the maids?" Sampson answers, "Ay, the heads of the maids, or their maidenheads," or hymens. This is comic and bawdy repartee, but just as the witty give-and-take of the first balcony scene leads Romeo and Juliet quickly into the marriage bed and total longing, so this repartee leads to a spectacular bloodbath on the stage. The bloodletting does not stop until Tybalt kills Mercutio, Romeo kills Tybalt, Romeo kills Paris, Romeo kills himself, Juliet stabs herself to death, and Romeo's mother dies of grief.

If Romeo and Juliet are the focus of love in the play, Juliet's cousin Tybalt is the focus of rivalry and vendetta. What sets off Tybalt is not simply Romeo's crashing of the Capulet party but ultimately the threat to the virginity of his thirteen-year-old first cousin, Juliet. With the knowledge that comes from previous contact in deadly rivalry, he recognizes Romeo at the party by his voice from behind the mask—a voice sounding praises of Juliet's beauty in an overheard soliloquy. Romeo is speaking to himself and to the audience, "Did my heart love till now?" (1.5.53), but Tybalt overhears him.

Tybalt immediately says to his squire,

> This, by his voice, should be a Montague.
> Fetch me my rapier, boy.

True vendetta always includes an element of intimacy, especially the extreme intimacy of loathing. And hate has its own imagination, just as passionate love does. It is just as self-flagellating and dark as romantic passion. Here, for example, Tybalt sees Romeo as a threat to the "honor of my kin" (maintaining honor often goes with murder in Shakespeare). But he also needs to see Romeo as devilish in his supposed "fleering" (grimacing, or laughing unpleasantly; possibly a reference to his mask) and "scorning" of "our solemnity" (1.5.58). This is hardly the case with moonstruck Romeo, yet Tybalt is certain (just as a jealous lover is always sure in his or her wrong belief). It is, however, hardly believable to Tybalt's uncle, Capulet, who chides his nephew for trying to turn his party into a bloodbath.

Capulet says of Romeo,

> 'A bears him like a portly gentleman. . . .
> > He shall be endured.
> What, goodman boy? I say he shall. Go to!
> Am I the master here, or you? Go to.   (1.5.67, 77–79)

Romeo is described as portly, probably because he carries himself with a good "port," or carriage, although the first actor to play the role of Romeo, the famous Richard Burbage (see Chapter 5), was a solid or portly man. Romeo is supposed to be pining away. "Goodman boy" is something of an oxymoron. "Goodman" suggests the head of a household, but a boy is just a boy. "Goodman" also has a slightly Puritan overtone as a means of address. And Puritans were often scapegoated on the Elizabethan stage, partly because although they were affluent they opposed on religious principle all plays and supposedly did not attend performances. "Goodman boy" and Capulet's later "saucy boy" (1.5.84) and "princox" (1.5.87) all seem fairly synonymous and mild insults designed to keep Tybalt in his place. Although they succeed in controlling him at the party, they make Tybalt more bloodthirsty on the hot streets of Verona. Insults foster rebellion. And no one is master of this intimate rivalry between houses—not the prince of a city-state where a wayward Friar acts out his fantasies of peace with the only children of major families; nor in the household of old man Capulet, where a much younger wife and mother gives way to a long-winded and bawdy nurse, and where a fairly modest party comes to resemble controlled chaos and near insurrection.

Paradoxically, it is the not-so-innocent bystanders who suffer most from the vendetta in the Verona of *Romeo and Juliet*. Benvolio, related to the Montagues, stands by with sword in hand while almost all his friends are killed. Mercutio, kin to the Prince, delivers his most famous line in his dying moments: "a plague o' both your houses" (3.1.90). Perhaps the most innocent bystander in the play is Paris, a relative of the Prince (like Mercutio) who is wooing Juliet, albeit unsuccessfully, from early in the play. Given the heated sex and violence in town, Paris is not only jeered contemptuously by Juliet at Friar Laurence's cell but then is dispatched by unequaled swordsman Romeo, whom he has importuned at the tomb of the Capulets. Once vendetta starts to rule in Verona, everything spins out of control until even the bystanders fall. "Oh, I am slain" in Paris's penultimate line is one of the most difficult to deliver in Shakespeare, because it might provoke—and has provoked in performance—grim laughter in the audience. Perhaps the best delivery of this line is to swallow the words in a groan of frustration.

CONTRARIETY IN *ROMEO AND JULIET*

The notion that to understand the universe one must simultaneously contemplate contraries goes back at least as far as the words of Heraclitus, the pre-Socratic philosopher of the sixth century B.C. who spoke of a harmony of opposites, or of discords, or of a discord of harmonies, as being at the center of the cosmic plan. Heraclitus' pagan philosophy and its descendants in neoplatonism influenced many Christian thinkers during the Renaissance, including many powerful leaders and many great intellectuals (e.g., Erasmus, Cornelius Agrippa, Castiglione, Paracelsus, Copernicus, Giordano Bruno, Sir Philip Sidney, Edmund Spenser, and Shakespeare).

Romeo and Juliet presents contraries in the action of (1) sex and violence, and (2) delay and rush, or stasis and excessive speed. It also presents individual paradoxes, such as the simultaneous good and bad of love and sex or of heroism and savagery. Contrariety appears in the paradoxes of oxymorons and other forms of self-contradiction among the principal characters. But it also informs larger issues that are uncovered when one does a double reading of the play: one, as a story of innocent young lovers; two, as a story of thrill-seeking quasi-genocides; one, as a story of an ill-fated municipality; two, as a story of the fall of a town that entertained willful licence in its beds and streets.

The great theorist of such yoked opposites in the play is Friar Laurence, who creates havoc out of essentially benevolent motives. He continually courts disaster with his feigned death potions, incompetent messengers, and sudden disappearances. He is a walking paradox, perhaps most centrally in not knowing that marriage will *not* bring peace but only the double self-slaughter of Romeo and Juliet. But he is also the great explainer of such self-generated paradox.

The fact that man, the ruler of nature and its gardener or custodian, is a walking self-contradiction is the Friar's central point. Man, he holds, is the final manifestation of contrariety in the sublunary world. Thus, at the very moment of Romeo's arrival in his cell, Friar Laurence picks up one of his cherished flowers and says,

Within the infant rind of this weak flower
Poison hath residence and medicine power:
For this, being smelt, with that part cheers each part;
Being tasted, slays all senses with the heart.
Two such opposèd kings encamp them still
In man as well as herbs—grace and rude will;
And where the worser is predominent,
Full soon the canker Death eats up that plant.
                    [capitals mine]   (2.3.23)

Canker worms (probably) eat a rose from inside, making it seem healthy until it disintegrates. Thus, the worms act like canker, or cancer. Note the ominous presence of personified Death, now as a threat to plants like rose bushes. Such a disease is a symbol for the Verona of this play. Non-rule, and thus licence, has hollowed out the city and has become its cancer.

As in *A Midsummer Night's Dream* and *Love's Labor's Lost*, Shakespeare has represented a popular philosophy in the very structure of his play, and thus he has everyone in the play rush to express it. Even the Nurse, not known for her intellect, gets to cry out "O woeful sympathy!" (3.3.85) in reference to Romeo and Juliet, but this also prefigures the audience's proper response to the tragic outcome of the play.

RUSH IN *ROMEO AND JULIET*

Around 1595, when he wrote *Romeo and Juliet*, Shakespeare was versed in the mystical thought evoked by a coin adopted by the Roman emperor Vespasianus. The coin had an image of the emperor's bust on one side, and on the reverse a dolphin wrapped around an anchor with the motto *festina lente*, or "hasten slowly" (see illustration). This may be the most famous emblem and motto of contrariety from Greek and Roman times.

An ideal ruler should hasten to act when necessary, but also he or she (especially in reference to Queen Elizabeth I) should slowly deliberate the effects of that action in advance. In some cases the deliberation and action should be simultaneous. The two equal and opposite movements could aptly be symbolized not so much by the speed of a dolphin and the staying power of an anchor, as by the acceleration of a dolphin (porpoises can suddenly fly through the water) and the deceleration of a boat created by the drag of a well-designed anchor. In this case, once again the sea or salt water is taken for the earthly medium, or the symbol for negotiation and change. Shakespeare represents an anchor in the constant deceleration of action in *A Midsummer Night's Dream*; in *Romeo and Juliet* he represents the acceleration of the dolphin, partly as a warning to Elizabeth I about balance in rule, and partly as a representation to all audiences of a symbol of unity in fragmentation and how thoughtful outcomes in marriage suit comedy, and how cruel sacrifices suit tragedy.

Romeo and Juliet's Verona is unhinged. What frames the haste in Verona are (1) the moderation and meditation—indeed, drowsiness—on the part of Prince Escalus; (2) the general lack of control of his household by Capulet I; and (3) the slow error of Romeo's adoptive "father," Friar Laurence, and Juliet's adoptive "mother," the unnamed Nurse. Thus when we first meet the Prince in the midst of the third straight bloodbath in the streets of his city, he seems to be contemplating something no more lethal than prison authorities who might take away the library privileges of gangland criminals and their leaders who are up to their elbows in blood.

Apparently on his third go-round, the Prince delivers his sentence:

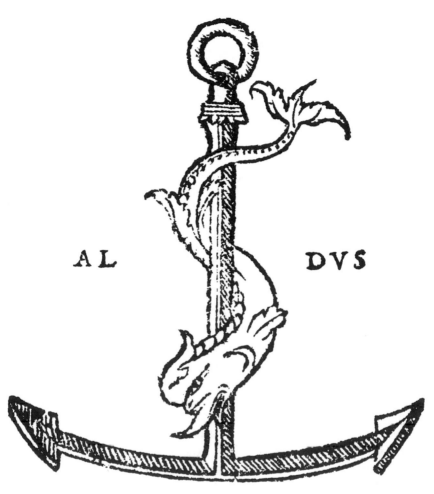

The Aldine symbol of the dolphin wrapped around the anchor: a visual yoked opposite. Accompanied by the motto *festina lente* ("hasten slowly"), the dolphin wrapped around the anchor was the symbol of the rule of the Roman emperors Augustus and Vespasianus. Without the motto, it was the symbol of the Aldine Press in Venice founded in the sixteenth century by Aldo Manuzio. Is the dolphin angry because he or she is stayed by the anchor? Photo Courtesy of the Newberry Library, Chicago.

Three civil brawls, bred of an airy word,
By thee, old Capulet, and Montague,
Have thrice disturbed the quiet of our streets
And made Verona's ancient citizens
Cast by their grave-beseeming ornaments
To wield old partisans in hands as old,
Cankered with peace, to part your cankered hate.
If ever you disturb our streets again
Your lives shall pay the forfeit of the peace.   (1.1.89)

The Prince focuses on the old men of the town ("ancient citizens") who have been forced to take off their dignified staffs and pendants and robes ("grave-beseeming ornaments") and dress for battle. They must take up, as they did long before (apparently in external wars), their long-staffed two-handled swords ("partisans") rusted with disuse ("cankered with peace"), to try to bring about peace ("to part your cankered hate"). One wonders where the Prince's guard figures in all this vigilante self-policing.

Because several words here have double meanings, such as *partisan* and *canker*, the Prince implies much more than any literal translation can indicate. For example, old Capulet and Montague are also venerable citizens involved—with their swords drawn—in very "partisan" (biased) activity. And *canker* here is not only the familiar worm but also cancer—rust and, indeed, the cancer of civic peace that invites the cancer of civil disturbance and gang warfare. Shakespeare often suggests in his plays and poems that through its permissiveness and greediness, peace creates not only prosperity but also civil war. Then the Prince, in the midst of condemning his own administration, boldly delivers to the great partisans (Capulet and Montague) the imminent sentence of death by banishing one family's son, Romeo, when Mercutio, his kinsman, and Tybalt, the leading young male of the Capulets, are killed in the next brawl on the next hot afternoon. This laxity of rule leads to the incredible haste of bloody action in the streets, right up to the death of Paris, another of the Prince's kinsmen.

Only at the end of the play does the Prince learn how disgracefully slow, how sadly decelerating, his regime was, and that his reluctance to act caused a great deal of the haste, making inevitable an unbelievable sacrifice of the city's youth. With sorrow he blames himself more clearly to the now thoroughly "scourged"—both officially whipped or lashed, and plagued—old Capulet and Montague:

> Where be these enemies? Capulet, Montague,
> See what a scourge is laid upon your hate,
> That heaven finds means to kill your joys with love.
> And I, for winking at your discords, too,
> Have lost a pair of kinsmen. All are punished.   (5.3.291)

Saying that Romeo and Juliet's love was ordained to make a mockery of their hate rubs salt in Capulet's and Montague's wounds. In the special circumstance of Romeo and Juliet, extreme love led to the extreme self-hate of suicide. Indeed, the two fathers are conscious of losing their "joys," the children they neglected, and the natural pleasures ("joys") of peace and old age that they should have otherwise enjoyed—not the least, no doubt, mutual grandchildren. But the notion that all are punished also comes home to the Prince, whose non-rule is best symbolized by the ruler's perpetual blinking of the eyes and "winking at your discords." It may be a minor element, but the play also seems to relate the tragedy of the drowsy Prince as well as of rushing old Capulet and fiery Mercutio.

Capulet narrowly avoids a brawl at his own party and rushes into treating his daughter both as a pawn in an arranged marriage to the rich and powerful Paris, and as an incompetent in conversation—though she is arguably the best poet in the play. Relying on insults in argument with her—"Mistress minion," "young baggage," "disobedient wretch," "hilding" (worn-out horse, or woman with a hint of aging prostitute) (3.5.151, 160, 168)—and leaving her to be raised by the bawdy Nurse, he produces a rebel of a child. Juliet becomes a thrill-seeker who prefers having her secret husband, Romeo, in love's embrace in her own room (initially while Paris and her parents are talking downstairs) to doing what the play calls out for them to do if they are to stay alive and produce a family. Elope. Elope to Mantua. After all, Juliet had once said that she would "follow thee my lord throughout the world" (2.2.148). But thanks to Capulet's non-rule and the lover's terrible rush, this is not to be.

If Friar Laurence is the spokesperson for contrariety in the play, Mercutio (whose name suggests the rush he analyzes) is the commentator on individual and civic precipitate action in the play. In the longest speech of the play he attributes all rushing into satisfaction of desires to the prodding of a faery queen named Mab, an immortal from Irish and English folklore who produces and controls human dreams. Since she is a queen of the faeries like Queen Titania in *A Midsummer Night's Dream* (an alternate name for the Olympian moon goddess Diana in Ovid), Shakespeare's Queen Mab is part of an elaborate double-edged compliment to Queen Elizabeth, who five years before the writing of this play had enthusiastically received the first three books of Edmund Spenser's great compliment to her, *The Faerie Queene.*

Why was Elizabeth pictured as the Queen of Faeries? Why did Elizabeth's favorite political poets, such as Sidney, Spenser, and Shakespeare, connect her with night-time universal goddesses of Olympian and Celtic myth? Apparently such a connection propagandizes Elizabeth as an inexorable force controlling vital men's and women's—especially poets' and even beasts'—imaginations. Calling the Queen moon goddess and queen of elves, trolls, and magical warriors remains a compliment even when we are asked to see her as quite mischievous, as in Mercutio's speech when as Queen Mab she spurs men, women, and even horses (1.4.89) into sudden ill-advised action. In a sense people are Elizabeth's horses. Metaphorically, horses become the dolphins of the land. They gallop for Queen Elizabeth.

Thus, at one remove, Queen Elizabeth, who would have attended this play at court (see Chapter 3), is represented as the great motivator of human dreams, taken both in the sense of the high imagination of night-time dreaming and in the sense of conscious ambition (dreams). Her mode, like Juliet's chariot of the sun, involves riding at full tilt. In her tiny carriage Queen Mab, according to Mercutio,

>   gallops night by night
> Through lovers' brains, and then they dream of love . . .
> O'er ladies' lips, who straight on kisses dream,

And

> Sometimes she driveth o'er a soldier's neck,
> And then dreams he of cutting foreign throats.   (1.4.70, 74, 82)

In these excerpts Mercutio seems to name Romeo's, Juliet's, and Tybalt's desires and their sudden afflictions. For example, are not Romeo's and Juliet's anxious brains and lips their leading sexual organs? And what victim's throat would be most foreign to Capulet Tybalt but that of the scion of the opposite House of Montague? He does not need a knightly crusade to distant beaches. His crusade is at home.

As Romeo approaches his friend after the balcony scene, for once Mercutio admits that Romeo's exaggerated mating urge may have psychic elements in it after all. Thus, he dissects for Benvolio the extreme idealism that spurs Romeo to unbridled desire—he guesses—still for Rosaline. Within earshot of his friend he says,

> Now is he for the numbers that Petrarch flowed in. Laura to his lady was a kitchen wench—marry, she had a better love to berhyme her —Dido a dowdy, Cleopatra a gypsy, Helen and Hero hildings and harlots, Thisbe a gray eye or so, but not to the purpose. (2.4.38)

Note the climactic reference to the ancient suicide of Thisbe (see Chapter 2). Mercutio here implies that maddening comparisons that are created by Petrarchan and Ovidian art send Romeo into the mania of haste that controls him. Art goads him to rush, even into unequal battles with love poets as distinguished as Petrarch.

Mercutio, moreover, analyzes rush into bloody combat. When Benvolio tries to convince him to go inside on a hot day that has "the mad blood stirring" (3.1.4), Mercutio attributes his own slightly mad tendencies to the mild-mannered pacifist, Benvolio. He says,

> Thou art like one of these fellows that when he enters
> the confines of a tavern, claps me his sword upon the table
> and says, "God send me no need of thee!" and by the operation
> of the second cup draws him on the drawer, when indeed there
> is no need.   (3.1.5)

Benvolio, baffled, asks, "Am I like such a fellow?" Of course he is not. Yet Mercutio has chosen this moment to make a wild attribution on the basis of what might happen if he went indoors with Benvolio to avoid a fight. He could drink and have a sudden mad fit and draw on a drawer of wine, who, if Benvolio killed him, could not draw any more wine to make him more belligerent. In a cosmic sense it would be superfluous to draw on the drawer, and thus he adds "there is no need." There is no need of fights, no need of swords, when one is having fun. One only needs the wine steward. It is another paradox. While Mercutio goes on to reduce the cause of fights to another absurdity, this story of unproductive slaughter encapsulates his understanding of the irrationality of rush into combat. He then promptly becomes another victim in a tragic city that gallops out of control until its scions, Romeo and Juliet, rush into suicide. Only in the final slaughter and self-slaughter can one reflect on all the events—all the rush—as part of a simultaneous ritual marriage and sacrifice to purify a sick city in the grips of unbounded haste.

NOTES

1. And even, ironically, of much of Shakespeare's blank verse (unrhymed iambic pentameter) in the generation after Shakespeare's.

2. Shakespeare's source, Brooke, also calls the Friar "ghostly father" (see Chapter 3).

3. The oath "Jesu Maria" was outlawed on the stage after the coronation of the Scottish King James I in 1603.

4. This contrariety is part of the universal mysticism of love poetry. It is even found in oxymoronic advertisements for cosmetics coming out of Madison Avenue, for example, in the lipstick color "fire and ice."

5. This scene was imitated probably by Shakespeare himself in *The Two Noble Kinsmen*, but also by John Ford and Richard Brome.

STUDY QUESTIONS

1. Consider the role of the prologue. Does that sonnet tell us what happens in the play? Or does it trick us into thinking that all is fated or determined by supernatural forces? In this context, how do you interpret "star-crossed"?

2. Critics have often dismissed *Romeo and Juliet* as a fledgling or immature Shakespearean tragedy. What strikes you as mature or highly developed in this play? Is there a tragedy of Friar Laurence in the play? Of Mercutio? Of Tybalt? Of old Capulet? Of Romeo? Of Juliet? Of the Prince? Of the Nurse? Discuss.

3. Do the elaborate descriptions of the time of the day in the play have a special significance? Discuss three examples.

4. There appear to be several instances of misrule in this play. Is there misrule in Juliet's home, the Capulet mansion? Explain.

5. How do Friar Laurence's remarks about his garden (2.3) apply to the play as a whole? Do his actions contradict or confirm his words?

6. How do the metaphors of the love poetry in the play, such as love as religion in Romeo and Juliet's first conversation, suggest a cult of love in the play? Where do you suppose Shakespeare stood on this issue? What can you conclude from evidence inside the work?

7. Do Romeo and Juliet in their poetry seem to dwell excessively on death and the afterlife? What does this mean? How does the form of the play help make this point?

8. How does Mercutio's poetry, especially in the Queen Mab speech (1.4.53ff.), undercut what the lovers say to each other? What is his general feeling about relations between the sexes and the ambitions of lovers? Does he regard sexual activity as bestial? Be specific.

9. How do Romeo and Mercutio behave with each other? Did Shakespeare depict true friendship (of Romeo and Mercutio) as well as true love (of Romeo and Juliet) in the play? Explain in detail.

10. How do you account for the importance of the Nurse in the play? What seems to be her relationship with the senior Capulets? With Juliet? What provokes Mercutio to be so rude with her—and her sexuality—when they meet?

11. Is there comedy in this play? Where? Is it merely comic relief, or does it have greater significance? Consider the scene with the musicians punning and worrying about pay (4.5.96–4.5.145). Is the Nurse's man, perhaps aptly named "Peter,"—a purely comic figure? Or is he a serious fool? Discuss.

12. Prepare a report on political disturbance in Shakespeare's Verona. There were bitter feuds between Guelph supporters of the Pope and his popular causes, and Ghibelline supporters of the Holy Roman Emperor and his aristocratic causes. These feuds were eventually won by the Guelphs. There were also feuds in the communes in northern Italy between white Guelphs and black Guelphs. Look up "Guelph" and "Ghibelline" in the index of an encyclopedia and give a report on their feuds. To reflect this struggle, might you dress up the Capulets and Montagues in black and white? Support your position.

TOPICS FOR WRITTEN OR ORAL EXPLORATION

1. Consider the role of Friar Laurence. Develop an argument that the Friar intentionally botches everything in the play (through secret weddings, wayward messengers, and potions) and thus brings about, perhaps with the collusion of Prince Escalus, a lasting peace in Verona.

2. Consider the presence of horror (or Gothic) imagery in the play, not only in the cemetery but in the speeches of Romeo, Juliet, and Friar Laurence. Develop an argument about Shakespeare as master creator of scary or panicky art (the sublime, art that terrifies pleasurably).

3. Some critics have argued that Shakespeare was a Roman Catholic. Explore this idea in relation to his largely favorable portrait of the Friar and the Friar's place in the society of Verona.

4. Consider that *Romeo and Juliet* has a significant Christian—even Roman Catholic—context. Why is there no reference to suicide as a mortal sin? How do you explain this absence in the play? Are Romeo and Juliet in any sense Christ-like and thus sacrificial victims in the play? Develop a carefully conceived argument on this subject with an eye to church doctrine.

5. Romeo seems to help bring about the death of a number of characters in the play: Mercutio, Tybalt, Paris, himself, Juliet, his mother. Develop an argument of Romeo as a promoter of genocide, an idealist in love and politics whose actions lead to his own and others' deaths.

6. Develop a portrait of the Nurse as a successful professional go-between or pimp (bawd) in both her speech and actions.

7. Develop a portrait of the Nurse as Juliet's unsuccessful mother.

8. Develop a portrait of old Capulet as representing dangerously ineffectual anger (or brief madness).

9. Develop a portrait of Tybalt as a gang leader. Examine his values—

military prowess, protection of women and of his own personal honor—in the context of what you know about gang warfare in big cities today.

10. Do a brief study of Queen Elizabeth, using sources in the library. Develop an argument about the fact that Mercutio's Queen Mab speech (1.40.53) may be a compliment to Queen Elizabeth from her favorite playwright.

11. Examine a single repeating image in the play—for example, mythological time, seafaring, or the idea of a personified male lover, Death—and develop an argument about the play as a whole on its basis.

12. Compose an argument about the Prince (perhaps entitled "Escalus the Weak and Drowsy") as an incompetent ruler.

13. Develop a portrait of a minor character who is nevertheless at the center of the action, such as Benvolio as peacemaker, Sampson as faithful retainer in a vendetta, or Capulet's wife as housewife and nag.

14. Support a thesis (perhaps entitled "Juliet the Sensible") that shows how the development of Juliet's understanding and love suggest that Shakespeare might have been an early feminist.

15. Develop an argument about Friar Laurence as an ineffectual father of Romeo. What does he do wrong, in your opinion? How? What are the consequences? Be specific.

SUGGESTED READINGS

The following are useful editions, biographical materials, and classical statements.

Bevington, David, ed. *The Complete Works of Shakespeare*, 4th ed. New York: HarperCollins, 1992; orig. 1973.

Bryant, Joseph, ed. *Romeo and Juliet*. Revised Signet ed. New York: New American Library, 1989.

Coleridge, Samuel Taylor. *Lectures 1808–1819 on Literature*, ed. R. A. Foakes, 2 vols. London: Routledge and Kegan Paul, 1987.

Evans, G. Blakemore, ed. *Romeo and Juliet*. The New Cambridge Shakespeare. Cambridge: Cambridge University Press, 1984.

Furness, Horace Howard, ed. *The New Variorum Edition of Shakespeare*. Vol 1., *Romeo and Juliet*. Philadelphia: Lippincott, 1871.

Gibbons, Brian, ed. *Romeo and Juliet*. Arden ed. London: Methuen, 1980.

Granville-Barker, Harley. *Prefaces to Shakespeare*, Vol. 2. Princeton: Princeton University Press, 1947.

Harbage, Alfred, ed. *The Complete Pelican Shakespeare*. Baltimore: Penguin, 1969.

Johnson, Samuel. *Johnson on Shakespeare*. The Yale Edition of the Works of Samuel Johnson, Vol. 9. New Haven: Yale University Press, 1958.

Romeo and Juliet: A Concordance to the Text of the Second Quarto of 1599. Oxford: Clarendon Press, 1972.

Schoenbaum, Samuel. *William Shakespeare: Records and Images*. London: Scolar Press, 1981.

Shakespeare, William. *The First Folio of Shakespeare*, 2nd ed. New York: W. W. Norton, 1996; orig. 1968.

Wilson, John Dover, and Arthur Quiller-Couch, eds. *Romeo and Juliet*, Vol. 28 of *The Works of William Shakespeare*. 38 vols., ed. for the Syndics of the Cambridge University Press. Cambridge: Cambridge University Press, 1923–1962.

2

Narrative Backgrounds to *Romeo and Juliet*

INTRODUCTION

Behind the elements of the story of Romeo and Juliet lie two classical works and two modern ones. In different ways, these four works led gradually to Arthur Brooke's *Romeus and Juliet* (see Chapter 3) and then to Shakespeare's *Romeo and Juliet*. Numerous stories contain the key elements of a shared "religion of love" followed by lovers' separation and subsequent demise resulting from a misunderstanding or misfortune. There are the classical tales of Hero and Leander or Orpheus and Euridice, or the medieval tales of the same lovers, or of Launcelot and Guinevere, Aucassin and Nicolette, Tristan and Isolde, Abelard and Heloise, Troilus and Criseyde, Floris and Blanchefleur, and many others. Missing from these romances are the sleeping potion and the double suicide at the tomb. These elements are present, however, in classical tales by Ovid and Xenophon of Ephesus. And they appear in the thirty-third tale of *il Novellino* of Masuccio Salernitano with a hint of family feuding. The balcony scenes, furthermore, are suggested by Geoffrey Chaucer's aubades (morning songs) in *Troilus and Criseyde*.

Three of these sources—excluding Chaucer—were brought together in Italy by Bandello to become what is known as the fictional tale of Juliet Capulet and Romeo Montague in Verona. Of course, if the story comes from high fiction—that is, work of the imagination that is not meant to be realistic, like *Star Trek*—it is "myth," not history. But if there were no lovers named Juliet Cappeletti or Romeo Montecchi in a strife-torn Verona, and no feud between their two houses—nor much civil disturbance at all—should we not want to preserve the fiction as symbolic truth? After all, we do just that with the idea of Bigfoot in the great Northwest, and the Loch Ness monster, and even Superman's second birthplace in Smallville, Illinois, and his ultimate home in Metropolis, Illinois. The narrative backgrounds of *Romeo and Juliet* have meaning when applied to the beautiful Italian city of Verona that comes to have historical weight through repeated mention in literature and through commercialization (see Chapter 7).

First, Ovid's story of Pyramus and Thisbe (8 A.D.?) relates the double suicide at a tomb of young lovers who are the only (?) children of warring families. Xenophon of Ephesus' *Ephesiaca*, or *The Ephesian Tale* (second or third century A.D.), relates the use of a sleep potion—producing the appearance of death—to avoid consummation of an unwanted marriage (and an illegal one, too, because the Juliet-figure, Anthia, is already married to her Romeo, Habrocomes). Geoffrey Chaucer in *Troilus and Criseyde* (1390?) develops the aubades, the witty scenes of morning song and departure, that Shakespeare subsequently used with a twist in the two balcony scenes he apparently added to the story. Finally, Masuccio Salernitano combines earlier elements to tell a more complete story of Romeo and Juliet—but before the present names were adopted and before the work was placed in Verona—in the thirty-third tale of his cycle of stories, *il Novellino* (1476).

THE PYRAMUS AND THISBE STORY FROM OVID'S *METAMORPHOSES*

Shakespeare's grammar and high school years—at Queen Elizabeth's New School in Stratford—were in good part devoted to the study of Latin rhetoric. As a result, in his literary education he was brought up with the great love poet of Augustan Rome, Publius Ovidius Naso (Ovid)—especially his narrative poem, *Metamorphoses*—rather than with English poets such as Chaucer and his descendants. Ovid's work in fifteen books and almost 12,000 lines of dactylic hexameter is in part a mythography of Olympian stories dating from the creation of the world up to Ovid's own time, which he pictures as the glorious reign of the first Roman emperor—and future god—Augustus. In fact, Ovid wrote the *Metamorphoses* in part to be a booster for Augustus' Olympian religious revival, which was an attempt to improve what the emperor thought was lacking in Roman morals. Thus, like Virgil's *Aeneid* from the same period, Ovid invokes for the first Roman emperor the grand old Olympian religion that was being challenged in Rome and elsewhere by a number of cults from the East. These cults offered the laity the possibility of a happy immortality of the soul.

Ovid does not suggest immortality of the souls of his protagonists as such—except in Hades—although his emphasis on the cult of Bacchus (or Dionysus, Bromios, Lyaeus, Liber, etc.) and deification of his wife, Ariadne, seems to provide an answer to the Eastern cults. Partly in keeping with his admiration for the pre-Socratic philosopher Pythagoras and the Pythagoreans, Ovid develops a notion of the origin of the species as a product of transformation or change (metamorphosis) that immortalizes humans and their achievements in the form of new flora and fauna—and even inanimates such as constellations or rock walls. Mortal humans become these permanent new species of animal, vegetable, or mineral as a result of their godlike (i.e., immortally stubborn and impetuous) activities.

This theory of the development of non-human dwellers of the world—the species—invites the poet to spiritualize virtually every aspect of existence. This is a poet's dream. People spiritualize inanimates every day when they kick chairs after clipping their ankles or talk to their cars when the red warning light goes on, but spiritualizing all of existence becomes in Ovid an overarching poetic purpose and program. This is where fiction comes in conflict with history and poetry with science.

Although Ovid can be profoundly ironic, he glorifies the activities of mortals—especially in the areas of love and invention—by showing their hubris (overweening pride), which has a divine spark. Gods and goddesses, like Juno and Jupiter, behave in a proud, jealous, greedy, and sometimes vengeful manner. But how else would one behave if one was only human and yet knew one was immortal? For actual mortals to behave in this manner merits their simultaneous death and transformation into a new species to ornament the earth and make it more enchanting.

The story of Pyramus and Thisbe, placed in the ancient Mesopotamian capital, Babylon, and its environs, tells how lovers impetuously took their own lives intending to rejoin their mates. It also explains why mulberry trees seem to bleed deep purple on the ground below them—as found on many springtime city sidewalks in Rome, New York, Babylon, or Chicago. They bleed for the double suicide of the two impetuous young urban lovers, Pyramus and Thisbe, scions of neighboring families who were apparently at war.

Shakespeare uses Ovid's rather abrupt account of Pyramus and Thisbe as the basis for the play-within-a-play at the center of *Romeo and Juliet*'s sister play, *A Midsummer Night's Dream*. However, Ovid's tale is also the basis for much of Shakespeare's love tragedy, notably *Romeo and Juliet*, in which even Mercutio refers to Thisbe as having a "gray eye or so, but not to the purpose" (2.4.42), because she cannot match Juliet in Romeo's estimation.

Ovid tells a story of family feuds, holes in garden walls, mistaken assumptions at a tomb on the outskirts of town, and a teenage double suicide. The story of Pyramus and Thisbe is a frame narrative (a story within a story) told by an unnamed Theban woman who refuses to go to the hilltops on the outskirts of Thebes and worship Dionysus or Bacchus, as the god of wine and tragedy requires. Rather, the woman and her sisters rebuke the hometown Theban god and his collective activities by staying at home, weaving and telling stories that subtly undercut Dionysus' religious revival in this town containing the scorched remains of his mother, the princess Semele.

In opposition to Dionysus, the narrator's tale glorifies human, not divine, love. The gods' only intervention inside of her story appears suddenly, almost inexplicably, in the final transformation of the suicides into the dark-red berries of the mulberry tree. Oddly, given a dry season or other causes, a mulberry tree may bear only white berries, so perhaps the tale glorifies the normal shift (metamorphosis) of the berries from white to dark red—Ovid says "black" in several ways—like that of unoxidized blood, when fully mature. After the sisters tell their stories, the vengeful spirit of Dionysus invades their home, transforms their looms into vines, and turns the sisters into bats—doomed forever to hide in houses and caves and come out only at night.

Shakespeare may have identified with Ovid because both men lived during periods of national consolidation of power and development of nascent empires. Possibly, like Ovid, Shakespeare was also a law-school dropout turned poet. Furthermore, Shakespeare would have known that Ovid had written the well-known but lost love tragedy of Augustan Rome, *Medea*. If Shakespeare borrows for *Romeo and Juliet* from *Metamorphoses* (1) Juliet's garden wall, (2) the use of formulaic chronographia (poetic description of time), and (3) the double suicide of the children of hostile neighbors (including a gutsy girl stabbing herself at an important family tomb)—which is represented as a notable human sacrifice deserving commemoration—he also, here and elsewhere, adopts what is called the Ovidian mode.

The Ovidian mode of fiction and poetry—growing largely out of readings of the *Metamorphoses*—pictures humans and gods in a passion-driven world. An Ovidian character often lacks the capability for self-reflection and is motivated primarily by sexual desire and the desire for revenge and fame. (These are the type of people Mercutio describes in his Queen Mab speech [1.4.53–95]). Beyond his use of the Ovidian mode, Shakespeare is also a profound reader of Ovid's characterization and his largely green world and ocean world habitats.[1] Ovid and Shakespeare both loved nature—including human nature—as few poets have.

At the opening of the inner play of Shakespeare's romantic comedy, *The Taming of the Shrew* (1594?), the wise servant Tranio warns his would-be studious master, Lucentio, not to be too disciplined, "Or so devote [himself] to Aristotle's checks / as Ovid be an outcast quite abjured" (1.1.32). In a complex joke Shakespeare has Tranio say that Aristotle's moral philosophy may be too full of "checks," or warnings and moral prescriptions, for young men to bear; Ovid, on the other hand, in seeming to approve of passionate achievement of goals (especially in love), may be more in keeping for his master, not to be "abjured," or sworn off. But in saying "outcast" Tranio also refers to the fact that for reasons possibly connected with his poetic emphasis on love and sex, Ovid was exiled by Augustus at the height of the poet's career in 8 A.D., around the time of his completion of the *Metamorphoses*. Even under the following regime of Tiberius, Ovid was not allowed to return to his beloved home, Rome, and he died an "outcast." However, his poetic output never stinted in the harsh social and geographic environs of what is now the area of Romania's leading port town (Constanta) and Black Sea resort. The Greek locals apparently adored this famous exile poet.

As for the following translation, I have written a very literal version in English of Ovid's story of Pyramus and Thisbe to bring out its antique qualities.[2] Using many more words than Ovid (who, like Virgil, Horace, and other Augustan poets, writes with supreme concentration and compactness), I have tried to clarify and catch the ancient Greek dramatic flavor of Ovid that might have appealed to Shakespeare. I have capitalized many generic words (such as "Night") that are not capitalized in the manuscripts, because I felt Ovid would want them spiritualized as they are elsewhere in the work. Although many translations and adaptations of Ovid's works were available to Shakespeare, most notably Arthur Golding's English translation of the *Metamorphoses* (1567), Shakespeare clearly shows in *A Midsummer Night's Dream* and *Romeo and Juliet* an acquaintance with the original in Latin. He even makes fun of mistakes a student of Latin might make, such as calling Pyramus and Thisbe's meeting place—Ninus' sepulchral mound (*Nini tumulum*)—"Ninny's tomb" (*A Midsummer Night's Dream* 3.1.92). Partly because of Shakespeare's sophistication in this regard, a number of scholars have been attracted to the story that Shakespeare was a schoolmaster up-country from London beyond the Cotswolds in his twenties. But probably he was an apprentice actor in London, and possibly an attender of law classes with many other future writers of Londinium or Augusta (the New Rome), such as Francis Bacon, John Donne, and John Webster.

FROM OVID'S STORY OF PYRAMUS AND THISBE IN
METAMORPHOSES (8 A.D.?)
(Book 4, lines 51–166; Latin text from William S. Anderson, ed.,
Ovid's Metamorphoses: *Books 1–5*, London and Norman: University
of Oklahoma Press, 1997)

[She considered what tale to tell, always of transformations]: Or how the tree that once bore white fruit now bears fruit black from the contact of blood; this one pleases her. This story, not yet commonly known, she spins out, while, at the same time, she weaves her woolen threads:

"Pyramus and Thisbe—he the most beautiful young man, she the most beautiful maiden who inhabited the East—lived in houses sharing a common garden wall in the city that Semiramis surrounded with walls of brick [probably a reference to the famous ceramic brick sculpture of figures—like lions—of ancient Babylon]. Their proximity provided the first steps of their acquaintance, which eventually grew into Love. They would have joined themselves to each other by right of the marriage torch, but their fathers vetoed it. But something fathers could hardly veto was the fact that, struck to their very souls, the lovers secretly burned with the flames of mutual passion. Without anyone else knowing, much less go-betweens, they talked to each other by nods and signs, and the more they smothered the fire of passion, the more it flamed up.

"There was a narrow crack in the shared wall between the gardens, a crack that occurred when it was being built. This crack, unnoticed for a long time—but Love is never blind—you lovers first found out and used as your channel of conversation. Through this crack, safely and privately, you exchanged Love talk in the quietest murmurs. Often when they had taken their positions, Thisbe on this side, Pyramus on that, when they had drawn in each others' mutual panting breath, they would say, 'Envious Wall, why do you obstruct us lovers? How small a favor it would have been to open wide enough to let us hold each other in love's embrace, or at least to open wide enough to let us kiss? But, O Wall, we are hardly ungrateful, we admit that you give us passage for words to reach loving ears.' So they talked on, frustrated, on opposite sides of the Wall. Toward Night they said 'Goodbye,' and although they could not reach each other with their lips, they each kissed either side of the Wall.

"When Dawn had extinguished the Night's fires [stars], and Sun with his rays had dried the frost on the grass, the lovers came together at their usual spots. In low murmurs, they complained about their fate, then decided that in the still of the Night they would try to sneak past their guardians out of doors. When they had managed to get beyond their own homes, they would go beyond the city walls, too. So that they would not miss each other wandering by error in the countryside, they would meet at the funeral monument of Ninus [tomb of the husband of Semiramis and founder of the Assyrian capital, Nineveh], hiding under its great tree. This tall tree hanging with snowy fruit, a huge mulberry bush, stood by an icy-cold fountain. The plan pleased them perfectly, and the daylight seemed to disappear very slowly. But at last Sun dove down beneath the waves and out from those waves appeared Night.

"Skillfully Thisbe opens the door on its hinges and steals out into the pitch black unnoticed. Reaching the sepulchral mound, her face hidden by a garment used as a veil, she sits down under the tree. Love was making her bold. But behold, a lioness, her chops smeared with the blood of slaughtered cattle, arrives to drink hard at the tree's fountain. Still a ways off, the Babylonian girl Thisbe sees the lioness by Moon's rays, and on terrified feet she escapes into a cave. As she ran her muffler slipped from her shoulders and remained on the ground.

"When the savage lioness had slaked her thirst with huge gulps of water, on the way back to the woods, the beast finds the garment—without the girl inside—and shakes its fabric to shreds with its bloody mouth.

"Pyramus exits the city a bit later and notices the prints of the ferocious animal in the deep dust and grows pale. But when he also sees the bloody muffler he says, 'One Night will lose two lovers, but of the two, she deserved more to live a long life: on my soul rests all the guilt. I have brought about your death, sorrowful girl, by ordering you to steal by Night into this dangerous place. Nor did I get here first. O come, all you lions dwelling beneath this cliff, and tear me to shreds. With your teeth, eat my guilty self. But it is a cowardly move just to pray for Death.'

"He grasps Thisbe's garment and carries it into the shade of the tree at which they mutually chose to meet. While he weeps over and kisses the well-known muffler, he says, 'Also drink my blood now.' As he said this, he took the sword that hung at his belt and stabbed himself up from below the rib-cage, and immediately, with his last strength, yanked the blade out of the hot wound. As he lay stretched out on his back on the dust, his blood spouted out high, as when water sprays up through a narrow hissing crack in a pipe, when there is some flaw in the lead, and gushes up breaking up the air. The tree's fruit, sprayed with the deadly gore, was now made thoroughly black. It watered the great root with blood and dyed the hanging mulberries in the hue of royal purple.

"Behold, here comes Thisbe, still in some terror but also in a fright that might she miss her lover. She looks for the young man both with her eyes and soul, longing to tell him of the dangers she had avoided. And although she knows the spot, even the shape of the tree, still the color of the berries throws her off somewhat. She is not certain if this is the place or not. While she wonders, she sees someone's arms and legs yanking about in the bloody dust. She goes whiter than the petals of flowering dogwood and shakes like the zephyrs of an offshore breeze that streak the sea's surface.

"In a moment she recognizes her lover and shrieking, claps her innocent arms, tears her hair, and hugs his lovely form, washing his wound with tears, mixing salt drops with blood, and kissing his cold lips. 'Pyramus, what accident has torn you from me? Answer me, Pyramus. Your dearest Thisbe is calling on you. Lift up your declining head and listen.' At Thisbe's name, Pyramus lifted his eyes already laden with death, and having seen her face, closed them again [forever].

"Now when she saw her own muffling veil and the ivory scabbard empty of its sword, she said, 'It was your own hand and your love that killed you, unhappy one. I too have a hand with strength for this one deed. I too have love that will give me strength for this one stroke. I will follow you in Death, and men will tell and retell the story that I was the most miserable cause and the companion of your fate. Whom only Death had the power to tear away from me, not even Death can take from me.

" 'O, most miserable fathers and mothers and relatives of both of us, be willing to do this one thing for us. Do not in envy deny us the prayer that we, whom certain Love, whom the last hour [death] has joined, should be buried together in the same tomb. And you, o tree, whose branches arch over one dead body, soon to be two, retain you the signs of our death and always give birth to fruit of a dark and gloomy color as a monument to our twin deaths.' She spoke and fitting the sharp point beneath her breast, she fell forward on the iron weapon still warmed by her lover's blood. Her prayers moved both the gods and the families, because the color of the fruit of the mulberry bush is black when it fully ripens, and the remains from both funeral piles [pyres] rest in one urn."

I have based my translation on the meticulously established text noted above, edited, with introduction and commentary, by William S. Anderson. We have one disagreement on 4.143, where Thisbe either says she is Pyramus' dearest or Pyramus is her dearest. I chose the former, unlike Anderson, and over some early manuscript evidence, because I felt that Thisbe's saying such a relatively bold thing seems to shock Pyramus into looking up practically from death's door. Thisbe is a girl after Juliet's heart.

XENOPHON OF EPHESUS' *AN EPHESIAN TALE*

Shakespeare and his contemporaries reveled in the gradual rediscovery of what are today called the Greek Romances, works of
sensational popular fiction that date mainly from the so-called New
or Second Sophistic period, roughly from the second to the fourth
centuries A.D. Written in rich literary Greek, they come mostly from
the eastern realms of the Roman Empire and the Mediterranean,
notably Alexandria at the mouth of the Nile River in Egypt. They
give that area of the world, with its islands—especially the Greek
archipelago—and cities and beautiful countryside, colorful but improbable symbolic meaning. A Greek Romance begins with "once
upon a time" meaning its opposite, "in no time and at no place,"
and it ends with the improbable "they lived happily ever after."

With heroes and heroines whose lives and chastity are always
threatened, Greek Romances are chock-full of the elements of high
fiction (fabulous, rather than realistic, storytelling): coincidences,
lost twins, lost rings, potion stories, dismemberment, premature
burial and other Gothic horrors, exorcism, and other magical and
symbolic elements. They hark back to the so-called Attic New Comedy of the fourth century B.C. of Menander and other playwrights
that Shakespeare enjoyed and imitated. He may have studied the
originals, but certainly he knew the translations and adaptations
of the Roman comic playwrights of the third and second centuries
B.C., Plautus and Terence.

Greek Romance, however, in its unflinching fantasy fiction that
foreshadows much of the fiction of popular culture in our day,[3]
also dates back to the most ancient Canaanite and Sumerian folk-
tales with their satisfying worlds of tests and ultimate justice, especially in love. This is the world of *The Ephesian Tale*.

Practically nothing is known about Xenophon of Ephesus. A notice in the *Suda* (the first encyclopedic dictionary in alphabetic
order; tenth or eleventh century) indicates that the author also
wrote a history of the city of Ephesus. This ancient Greek Ionian
city—lying on the western Mediterranean shore of Turkey—was,
from its foundation in the second millenium B.C., famous for its
devotion to the cult of an Asian Artemis (the Latin Diana) or god-

dess of chastity (probably identical with the Egyptian Isis). Xenophon's history is lost, but the emphasis in his Ephesian tale on chastity (especially marital chastity, or fidelity, in the face of death of the beloved) may reflect aspects of the cult of that many-breasted goddess of chastity. The work may be a gospel of sorts, helping to promote the Diana-cult's theological positions. The notice in the *Suda*, however, also indicates that Xenophon's romance occurred in ten books whereas only five are extant today. His name is probably a nom de plume in homage to the military historian and polemicist of fifth-and fourth-century Greece, Xenophon (427?–355 B.C.).

What Shakespeare drew on for *Romeo and Juliet*, directly or indirectly, is the story of the potion that Anthia—already married to her true love, Habrocomes—swallows to give her all the appearances of death. This state allows her to avoid a wedding night with Perilaos (so close in sound to "Paris"), her amorous benefactor, but leads to some odd and dangerous moments with brigands in the cemetery when she awakens. As in most Greek Romances, plot comes before character.

Note that the mechanics of marrying "by right of the marriage torch" are given in some detail. Shakespeare might have also drawn on (1) the tricky dealings of Eudoxos, the Ephesian physician (a little like Friar Laurence), (2) Anthia's huge expenditure for what she thinks is poison (like Romeo's with the Apothecary) and (3) Habrocomes' fears of necrophilia (corpse-loving) among the grave robbers (like Romeo's stated fears about a necrophiliac Death).

FROM XENOPHON OF EPHESUS' *EPHESIAN TALE OF ANTHIA AND HABROCOMES* (SECOND OR THIRD CENTURY A.D.)
(The end of Book Three; text from *Three Greek Romances*, translated with an introduction by Moses Hadas, The Library of Liberal Arts, New York: Bobbs and Merrill, 1964 [orig. New York: Doubleday, 1953], pp. 98–101)

At the time when Anthia was rescued from the robber band there came to Tarsus an elderly Ephesian, Eudoxos by name and a physician by profession; sailing toward Egypt, his ship had been wrecked near the Cilician shore. This Eudoxos went about soliciting all the gentry of Tarsus, asking some for clothing and others for money, and recounting his misfortunes to each. He approached Perilaos also, and told him that he was an Ephesian and a physician. Perilaos took him up, and brought him to Anthia, thinking that she would be overjoyed to see a man from Ephesus. She gave Eudoxos a friendly welcome, and inquired whether he had any news to tell of her own people. He said that he had been long absent from Ephesus and so had no tidings; nonetheless Anthia took pleasure in his society, for it brought to her mind memories of people at home. And thus Eudoxos became a familiar of the household and frequently addressed himself to Anthia; he enjoyed all the resources of the house, but always besought her to have him sent back to Ephesus, for he had a wife and children in that city.

Now when all preparations had been completed for the marriage of Perilaos and the day was at hand, a sumptuous feast was prepared for them and Anthia was decked out in bridal array. But neither by night nor by day had she surcease of tears; always she had Habrocomes before her eyes. Many thoughts coursed through her mind—her love, her oaths, her country, her parents, her constraint, her marriage. And when she found herself alone she seized the occasion and tore her hair and said, "Ah, wholly unjust am I and wicked, for I do not requite Habrocomes' loyalty to me. To remain my husband, he endured fetters and torture, and now may somewhere lie dead; but I am oblivious to all these things, and am being married, wretch that I am, and someone will chant the hymeneal [bridal song] over me and I shall go to the bed of Perilaos. But ah, Habrocomes, dearest soul of all, do not afflict yourself over me; never willingly would I wrong you. I come to join you, and until death will remain your bride."

Thus she said and when Eudoxos, the Ephesian physician, came to her, she led him aside to a certain vacant chamber, and fell at his knees and petitioned him not to reveal anything she would say to anyone, and exacted an oath by their ancestral deity, Artemis, that he would help her in whatever way she should request. Eudoxos raised her up as she wailed disconsolately, and bade her take heart, and promised upon oath that he would do everything. She told him then of her love for Habrocomes, of the oaths she had sworn to him, and of their engagements in regard to chastity. And then she said, "If it were possible for me, being alive, to recover Habrocomes alive, or else to flee from this place in secret, I should take counsel for such courses. But since Habrocomes is dead and it is impractical for me to escape and impossible to abide the approaching marriage—for I will neither transgress my pledges to Habrocomes nor will I despise an oath—do you then be my helper; find me somewhence a drug which will release wretched me from my tribulations. In return for this service you will receive much recompense from the gods, whom I shall ardently and frequently beseech on your behalf before my death, and I myself will give you money and arrange your return to Ephesus. Before anyone discovers anything that has transpired, you will be able to take ship and sail to Ephesus. And when you arrive there inquire for my parents, Megamedes and Evippe, and give them a report of my death and all that happeneed on my travels; say, too, that Habrocomes has perished.''

When she had so spoken she writhed at his feet and implored him not to refuse to give her the poison. Then she produced twenty minae of silver and her necklaces (all things she had in abundance, for all Perilaos' property was at her disposal) and gave them to Eudoxos. He deliberated for a long while: he pitied the girl for her misfortunes, he yearned to return to Ephesus, he coveted the money and the jewels; and so he promised to give her the drug, and went off to fetch it. She, in the meantime, was sunk in grief. She lamented her youth and was anguished at the thought of her untimely death; and frequently she called upon Habrocomes as though he were present. After no long while Eudoxos arrived bringing a drug, not lethal, however, but only hypnotic, so that no real harm should come to the girl and he himself meanwhile make arrangements for travel and be on his way. Anthia received the potion, thanked him warmly, and dismissed him. He then took ship and sailed away, and Anthia awaited a suitable moment for imbibing the poison.

Now was night fallen, and the bridal chamber was made ready, and those charged with the duty came to lead Anthia forth. She did go forth, all unwilling and suffused with tears, and she held the drug hidden in her hand. When she drew near the bridal chamber the members of the household chanted the propitious hymeneal, but Anthia grieved and wept, saying, "Just so, upon a time, was I led to my bridegroom Habrocomes, and the torches of love escorted us, and the hymeneal was sung for our propitious union. And now what will you do, Anthia? Will you wrong Habrocomes, your husband, who loves you, who has died because of you? Nay I am not so cowardly nor have my misfortunes made me so fearful. It is resolved: I shall drink the drug. Habrocomes must be my only husband; him do I desire though he is dead." This she said, and she was conducted in to the bridal chamber.

And now she found herself alone, for Perilaos was still feasting with his friends. She pretended that the agitation had made her thirsty, and bade one of the servants to bring her water to drink. And when the cup was brought, she took it, when no one was by, and cast the drug into it, and she wept, saying, "Ah, dearest soul, Habrocomes, lo, I discharge my promises to you, and I embark upon my journey to you, an unhappy journey but an inevitable one. Receive me gladly, and make my sojourn there with you a happy one." When she had so spoken she drank up the drug. Immediately sleep held her fast and she fell to the ground; the drug had accomplished its full task.

When Perilaos entered the chamber, as soon as he caught sight of Anthia lying unconscious, he was stunned and cried out. There was a great tumult among the whole household, and mingled emotions—lamentations and horror and stupefaction. Some were moved by pity for the girl seemingly dead, others sympathized with Perilaos' affliction, all bewailed what had happened. Perilaos rent his garments and threw himself upon the body, saying, "Ah, my dearest girl: before your marriage, alas, you have left your lover behind, his destined bride of but a few days. . . . Is it the tomb to which we shall bring you as a bridal chamber? Happy indeed that Habrocomes, whoever he was, truly blessed is he, receiving such a gift from his beloved." So he lamented, and he held all her body close, and caressed her hands and feet saying, "My poor bride, my more unhappy wife." Then he adorned her, wrapping rich robes about her body and decking it with much gold. The sight of her was too much for his endurance, and when day dawned, he placed Anthia (who lay unconscious) upon a bier and conveyed her to the cemetery near the city. There he deposited her in a funerary chamber, having immolated many victims and consumed many garments and other attire in flames.

When he had completed the customary rites, Perilaos was conducted back to the city by his household. Anthia, who had been left in the tomb, recovered her consciousness, and when she realized that the potion had not been lethal she groaned and wept, saying, "Ah, drug that has decieved me, that has prevented me from pursuing my happy journey to Habrocomes. Wholly hapless as I am, I am balked even in my yearning for death. But it is yet possible for me to remain in this tomb and by starvation bring the work of the drug to accomplishment. From here, none shall remove me, nor would I look upon the sun, nor shall I rise to the light of day." Thus saying she made her heart firm and awaited death with fortitude.

THE FAREWELL SCENES FROM GEOFFREY CHAUCER'S *TROILUS AND CRISEYDE*

Shakespare responded to the works of Geoffrey Chaucer throughout his career as a poet and playwright. Above all, he made use of Chaucer's two extended romances, *The Knight's Tale* (from *The Canterbury Tales*) and *Troilus and Criseyde*, one of the greatest narrative poems in English. Shakespeare would have known that his contemporary, Sir Philip Sidney, had said, in evaluating the supposed failure of his own and his contemporaries' poetic efforts in England in relation to Chaucer in his *Defence of Poesie*, "I know not whether to marvel more, either that he in that misty time could see so clearly, or that we in this clear age go so stumblingly after him." Here Sidney parodies Chaucer's own persona (fictive authorial mask) stumbling behind in love's dance, like Sidney and his contemporary poets behind Chaucer.

From *The Knight's Tale*, Shakespeare took part of the plot and characterization of *A Midsummer Night's Dream* and essentially the whole of what I would argue was Shakespeare's last completed work, *Two Noble Kinsmen* (1612). From Chaucer's *Troilus and Criseyde*, he took Chaucer's witty attacks on the dawn and daylight for the balcony scenes of *Romeo and Juliet*. He also took the whole of Chaucer's *Troilus and Criseyde* story for his bitter play *Troilus and Cressida*, with assists from Homer's *Iliad* and *Odyssey* and Robert Henryson's *Testament of Cresseid* (c.1480).

Of course Troilus and Criseyde, Chaucer's extramarital "courtly" lovers, are older—even more sophisticated—than Shakespeare's Romeo and Juliet, and some of their shared poetry betrays anxiety about their new relationship, not just their future parting. Unlike Shakespeare, Chaucer paints an uneasiness in their love that partly predicts the infidelity of Criseyde's part and the final abstraction from the scene on Troilus' part in the apotheosis (rising up as if to become a god) following his death. The notion of Day arriving in their bedroom as a thousand-eyed monstrous spy or hostile witness passes on this tension to the reader. Romeo and Juliet see nothing wrong with what they are doing, and thus Romeo's bravado at getting caught and facing death is a little different from Troilus' (see Book Three, stanza 217).

Shakespeare, however, made good use of Chaucer's nightingale and lark and other bird imagery, either from hawking or listening at dawn; Troilus' scolding the day and the sun; and the general sense in Chaucer of witty sadness at parting and the consciousness of Lady Fortune's rule of the universe. Shakespeare also gave Juliet, as Chaucer does with Criseyde, a more than equal voice to Romeo's in the aubades. Juliet's "Parting is such sweet sorrow" (2.2.185) could serve to describe the following scenes of Chaucer's great completed masterpiece.

FROM CHAUCER'S *TROILUS AND CRISEYDE* (CA. 1390)
(From Books Three and Four; text from Robert Kilburn Root, ed., *The Book of Troilus and Criseyde*, Princeton: Princeton University Press, 1926. Copyright renewed 1954 by Princeton University Press. Modern English rendering by the editor.)

3.1190 (Criseyde as a Lark in Bed with Troilus)

171

What mighte or may the sely larke seye,
Whan that the sperhauk hath it in his foot?
I kan no more, but of thise ilke tweye,—
To whom this tale sucre be or soot,—
Though that I tarie a yer, som tyme I moot,
After myn auctour, telle of hire gladnesse,
As well as I have told hire hevynesse.

[What can the silly, unlucky lark do or say when the sparrow hawk has it in his claws? I only know the story of these two lovers—to whom this account may be sugar or bitter soot. And even though I spend a whole year on it, I need some time, always in synch with my author [auctour or source], *to tell the story of their great happiness, as well as I have already done of their sorrow.]*

3.1233 (Criseyde as the Nightingale)

177

And as the newe abaysed nyghtyngale,
That stynteth first whan she begynneth to singe,
Whan that she hereth any herde tale,
Or in the hegges any wyght sterynge,
And after, siker, doth hire vois out rynge;

Right so Criseyde, whan hire drede stente,
Opned hire herte, and tolde al hire entente.

[And as the suddenly skittish nightingale, who freezes when she begins to sing if she hears any shepherd speak, or any creature stirring in the hedges, yet later, feeling safe, sings out with full voice, just so Criseyde, when her fear disappeared, she opened her whole heart and told all her meaning.]

3.1415–1528 (The First Farewell of Troilus and Criseyde)

Following the crowing of the cock after their first night of love, Criseyde complains about the dawn. Then Troilus speaks, rather than sings, his aubade (lover's morning poem to the beloved) to Criseyde, and they trade complaints:

203

Whan that the cok, comune astrologer,
Gan on his brest to bete, and after crowe,
And Lucifer, the dayes messager,
Gan for to rise, and oute hire stremes throwe,
And estward roos, to hym that koude it knowe,
Fortuna Major, that anoon Criseyde,
With herte soor, to Troilus thus seyde:

[When the rooster, the world-wide astrologer, began to beat his chest and crow, then Lucifer the morning star [also Venus] began to rise, and throw out her rays of light—and, for someone in the know [an astrology buff], up rose also in the east Major Fortune [an astrological sign in the form of a group of six stars]—then right away Criseyde, with a sore heart, said to Troilus:]

204

"Myn hertes lif, my trust and my plesaunce,
That I was born, allas, what me is wo,
That day of us moot make disseveraunce!
For tyme it is to ryse and hennes go,
Or ellis I am lost for evere mo.
O nyght, allas, why nyltow overe us hove,
As longe as whan Almena lay by Jove?

["My heart's life, my trust and my pleasure, how awful it is to have been born now that Day must split us up. For it is time to get up and go from here, or else I am lost forever. O Night, alas, why wouldn't you

hang over us, as long as when Alcmena lay with Jove [three courses of the moon in one night]*?]*

205

"O blake nyght, as folk in bokes rede,
That shapen art by god this world to hide
At certeyn tymes with thi blake wede,
That under that men myghte in rest abide,
Wel oughten bestes pleyne, and folk the chide,
That there as day with labour wolde us breste,
That thow thus fleest, and deynest us nat reste.

[*"O black Night, as people read in books, who art designed by God to hide the world at certain times with your black garments so that under that* [darkness] *men might remain resting. Well should animals complain and humans scold you, because when Day wants to break our backs with work, you sneak away and don't allow us to rest.]*

206

"Thow doost, allas, to shortly thyn office,
Thou rakel nyght, ther god, maker of kynde,
For thow so downward hastest of malice,
The corse and to oure hemysperie bynde,
That nevere mo under the ground thow wynde!
For thorugh thy rakel hying out of Troie,
Have I forgon thus hastili my joie."

[*"Alas, you do your office too quickly. Stubborn Night, may God, maker of all nature, curse you and bind you up to our hemisphere so that you can never again go beneath the earth! For, thanks to your stubborn rushing out of Troy, I must so quickly lose my joy."]*

207

This Troilus, that with tho wordes felte,
As thoughte hym tho, for pietous distresse
The blody teris from his herte melte,
As he that nevere yit swich hevynesse
Assayed hadde, out of so gret gladnesse,
Gan therwithal Criseyde, his lady deere,
In armes streyne, and seyde in this manere:

[Troilus, with these words felt—as he then thought with pitious dis-
tress—the bloody tears melt from his heart, so that he never yet suffered
such heaviness out of such great gladness. He gripped Criseyde, his dear
lady, tight in his arms and said:]

208

"O cruel day, accusour of the joie
That love and nyght han stole and faste iwryen,
Acorsed be thi comyng into Troye,
For every bore hath oon of thi bryghte eyen!
Envyous day, what list the so tespien?
What hastow lost? what sekist thow in this place?
Ther god thi light so quenche for his grace!

["O cruel Day, hostile witness of the joy that Love and Night have stolen
and carefully hidden, cursed be your coming into Troy, for every open-
ing in the house has one of your bright eyes. Envious Day, what makes
you want to look around so much? What have you lost? What are you
looking for in this house? May God for his grace put out your lights
[blind you]!]

209

"Allas, what han thise loveris the agilt,
Dispitous day? thyn be the pyne of helle!
For many a lovere hastow slayn, and wilt;
Thi pourynge in wol no wher late hem dwelle.
What profrestow thi light here for to selle?
Go selle it hem that smale selys grave;
We wol the nought, us nedeth no day have."

["Alas, how have these lovers sinned against you, contemptuous Day?
May you suffer the pains of hell! For many a lover you have murdered,
and will again. Your pouring in (of light) will nowhere let them live.
Why offer your light to sell in here? Go sell it to some jeweler who en-
graves tiny seals."]

210

And ek the sonne, Titan, wolde he chide,
And seyde: "O fool, wel may men the dispise,
That hast al nyght the dawyng by thi syde,
And suffrest hire so soone up fro the rise,
For to disesen loveris in this wyse.

What! hold thy bed ther, thow and ek thi Morwe,
I prey to god, so yeve yow bothe sorwe!"

[And also he would chide the Titan Sungod, and said, "O fool, well may men despise you who have the beautiful Dawn all night by your side and yet you force her to get up so early and leave you just to disturb lovers in this way. What ho, stay in your bed there, both you and your morning [Dawn], I pray God give you both deep sorrow!"]

211

Therwith ful soore he syghte, and thus he seyde:
"My lady right, and of my wele or wo
The welle and roote, O goodly myn Criseyde,
And shal I rise, allas, and shal I so?
Now fele I that myn herte moot a-two.
For how sholde I my lif an houre save,
Syn that with yow is al the lif ich have?

[He sighed heavily and said, "My true lady, the very well and root of my health or destruction, o my Criseyde, and shall I get up alas? Shall I? And now I feel that my heart might break in two, for how should I save an hour of my life when all the life I have is here with you?]

212

"What shal I don? for certes I not how,
Ne whanne, allas, I may the tyme see,
That in this plit I may ben eft with yow;
And of my lif, god woot how that shal be,
Syn that desir right now so streyneth me,
That I am dede anon, but I retourne.
How sholde I longe, allas, fro yow sojourne?

["What will I do? For I sure don't know how—nor when—I can see the time that I'll be with you like this again. And God knows about my fragile life, because desire right now grips me so hard that I'll soon be dead unless I get back to you. How could I possibly live away from you for long?]

213

"But natheles, myn owen lady bright,
Yit were it so that I wiste outrely,
That I, youre owen servant and youre knyght,

Were in youre herte iset as fermely
As ye in myn,—the which thyng, trewely,
Me levere were than thise worldes tweyne,—
Yit sholde I bet enduren al my peyne."

*["But nevertheless, my own bright lady, yet were it so that I would know
for sure that I, your own servant and your knight, were set as firmly in
your heart as you are in mine—the which knowledge truly I would
rather own than two whole worlds such as this one. Then should I better
endure all my pain."]*

214

To that Criseyde answerde thus anon,
And with a sik she seyde, "O herte deere,
The game, ywys, so ferforth now is gon,
That erst shal Phebus fallen fro his spere,
And everich egle ben the haukes feere,
And every roche out of his place sterte,
Or Troilus out of Criseydes herte.

*[On this cue, Criseyde answered quickly. With a sigh, she said, "Dear
heart, O, the game certainly is so far gone that Phoebus Apollo will fall
from his sphere and every eagle will become the hawk's best friend, and
every huge rock will jump out of his place before Troilus will jump from
from Criseyde's heart.]*

215

"Ye ben so depe inwith myn herte grave,
That, though I wolde it torne out of my thought,
As wisly verray god my soule save,
To dyen in the peyne, I koude nought.
And, for the love of God that us hath wrought,
Lat in youre brayn non other fantasie
So crepe, that it cause me to dye.

*["You have been so deeply engraven in my heart, that though I would
turn you out of my thoughts, as God save my soul, even to die in the
pain I could not. And for love of the God who made us all, let no other
fancy creep into your brain, since it might cause me to die.]*

216

"And that ye me wolde han as faste in mynde
As I have yow, that wolde I yow biseche;
And if I wiste sothly that to fynde,
God myghte nat a poynt my joies eche.
But, herte myn, withouten more speche,
Beth to me trewe, or ellis were it routhe;
For I am thyn, by god and by my trouthe.

*["Let me beseech you to hold me just as firmly in mind as I hold you;
and if I find this to be true, God could not add a pin to my joys. But,
dear heart, no more speech. Just be true to me, or else it were a terrible
shame, for I am yours by God and my truth.]*

217

"Beth glad, forthy, and lyve in sikernesse;
Thus seyde I nevere or now, ne shal to mo;
And if to yow it were a gret gladnesse
To torne ayeyn soone after that ye go,
As fayn wolde I as ye that it were so,
As wisly god myn herte brynge at reste";
And hym in armes tok and ofte keste.

*["Be glad then and live in certainty; these things I never said before nor
shall to others. And if for you it would be a great thing to turn around
and come right back, as much would I want it as you, as the all-
knowing God oversees my death." And she took him into her arms and
kissed him again and again.]*

218

Ayein his wil, sith it mot nedes be,
This Troilus up ros, and faste hym cledde,
And in his armes took his lady free
An hondred tyme, and on his wey hym spedde;
And with swich voys as though his herte bledde,
He seyde: "fare wel, dere herte swete,
Ther God us graunte sownde and soone to mete."

*[Against his will, since it must be, Troilus got up and quickly dressed,
and in his arms he took his lady free a hundred times, and rushed on
his way. And with such a voice as though his heart bled, he said, "Fare-*

*well, dear sweet heart, may God grant us sound health and also another
meeting soon."]*

219

To which no word for sorwe she answerde,
So soore gan his partyng hire distreyne;
And Troilus unto his paleys ferde,
As wobygon as she was, soth to seyne.

*[To this, for sorrow, she answered no word, so sorely did his parting
grasp her. And, truth to tell, Troilus walked to his palace, just as woe-
begone as she was.]*

3.1685–1715 (Troilus and Criseyde's Second Farewell and the Many to Follow)

243

But cruel day, so weylawey the stounde,
Gan for taproche, as they by sygnes knewe,
For which hem thoughte feelen dethis wownde;
So wo was hem, that changen gan hire hewe,
And day they gonnen to despise al newe,
Callyng it traitour, envyous, and worse;
And bitterly the dayes light thei corse.

*[But cruel day—alas, the time of pain—began to approach, as they
knew so well by the signs, for which they thought they felt death's
wound, so miserable they were, that their very color changed. And they
despised Day once anew, calling it traitor, envious, and worse. And
bitterly the day's light they curse.]*

244

Quod Troilus, "allas, now am I war
That Pirous and tho swifte steedes thre,
Which that drawen forth the sonnes char,
Han gon some bi-path in dispit of me;
That maketh it so soone day to be;
And, for the sonne hym hasteth thus to rise,
Ne shal I nevere don hym sacrifice."

[Said Troilus: "Alas, now I know that Pyrois [one of Apollo's four immortal horses] *and the other three swift steeds that draw the chariot of
the sun have taken a short cut to spite me—that make day so soon; and*

as for the Sun, he rushes thus to get up; never again will I do him any sacrifice"]

245

But nedes day departe hem moste soone,
And whan hire speche don was and hire cheere,
They twynne anon as they were wont to doone,
And setten tyme of metyng eft yfeere.
And many a nycht they wroughte in this manere.
And thus Fortune a tyme ledde in joie
Criseyde and ek this kynges sonne of Troie.

[But Day must split them up right away. When their speech was over and their fond looks, they twine themselves in each other once again, as they were wont to do, and set the time of their next meeting together. And many a night they worked in this manner, and thus Lady Fortune for a time led in joy Criseyde and also this son of the king of Troy.]

4.1687–1694 (Troilus and Criseyde's Final Farewell)

Criseyde speaks,

241

"And fare now wel, for tyme is that ye rise."

["And so, farewell, for it is time you get up."]

242

And after that they longe ypleyned hadde,
And ofte ykist, and streite in armes folde,
The day gan rise, and Troilus hym cladde,
And rewfullich his lady gan byholde,
As he that felte dethes cares colde.
And to hire grace he gan hym recomaunde;
Wher hym was wo, this holde I no demaunde.

[And after they had long complained and often kissed and directly in arms folded themselves, the day began to rise, and Troilus got dressed and ruefully he looked at his lady just as one who felt Death's freezing cares, and to her grace he recommended himself. There is no question that he was miserable.]

THE THIRTY-THIRD-NOVEL FROM MASUCCIO SALERNITANO'S *IL NOVELLINO*

Always on the lookout for material for plots of plays, Shakespeare was not only familiar with (1) *The Decameron* (1354) of Giovanni Boccaccio, a cycle of one hundred stories delivered by ten people ostensibly escaping the black plague, but also (2) the cycles of stories of Boccaccio's English and Italian disciples—including, among others, Chaucer and Masuccio Salernitano (of Salerno on the Amalfi coast below Naples). Masuccio, who was appointed secretary to Prince Roberto di Sanseverino of Salerno in 1463, produced his version of the lovers' tragedy and urban woes as the thirty-third of fifty stories in his cycle, narrated in five days in units of ten. Making appeals to his patron (and his purported capacity for love), the Duke of Amalfi (just as Shakespeare did, I believe, to Queen Elizabeth), Masuccio presents the bare bones of the plot of *Romeo and Juliet*. He includes the furtive marriage of aristocratic young lovers, the exile of the hero, the avoidance of the heroine's forced second marriage through the use of a sleep potion to feign death, the missed messages, and the ostensible suicides at the end. Masuccio places the story in and around Siena and Alexandria—not Verona and Mantua—and names his lovers Mariotto and Gian-Giannozza.

Notice the superior wisdom and marriage arrangement of the girl, including the motive to the furtive marriage (in this case with the help of an Augustinian, not a Franciscan, friar with magical skill). Note also the exile of the hero following a death (due here to a head blow on an enemy with a stick), the emphasis on Lady Fortune as a force in their affairs, and the crossing of messengers as in Greek New Comedy and in Greek Romance. Masuccio's tale is told with skill and economy—exactly what Shakespeare loved about the Italian cycles, related as they are to Greek Romance and many medieval genres. Note that the plot-description has Gian-Giannozza die on Mariotto's body, as does Juliet; but Masuccio's actual story has her die of starvation and grief in a convent (which forms the basis of one of Friar Laurence's proposals).

FROM MASUCCIO SALERNITANO'S THIRTY-THIRD NOVEL FROM *IL NOVELLINO* (1476)

(Translated from the Italian into English, with an introduction and full bibliography by Maurice Jonas, and published by Davis & Orioli, London, 1917. Text modernized and Americanized by the editor.)

Argument [plot]

Mariotto of Siena, enamored of Gian-Giannozza, flies to Alexandria as a murderer. Giannozza feigns to be dead, and rising from her tomb, goes to find her lover. He, learning of her death, returns to Siena to die. He is recognized, arrested, and beheaded. The lady does not find him in Alexandria, returns to Siena, and finds her lover beheaded. She dies with grief upon his body.

To my illustrious lord, the Duke of Amalfi.

Introduction

The more diverse and unhappy are the varied chances of love, the more does it behoove tender and gentle lovers to relate them in their writings. Because, my illustrious lord, I have known you for a long time not only caught in the nets of love but as a prudent lover, it has now pleased me to give you a full relation of a pitiful misfortune of two unhappy lovers, so that with your habitual prudence and perfect wisdom, you may give a just judgment in your opinion, after considering every circumstance, as to which of the two most fervently loved.

The Tale

In these days, the following tale was related in a company of fair ladies by a citizen of your town of Siena of little standing:

Not long ago, there was in Siena a youth of good family, courteous and handsome, Mariotto Mignanelli by name. He, being deeply enamored of a lovely girl, called Giannozza, daughter of a notable citizen of the house of Saraceni, in course of time grew to be beloved by her with equal ardor.

After he had fed his eyes for a long time on the sweet flowers of love, and each of them desiring to taste its sweetest fruits, and having sought many ways to do so, and found none prudent, the maiden, who was no less wise than beautiful, determined to take him for her husband, so that, if by contrary fate their enjoyment was cut short, they might have a shield to cover the wrong done.

To complete the matter with action, they bribed an Augustine friar and, by his aid, secretly married. With this clever excuse, they entirely satisfied their longing desires.

When they had enjoyed for some time the fruits of this furtive but partly lawful love, it happened that wicked and hostile fortune reversed all their present and future desires.

One day, Mariotto having words with an honorable citizen, from words came deeds, and the quarrel grew to such an extent that Mariotto wounded him with a stick on his head and from this wound, he, in a brief time, died.

For this crime, Mariotto hid himself. When the Court had made a diligent search for him and neither the lord of the town nor the mayor had succeeded in finding him, he was not only condemned to perpetual exile, but publicly proclaimed a rebel.

How great was the supreme grief of the two most wretched lovers, so lately wed, and how bitter their tears at the thought of what they believed to be their endless separation, he alone who has been pricked by such wounds can truly tell. So deep and bitter it was, that at their last parting, they seemed for a long while to have died in each other's arms.

Yet, subduing his grief a little, and hoping in time to return to his native country, Mariotto determined to go to Alexandria, where he had an uncle named Ser Nicolo Mignanelli, a man engaged in great business and a well-known merchant.

In a quiet fashion, knowing that they could visit each other, though from afar, with letters, but with infinite tears, the loving couple parted.

The unhappy Mariotto set forth, having told his brother all his secrets and warmly entreated him above all things to keep him minutely and constantly informed of all that befell his Giannozza.

With the instruction that had been given him, he entered on his journey and made for Alexandria. In due time, he arrived there and found his uncle, who received him with joy and affection. Having heard all that had happened, like a wise man, grieving not so much for the murder that had been committed as for the offence given to such an important family, and knowing that to repent for what is past is next to useless, he strove with Mariotto to find a way out and think in time to provide a suitable remedy.

He engaged him in his business and kept him with him with great kindness and almost constant tears, for there was hardly a month that Mariotto did not receive many letters from his Giannozza and his brother, which, in their sad plight and separation, were a wonderful comfort to each of them.

Such was the state of affairs when it happened that the father of Giannozza, being entreated and importuned by many to marry her, she was so pressed by him to take a husband that she could no longer refuse.

Her afflicted mind was so distraught by the continual struggle that she would have preferred death to such a life.

Having lost all hope of the return of her dear, secret husband, and knowing that to reveal the truth would have availed her nothing, but rather brought her greater reproof, she determined, by a means not only strange, but dangerous and cruel, and perhaps never before heard of, by placing her honor and life in danger, to atone for so many failures.

Helped by her great courage, she replied to her father that she would satisfy his wishes.

At once, she sent for the friar, who was the first weaver of the plot, and very cautiously explained to him what she meant to do, and begged him to favor her with his aid. He listened to her story and, as friars are wont, showed himself a little surprised, timid, and slow to action. But she, by her bravery and the magic of St. John of the Golden Mouth, made him bold and eager to follow up the enterprise.

Such was her eagerness that the friar swiftly departed and he himself, being experienced in the matter, made up a certain water with certain concoctions of various powders that, when the draught was ready and she had drunk it, it would not only make her sleep for three days, but seem to be really dead.

He sent it to the lady, who had first fully informed Mariotto by a courier of what she meant to do. When she learned from the friar what she had to do, with great joy she drank that draught. After a little while, she sank into such a swoon that she fell, as if dead, upon the ground.

Her maids, shrieking loudly, made the old father and many others rush to her aid at the cry, to find his only and so dearly beloved daughter dead. With grief that he had never before felt, he hastily summoned the physicians, beseeching them to call her back to life; but none were able, and all certainly believed that she had died in the swoon.

All day and the following night, they patiently watched her and saw no sign but of death.

With infinite grief of the afflicted father, and with tears and laments of her family and friends, and of all the Sienese in general, she was buried the next day, with pompous funeral ceremonies, in an honorable tomb in the church of St. Augustine.

But, in the middle of the night, she was taken by the venerable friar, with the aid of a companion, as they had established, from the tomb and brought to his room.

The hour was drawing near when the potion would have run its course, and they, with heat and other necessary means, brought her back to life.

She recovered herself, and in a few days, disguised as a monk, went with the good friar to Porto Pisano, where the galleys of Aigues-Mortes, making for Alexandria, had to touch. Finding that they sailed to Alexandria she embarked. But as sea journeys, through unfavorable winds or new needs of merchandise, are usually much longer than travelers would wish, it happened for various reasons that the galleys delayed their arrival for some months beyond the appointed time.

Now Gargano, the brother of Mariotto, following the instructions that his dear brother had left him, at once, with several letters entrusted to merchants, informed the unhappy Mariotto in detail of the sudden death of his dear Giannozza, and of how she had been mourned for, and where she had been buried, and how, not long after, the old and loving father had departed this life from his great grief.

Adverse and wicked fortune was much more favorable to this news than to the messages which Giannozza had sent. And perhaps because the bitter and bloody death that befell those lovers caused it to happen, the messenger of Giannozza, on a boat sailing for Alexandria with grain, was taken prisoner by the corsairs and slain.

Mariotto had no other news than from his brother. Believing all the bitter tidings to be most certain, and grieving, and afflicted with good cause (think, if you have any pity in your heart), he sorrowed so greatly that he determined to live his life no longer.

The entreaties and consolation of his dear uncle were of no avail. After long and bitter weeping, he determined to return to Siena for the last time, and, if fortune would favor him at all, keep his return secret and cast himself, in his disguise, at the foot of the tomb where he believed his Giannozza to be buried, and there to weep as if their lives were ended.

But if by misfortune he was recognized, he thought he would gladly be condemned as a murderer, knowing that she was already dead whom he loved more than himself and who loved him with equal love.

Having determined upon this course, he awaited the departure of the Venetian galleys for the West, without saying a word to his uncle. He embarked, and, with great joy, hastened to his predestined death. Having arrived at Naples, from there by land he proceeded to Tuscany with all haste.

Disguised as a pilgrim, he entered Siena, known by none, and betook himself to an unfrequented inn. Without making himself known to his friends, at a suitable hour, he went to the church where his Giannozza was buried, and before her tomb bitterly wept.

Willingly, if he could, would he have entered the tomb, so that he might have as his companion in death forever that delicate body which in life he was not allowed to enjoy. All his thoughts were intent on this.

Without abating his accustomed grief and constant tears, he cautiously procured certain tools. One evening at vespers, he hid himself inside the church. During the night, he worked so hard that he placed the lid of the sepulchre on props, and was going to enter into it, when the sacristan, going to ring the bell for matins, heard a certain noise. He went to see who it was, and found Mariotto at his work, as we have related.

Thinking him a thief who would be robbing the dead bodies, he cried out, "Thief, thief!" All the friars ran up and seized him, and opened the doors. Many laymen entered the church and found the wretched lover, who, though he was clothed in vile rags, was at once recognized to be Mariotto Mignanelli.

He was detained in the church. Before dawn, all Siena was full of the news, which reached the ears of the Court, who ordered the mayor to go and arrest him and quickly do that which the laws and the State commanded.

So, a prisoner in fetters, Mariotto was led to the palace of the mayor. When he was flogged, without needing long tortures, he faithfully confessed the cause of his desperate return. Though all alike had the greatest pity for him, and amongst the women he was bitterly wept for and thought the only perfect lover in the world, and each of them would have willingly redeemed him with her own life, yet he was at once condemned by the law to be beheaded. When the time arrived, without his friends or parents being able to aid him, the sentence was carried out.

The unhappy Giannozza, with the escort of the said friar, after many and varied troubles, arrived in Alexandria at the house of Ser Nicolo. When she made herself known to him and told him who she was and why she had come, and related to him all that had befallen her, he was at once filled with grief and amazement. After honorably receiving her and having made her dress again in woman's clothes and bid the friar farewell, how and in what despair at the news he had received, he told her Mariotto had left, unbeknown to all; and how he himself had wept for Mariotto as though he were dead.

Consider well, you who have the power of thought, if the great grief [of] Giannozza grew less, when she thought of this and all the other woes that had befallen herself and her lover. But, recovering herself a little, she took counsel with her new-found father. After many discussions— bathed in warm tears, she and Ser Nicolo determined to go as swiftly as possible to Siena, and whether they found Mariotto alive or dead, at least to vindicate the lady's honor with such remedies as their extreme necessity allowed.

So when they had arranged affairs as best they could, the lady dressed again as a man, and, wind favoring them, in a short time sailed to the Tuscan shores and disembarked at Piombino. From there, they secretly went to a farm of Ser Nicolo, near Siena. Asking the news, they found that their Mariotto had been beheaded three days before.

On hearing the bitter tidings, although they had always thought it certain, yet being now most sure of it, how each and either remained as if dead, the sad case itself will amply show.

The laments of Giannozza and her bitter cries of "alas!" were so passionate that a heart of marble would have been moved to pity. Yet she was constantly comforted by Ser Nicolo. With many wise counsels, full of kindness, they determined after such a loss only to think of the honor of their great house. The poor maiden decided secretly to shut herself up in a pious convent, and there bitterly weep over her misfortunes, the death of her lover, and her own misery as long as she lived.

This she very cautiously did and completely carried out her intention. She let no one know but the abbess. With intense grief and tears of blood and little food and no sleep, continually calling for her dear Mariotto, in a very short time ended her wretched days.

NOTES

1. Thus, exactly what Ovid was up to in his not-so-innocent seamstress' story of Pyramus and Thisbe, with all its apostrophes (poetic calling on elements not present, or even inanimate, such as "Wall") with its epic "Babylonian girl," with its image of a lioness shaking a cloak or veil or muffler without Thisbe in it, with its epic simile of artificial water pipes, and its black-berried mulberry tree/bush, Shakespeare may have known better than we do.

2. A metaphrase (word for word) rather than a paraphrase (looser version in other, usually modern, words).

3. Modern fiction, from Tarzan and the Western to comic strips like *Superman, Wonder Woman, Batman, The Shadow*, and *Spiderman*; as well as movie shoot-em-ups starring Clint Eastwood, Sigourney Weaver, Steven Seagal, Arnold Schwarzenegger, Sylvester Stallone, and others.

STUDY QUESTIONS

1. The tale of Pyramus and Thisbe in Ovid's *Metamorphoses* sentimentalizes the lovers; they are young and impetuous and have bad luck with a lioness. Does Shakespeare shift the blame for his lovers' fate to the lovers themselves in *Romeo and Juliet*? If so, how?

2. The image of the lioness shaking Thisbe's cloak may be naturalistic, but it is ironic that Ovid adds "without Thisbe in it." This is Ovidian understated irony. Where do you find such irony in Shakespeare's play? For example, is there Ovidian irony in the Prologue? Recall that the Prologue—possibly delivered by Shakespeare himself in the original performance—was probably the part of a very old man.

3. Ovid's story of Pyramus and Thisbe is framed by a narrative in which the sisters are seen as irreligious in replacing the true religion of Dionysus with the false religion of love. Is there any hint that this is the case with Romeo and Juliet, that their idea of love is replacing the Christian god? Consider the shared sonnet when they first meet. Where else is the same tendency evident? Develop your thoughts with precise discussion of the evidence. Include specific quotes.

4. Compare the extraordinary number of references to birds in Chaucer's aubades and Shakespeare's balcony scenes of *Romeo and Juliet*. Develop a paper on the subject entitled "Chaucer's and Shakespeare's Aviaries," and present it to the class with pertinent recorded bird songs, if you can locate them.

5. You know something of Troilus and Criseyde and Romeo and Juliet. Research the love of Tristan and Isolde in Gottfried von Strassburg's *Tristan*, and develop a report on the subject.

6. Masuccio Salernitano's thirty-third novella places much of the action in Siena. Look up Siena in encyclopedias, and write a report on why it might be a more likely location of the vendetta that was placed by later authors in Verona. Recall that in Franco Zeffirelli's movie version of *Romeo and Juliet* (1972), he placed the central scene of strife in the Campo (central square and racetrack) in Siena.

7. Research and write a report on the career of Ovid and his relationship with Caesar Augustus.

8. Research and write a report on the career of Geoffrey Chaucer and three kings of England: Edward III, Richard II, and Henry IV.

9. Research and write a report on the careers of Masuccio Salernitano, the Prince of Salerno, and the Duke of Amalfi.

10. Research and write a report on Giovanni Boccaccio, Masuccio's story-telling predecessor in the Naples area of southern Italy.

TOPICS FOR WRITTEN OR ORAL EXPLORATION

1. Create your own play entitled *Pyramus and Thisbe*. Is it possible to include many of the elements of *Romeo and Juliet* merely by amplification (fictional enlargement)? This might have been one of Shakespeare's exercises in Latin at the New School thanks to a Latin composition manual that Chaucer also knew, Geoffrey of Vinsauf's *Poetria Nova*. Present your piece to the class, and have classmates critique it.

2. The fabric of Ovid's poetry is Olympian myth. Could the same be said of Shakespeare's—even though Shakespeare and his play are apparently Christian? Is there a pagan element in Shakespeare's characters' references to wheels of fortune; Apollo, the sun-god; Aurora, the goddess of dawn; or Diana, the goddess of the hunt and the moon? Select three examples from both Ovid and Shakespeare, and compare them. Take a position on Shakespeare's "paganism," and develop a thesis on the subject.

3. Read the first four books of Ovid's *Metamorphoses*. Develop a paper on the importance of Shakespeare's use of Ovid's figures, from Apollo and Phaeton, to Diana and Actaeon, to Dionysus and Pyramus and Thisbe, to Shakespeare's Romeo and Juliet. Be specific and argumentative.

4. *The Ephesian Tale* is supposed to have come out of the Second Sophistic period of Greek literature, indicating a period of word-magicians. Look for high rhetorical moments in the passage quoted from Xenophon's work. What conclusion do you make about those speeches designed to enlist your sympathy? Subtitle your paper "Xenophon of Ephesus' Versions of Pathos (When Art Causes Sadness or Tears)" and develop an argument on the subject.

5. Develop a comparative essay on Eudoxus, the doctor figure of *The Ephesian Tale*, and Friar Laurence. Are they both welcome outsiders in very awkward positions? Are they both more doctor or magician? Take a position and develop a thesis in a well-evidenced paper.

6. Research the nature of the formerly aristocratic sport of hawking. Explain how the references to hawking in Chaucer and in *Romeo and Juliet* combine to give a medieval aristocratic flavor to Chaucer's poem and to Shakespeare's play.

7. Chaucer's Troilus and Criseyde in bed say a number of things to each

other that are the product of sexual politics, such as Troilus' stating that he does not know if Criseyde loves him or not (3.213). Compare Romeo and Juliet in the two balcony scenes. Do they engage in sexual politics? Come to a conclusion and write it up in a coherent comparative piece.

8. Masuccio's thirty-third tale contains a number of direct references to his patron, the Duke of Amalfi, and his ability to love as well as his nobility. Is the effect one of elaborate compliment, or is there more to it? Discuss Masuccio's asides and references in a paper that also explores the system of patronage of artists during the Renaissance.

9. Does Masuccio's mention of Alexandria give his story a high romantic (or purely fictional) quality, as if it were a version of Greek Romance? Do some research on what Alexandria "means" in Greek Romance, and show how different it is from Shakespeare's Mantua. Develop a thesis on the subject in a comparative paper.

SUGGESTED READINGS

Anderson, William S., ed. *Ovid's* Metamorphoses: *Books 1–5*. London and Norman: University of Oklahoma Press, 1997.

Bate, Jonathan. *Shakespeare and Ovid*. Oxford: Oxford University Press, 1994; orig. Oxford: Clarendon Press, 1993.

Benson, Larry, ed. *The Riverside Chaucer*, 3rd ed. Based on the edition by F. N. Robinson. Boston: Houghton Mifflin, 1987.

Boccaccio, Giovanni. *The Decameron*, 2nd ed. Trans. and ed. by H. McWilliam. London and New York: Penguin, 1995.

Coghill, Nevill, trans. and ed. *Chaucer's Troilus and Criseyde*. New York: Penguin, 1971.

Frantzen, Allen J. *Troilus and Criseyde: The Poem and the Frame*. Twayne's Master Studies no. 113. New York: Twayne, 1993.

Gordon, Robert Kay, trans. and ed. *The Story of Troilus*. New York: Dutton, 1964.

Hadas, Moses, trans. and ed. *Three Greek Romances*. The Library of Liberal Arts. New York: Bobbs Merrill, 1964; orig. New York: Doubleday, 1953.

Hughes, Ted, and Christopher Lebrun. *Shakespeare's Ovid (Metamorphoses, Selections)*. London: Eritharmon, 1994.

Krapp, George Philip, ed. *Chaucer's Troilus and Criseyde (Rendered into Modern English)*. New York: Random House, 1972.

Root, Robert Kilburn. *The Book of Troilus and Criseyde*, 2nd ed. Princeton: Princeton University Press, 1930; orig. 1926.

Windeatt, B. A. *Chaucer's Troilus and Criseyde*. London: Longman, 1990.

3

The Narrative Source of *Romeo and Juliet*

INTRODUCTION

The tale of Romeo and Juliet progresses toward Shakespeare's plot in an Italian version by Luigi da Porto. In this version the lovers first appear in Verona with the names Romeo and Giulietta, now scions of warring families with actual Veronese family names, Montecchi and Cappelletti. Matteo Bandello, the bishop of Agen, polished da Porto's story for his storybook *Novelle* (1554–1573), which was based on Boccaccio's *Decameron* (1354). The sole incontestable source for Shakespeare's planning and writing of *Romeo and Juliet* is the Elizabethan sailor and narrative poet, Arthur Brooke's version of Pierre Boaistau's translation of Bandello's story, now called *The Tragedy of Romeus and Juliet*, published in 1562. Brooke also refers to a lost play about Romeo and Juliet that he might have seen at Cambridge or Oxford or on the continent.

Given Brooke's additions, such as the Apothecary (druggist) and his extension of speeches and Chaucerian moralization, Brooke's work is by far the most developed version (before Shakespeare's) of the story of the young Veronese lovers and their double suicide. Both sources of *Romeus* may have been available to Shakespeare, but he seems to have used only Brooke and suggestions from elsewhere (see Chapter 2), some of which might have come from the other, lost play.

In adapting the romance to the stage Shakespeare echoes the words and events of Brooke, yet through a sort of creative mistranslation he changes every speech and event for heightened dramatic effect and thematic reinforcement. For example, even though Brooke gives Shakespeare versions of the twelve main events of *Romeo and Juliet*, Shakespeare makes them entirely new.

The four central themes of Shakespeare's play also appear in undeveloped form in *Romeus and Juliet*. First, there is Romeus' unnamed first love, her sudden replacement by Juliet, and the shared desperation of the young lovers. Shakespeare reduced Juliet's age from fifteen to thirteen, leaving Romeus (now Romeo) at about eighteen to twenty years of age. But the playwright removed the sense of grief from the shared love of his principals, relegating all painful or bitter love in Brooke to Romeo's love for Rosaline, not Juliet (see Chapter 4). Though their feelings are strained and idealistic and contain a Gothic or horror element, Shakespeare's Romeo and Juliet are quite positive about their love. It contains little grief except for brief misunderstandings and the thought of separation. If Juliet suddenly "hates" Romeo when she hears he has killed her favorite cousin, Tybalt, she regrets her words immediately when the Nurse makes the mistake of agreeing with her.

Second, the vendetta between the Capulets and Montagues is developed in Brooke over several months of narrative time, especially in his characterization of the firebrand, Tybalt; but Shakespeare developed a much larger role for Tybalt that intersects with the love plot on several occasions for effect, and he reduced the time from about nine months to five days. Shakespeare's characterization of Tybalt can actually dominate a production of *Romeo and Juliet*, as proven in 1971 when Michael York as Tybalt stole the show in Franco Zeffirelli's movie version (see Chapter 5); in contrast, Brooke's Tybalt only appears in a single scene of bravery, heroic sarcasm, and doomed dueling and as a corpse in the Capulet family crypt.

Third, in multiple scenes Shakespeare developed dramatic foils (opposite characters) for Tybalt in Mercutio, Benvolio, and the Capulet men, Sampson and Gregory, who do not appear in Brooke. Brooke's Mercutio is a more courtly figure who appears (with mysteriously cold hands) only once, sitting at a table at the Capulet ball. Brooke also suggests the mystical notion of the yoking of contraries in the concoctions of Friar Laurence—he is a full-fledged white magician (a creator of magical potions for the good). Shakespeare, however, noted Brooke's other references to the sacred doctrine of contrariety, of medicine and poison, of rule and non-rule, and of the sea as giver and taker away of life.

Fourth, there is an overpowering sense of rush in Brooke's story. This is underscored by continual evocation of the time (often involving seascapes, as in Homer's *Odyssey*), even though Brooke's story covers a significantly longer period.[1] With its continual references to fate and fortune and predestination and free will, as well as its chronographia, Brooke's romance never lets the reader feel easy about the future. Nonetheless, in contradiction to his own preface (which contains a diatribe against passionate excess and intrigue), Brooke treats his Nurse and Priest and the marital love of his principals sympathetically. In fact, beyond a wealth of characterization, Shakespeare's only notable thematic addition to the story is the witty formulation of love psychology and sexual politics implicit in the sophisticated English sonnets of Philip Sidney, Edmund Spenser, and Shakespeare himself—most of which were composed around the time of the writing of his play (see Chapter 4).

Again, however, there is a connection with Brooke. Brooke published his *Tragedy of Romeus and Juliet* with an eccentric printer and amateur versifier named Richard Tottel, who had recently completed editing a collection of sonnets and songs by members of Brooke's generation. This collection was eventually published as *Tottel's Miscellany* (1557). It is apparent that many of the sonnets (translations and adaptations, often of the Italian Petrarch) by Sir Thomas Wyatt and Henry Howard, Earl of Surrey, were "regularized" by Tottel, who had the mistaken notion that poetry was trying to effect an absolutely regular beat and regular rhyming—not only in sound but in sight, such as "feast" to be rhymed not with "guest" but "geast." This is possible only in Middle English (1150–1450), where it might also rhyme.

Without a manuscript of Brooke, it is impossible to gauge what ill effect Tottel's efforts might have had on Brooke's text (which must have horrified Tottel in its irregularity, not only of rhythm but of rhyme). Brooke seems to have loved the slant, or approximate rhyme, of "guest" and "feast," using it three times in the work. His rhythm, so-called poulter's measure, is designed to have the memorable—and easily memorized—rambling effect of the ballad with its widely variable syllable count and its sudden, song-like accents.

The term "poulter's measure"—a poulter was a poultry retailer—was originally a joke-name based on the fact that if one bought a dozen eggs in Tudor England a thirteenth was free, like the later "baker's dozen." Thirteener, or poulter's measure, meant couplets (two rhymed lines), the first with six accents or strong beats, the second with seven (often with twelve beats, then fourteen). There were emphatic pauses (cesuras) in each line, the first with three pause three accents, the second with four pause three accents. This resembles the standard ballad rhythm, as in Samuel Coleridge's famous *Rime of the Ancient Mariner*: "Water, water, everywhere / And not a drop to drink."

One of Brooke's most influential moments occurs when young Juliet is worried that the older Romeus is a dangerous serial lover (like Theseus). This is an idea that Shakespeare's Juliet does not share except momentarily, but it is developed at length in *Romeo and Juliet*'s comic twin, *A Midsummer Night's Dream*. Brooke's Juliet says to herself in an elaborate complaint after the lovers have met with Mercutio,

> What if his subtle brain to feign have taught his tongue,
> And so the snake that lurks in grass thy tender heart hath
>   stung?   (385)

The comparison of Romeus to the devil in the garden is implicit following the pauses before "to feign" (both "to love" and "to pretend"—and internally rhymed with "brain"—and before "thy tender heart," a reminder of Juliet's youth and sensitivity. The second line with its four/three accentuation and its mass of one-syllable words is terribly long for effect. That is to say, on a stop-watch the words would take more seconds than normal to read aloud because of pauses between single-syllable words and the pronunciation of the triple and double consonants in "lurks," "tender," and "stung." The line's length thus imitates the slow action of a snake in the grass; one finds echoes of this in Spenser and even the romantic poet Blake. And the line emphatically reminds us of Juliet's fear of betrayal.

This kind of rambling poetry, which was ridiculed among the next generation of poets, is powerful and should be read aloud to savor its full effects. This was done often in Shakespeare's day, given the price of books. Its singsong quality reminded the audience of the heroic ballads that first glorified love, affection, and lovers put upon by society and vendetta in the late medieval era. Brooke is by no means the unsophisticated poet that his Chaucerian archaisms (antique terms like "eyne" for eyes, "eke" for also) and rambling poulter's measure might suggest to modern ears. The fact that his themes are shared so often by Shakespeare results from the poets' common narrative and thematic sources in Ovid and Chaucer.

SELECTIONS FROM THE NARRATIVE SOURCE
OF *ROMEO AND JULIET*

I have modernized Brooke's text and removed his editor's (Tottel's) slashes for pauses and many of his spurious sight rhymes. My notes are in the form of glosses bracketed within the text. Line numbers are provided for easy reference. Numbered heads reflect the twelve events in Shakespeare's play.

FROM ARTHUR BROOKE'S *ROMEUS AND JULIET* (1562)
(London in Fleet Street, within the Temple Bar, at the Sign of the
Hand and Star, by Richard Tottill the xix day of November,
An. Do. 1562)

To the Reader

. . . And to this end, good Reader, is this tragical matter written, to describe unto thee a couple of unfortunate lovers, thralling [enslaving] themselves to unhonest desire; neglecting the authority and advice of parents and friends; conferring their principal counsels with drunken gossips and superstitious friars (the naturally fit instruments of unchastity); attempting all adventures of peril for th'attaining of their wished lust; using auricular confession, the key of whoredom and treason, for furtherance of their purpose; abusing the honorable name of lawful marriage to cloak the shame of stolen contracts; finally by all means of unhonest life hasting to most unhappy death. . . .

The Argument

1   Love hath inflamed twain [two] by sudden sight,
    And both do grant the thing that both desire.
    They wed in shrift [confessional] by counsel of a friar.
    Young Romeus climbs fair Juliet's bower by night.
5   Three months he doth enjoy his chief delight.
    By Tybalt's rage provoked unto ire [anger],
    He payeth death to Tybalt for his hire [service].
    A banished man he 'scapes by secret flight.
    New marriage is offered to his wife.
10 She drinks a drink that seems to reave [take away] her breath:
    They bury her that sleeping yet hath life.

Her husband hears the tidings of her death.
He drinks his bane [poison]. And she with Romeus' knife,
When she awakes, herself, alas! she slayeth.

Romeus and Juliet

1   There is beyond the Alps, a town of ancient fame,
     Whose bright renown yet shineth clear: Verona men it name;
     Built in a happy time, built on a fertile soil,
     Maintained by the heavenly fates, and by the townish toil
        [work]. . . .
25   There were two ancient stocks [families], which Fortune high
        did place
     Above the rest, indued [endowed] with wealth, and nobler of
        their race,
     Loved of the common sort, loved of the prince alike. . . .
30   The one was cleped [called] Capulet, and th'other Montague.
     A wonted [usual] use it is, that men of likely sort, similar
     (I wot [know] not by what fury forced) envy each other's port
        [carriage].
     So these, whose equal state bred envy pale of hue,
     And then, of grudging envy's root, black hate and rancor
        [bitterness] grew.

   [1. Romeus Reveals His Love of the Unnamed Woman (Shakespeare's
       Rosaline) to an Unnamed Friend (Shakespeare's Benvolio?)]

53   One Romeus, who was of race a Montague,
     Upon whose tender chin as yet no manlike beard there grew,
55   Whose beauty and whose shape so far the rest did stain,
     That from the chief of Verona youth he greatest fame did gain,
     Hath found a maid so fair (he found so foul his hap [chance]),
     Whose beauty, shape, and comely grace, did so his heart entrap
     That from his own affairs, his thought she did remove . . .
101 But one among the rest, the trustiest of his feres [fellows],
     Far more than he with counsel filled, and riper of his years,
     'Gan sharply him rebuke, such love to him he bare,
     That he was fellow of his smart [pain], and partner of his care.
105 "What mean'st thou, Romeus," quoth he, "what doting [fond]
        rage
     Doth make thee thus consume away the best part of thine age,
     In seeking her that scorns, and hides her from thy sight . . . ?
131 But if unto thy will so much in thrall [slavery] thou art,
     Yet in some other place bestow thy witless wand'ring heart.

Choose out some worthy dame, her honor thou and serve,
Who will give ear to thy complaint, and pity ere [before] thou
    sterve [die]. . . .''

[2. At Capulet's Feast, Romeus Meets Juliet]

155   The weary winter nights restore the Christmas games,
And now the season doth invite to banquet townish dames.
And first in Capel's house, the chief of all the kin
Spar'th for no cost, the wonted [usual] use of banquets to
    begin,
No lady fair or foul was in Verona town,
160   No knight or gentleman of high or low renown,
But Capulet himself hath bid unto his feast,
Or by his name in paper sent, appointed as a guest.
Young damsels thither flock, of bachelors a rout [crowd],
Not so much for the banquet's sake, as beauties to search out.
165   But not a Montague would enter at his gate,
(For as you heard, the Capulets and they were at debate [war])
Save Romeus, and he, in mask with hidden face,
The supper done, with other five did press [crowd] into the
    place. . . .
197   At length he saw a maid, right fair, of perfect shape,
Which Theseus [detective hero of Athens and serial lover] or
    Paris [Trojan ravisher of Helen] would have chosen to their
    rape.
Whom erst [before] he never saw; of all she pleased him most;
200   Within himself he said to her, ''Thou justly may'st thee boast
Of perfect shape's renown, and beauty's sounding praise,
Whose like he ne [nor] hath, ne [nor] shall be seen, ne [nor]
    liveth in our days.''
And whilst he fixed on her his partial pierced eye,
His former love, for which of late he ready was to die,
205   Is now as quite forgot, as it had never been. . . .
223   Whilst Juliet, for so this gentle damsel hight [is called],
From side to side on every one did cast about her sight:
At last her floating eyes were anchored fast on him. . . .
249   The whilst our Romeus a place had warely [secretly] won,
Nigh to the seat where she must sit, the dance once being
    done.
Fair Juliet turned to her chair with pleasant cheer [face]
And glad she was her Romeus approached was so near.
At th'one side of her chair her lover Romeo,
And on the other side there sat one called Mercutio;

255   A courtier that each where was highly had in price,
　　　For he was courteous of his speech, and pleasant of device
　　　　[tricky speech].
　　　Even as a lion would among the lambs be bold,
　　　Such was among the bashful maids Mercutio to behold.
　　　With friendly grip he seized fair Juliet's snowish hand:
260   A gift he had that Nature gave him in his swathing band
　　　　[swaddling clothes, i.e., from infancy],
　　　That frozen mountain ice was never half so cold,
　　　As were his hands, though ne'er so near the fire he did them
　　　　hold.
　　　As soon as had the knight the virgin's right hand raught
　　　　[grasped],
　　　Within his trembling hand her left hath loving Romeus caught.
265   For he wist [knew] well himself for her abode most pain,
　　　And well he wist [knew] she loved him best, unless she list
　　　　[wanted] to feign.
　　　Then she with tender hand his tender palm hath pressed;
　　　What joy, trow [believe] you, was grafted, [engrafted] so in
　　　　Romeus' cloven [cut] breast . . . ?
284   "What chance," quoth he, "un'ware to me, O lady mine, is
　　　　hapt [chanced],
　　　That gives you worthy cause my coming here to bliss?"
　　　Fair Juliet was come again unto herself by this:
　　　First ruthfully [with pity] she looked, then said with smiling
　　　　cheer:
　　　"Marvel no whit, my heart's delight, my only knight and fere
　　　　[fellow],
　　　Mercutio's icy hand had all-to frozen mine,
290   And of thy goodness thou again hast warmed it with thine. . . ."
309   Even with his ended tale, the torches' dance had end,
　　　And Juliet of force [necessarily] must part from her new chosen
　　　　friend.
　　　His hand she clasped hard, and all her parts did shake,
　　　When leisureless with whisp'ring voice thus did she answer
　　　"You are no more your own, dear friend, than I am yours,
　　　My honor saved, pressed t'obey your will, while life
　　　　endures. . . ."

[Juliet with the Nurse]

344   An ancient dame she called to her, and in her ear 'gan round.
　　　This old dame in her youth had nursed her with her milk,
　　　With slender needle taught her sew, and how to spin with silk.

"What twain are those," quoth she, "which press [crowd] unto
the door,
Whose pages in their hand do bear two torches light before?"
And then as each of them had of his household name,

350 So she him named yet once again, the young and wily dame.
"And tell me, who is he with visor in his hand,
That yonder doth in masking weed [clothing] beside the
window stand?"
"His name is Romeus," said she, "a Montague,
Whose father's pride first stirred the strife which both your
households rue [regret]."

355 The word of Montague her joys did overthrow,
And straight instead of happy hope, despair began to grow.
"What hap [chance] have I," quoth she, "to love my father's
foe?
What, am I weary of my weal [health]? What, do I wish my
woe?"

[3. Later, Juliet and Romeus Meet and Vow to Marry]

467 Impatient of her woe, she happed [chance] to lean [rest] one
night
Within her window, and anon [soon] the moon did shine so
bright
That she espied [saw] her love: her heart revived sprang
[leapt]. . . .

491 "O Romeus, of your life too lavas [careless] sure you are,
That in this place, and at this time, to hazard it you dare.
What if your deadly foes, my kinsmen, saw you here
Like lions wild, your tender parts asunder would they tear. . . .

535 But if your thought be chaste, and have on virtue ground,
If wedlock be the end and mark which your desire hath found,
Obedience set aside, unto my parents due,
The quarrel eke [also] that long ago between our households
grew,
Both me and mine I will all whole to you betake [give],

540 And following you whereso you go, my father's house forsake.
But if by wanton love and by unlawful suit
You think in ripest years to pluck my maidenhood's dainty
fruit,
You are beguiled; and now your Juliet you beseech
To cease your suit, and suffer her to live among her likes. . . ."

553 "Since, lady, that you like to honor me so much
As to accept me for your spouse, I yield myself for such.

In true witness whereof, because I must depart,
Till that my dead do prove my word, I leave in pawn my heart.
Tomorrow eke [also] betimes [early] before the sun arise,
To Friar Laurence will I wend [go] to learn his sage advice.
He is my ghostly [spiritual] sire. . . ."

[4. Carrying Out the Marriage with the Help of the Friar]

565 This barefoot friar girt with cord his grayish weed [clothing],
For he of Francis' order was, a friar, as I rede [read].
Not as the most was he, a gross unlearned fool,
But doctor of divinity proceeded he in school.
The secrets eke [also] he knew in Nature's works that lurk;
570 By magic's art most men supposed that he could wonders
work. . . .

[Nurse Speaks to Romeus]

652 And how she gave her suck in youth, she leaveth not to tell.
"A pretty babe," quod she, "It was when it was young,
Lord, how it could full prettily have prated [prattled] with it
[its] tongue.
655 A thousand times and more I laid her on my lap,
And clapped her on the buttock soft, and kissed where I did
clap.
And gladder then was I of such a kiss, forsooth,
Than I had been to have a kiss of some old lecher's mouth."
And thus of Juliet's youth began this prating [prattling] nurse,
660 And of her present state to make a tedious, long discourse. . . .

[Friar Laurence Marries Romeo and Juliet]

755 "Fair lady Juliet, my ghostly [spiritual] daughter dear,
As far as I of Romeus learn, who by you standeth here,
'Twixt you it is agreed, that you shall be his wife,
And he your spouse in steady truth, till death shall end your
life.
Are you both fully bent [determined] to keep this great behest
[requirement]?"
760 And both the lovers said, it was their only heart's request. . . .
773 Then Romeus said to her, both loth [unwilling] to part so
soon,
"Fair lady, send to me again your nurse this afternoon.
Of cord I will bespeak [speak of] a ladder by that time;
By which, this night, while others sleep, I will your window
climb.

[Romeus Comes to Juliet]

830 So light he wox [became], he leapt the wall, and there he spied
       his wife,
     Who in the window watched the coming of her lord;
     Where she so surely had made fast the ladder made of cord,
     That dangerless her spouse the chamber window climbs,
     Where he ere [before] then had wished himself above ten
       thousand times. . . .

919 Thus pass they forth the night, in sport, in jolly game;
     The hastiness of Phoebus' steeds in great despite they blame.
     And now the virgin's fort hath warlike Romeus got,
     In which as yet no breach was made by force of cannon shot,
     And now in ease he doth possess the hoped place:
     How glad was he, speak you that may your lover's parts
       embrace.

925 The marriage thus made up, and both the parties pleased,
     The nigh [near] approach of day's return these seely [pitiful]
       fools diseased [upset]

[5. The Brawl]

955 The prince could never cause those households so agree,
     But that some sparkles of their wrath [anger] as yet remaining
       be. . . .

960 The morrow after Easter day the mischief new begun.
     A band of Capulets did meet—my heart it rues [regrets]!—
     Within the walls, by Purser's gate, a band of Montagues.
     The Capulets, as chief, a young man have chose out,
     Best exercised in feats of arms, and noblest of the rout
       [crowd],

965 Our Juliet's uncle's son, that cleped [named] was Tybalt;
     He was of body tall and strong, and of his courage halt [valid].
     They need no trumpet sound to bid them give the charge,
     So loud he cried with strained voice and mouth outstretched
       large [wide]:
     "Now, now," quod he, "My friends, ourself so let us wreak
       [inflict],

970 That of this day's revenge and us our children's heirs may
       speak.
     Now once for all let us their swelling pride assuage [calm];
     Let none of them escape alive." Then he, with furious rage,
     And they with him, gave charge upon their present foes,
     And then forthwith, a skirmish [battle] great upon this fray
       arose.

975 For, lo, the Montagues thought: shame away to fly,
And rather than to live with shame, with praise did choose to
   die. . . .

994 Eke [also], walking with his friends, the noise doth woeful
   Romeus hear.
With speedy foot he runs unto the fray [battle] apace;
With him, those few that were with him he leadeth to the
   place.
They pity much to see the slaughter made so great,
That wetshod they might stand in blood on either side the
   street.
"Part, friends," said he. "Part, friends—help, friends, to part
   the fray [battle]. . . ."

1005 Then leapt he in the throng [crowd], to part and bar the blows
As well of those that were his friends, as of his deadly foes.
As soon as Tybalt had our Romeus espied [seen],
He threw a thrust at him that would have passed from side to
   side;
But Romeus ever went, doubting [fearing] his foes, well armed,

1010 So that the sword, kept out by mail [chain armor], hath
   nothing Romeus harmed.
"Thou dost me wrong," quoth he, "for I but part the fray
   [battle];
Not dread, but other weighty cause my hasty hand doth stay
   [stop].
Thou art the chief of thine, the noblest eke [also] thou art,
Wherefore leave off thy malice now, and help these folk to
   part,

1015 Many are hurt, some slain, and some are like to die."
"No, coward, traitor boy," quoth he, "Straightway I mind to
   try
Whether thy sugared talk, and tongue so smoothly filed,
Against the force of this my sword shall serve thee for a
   shield?"
And then at Romeus' head a blow he strake [struck] so hard,

1020 That might have clove [cut] him to the brain but for his
   cunning ward [counter]. . . .

1033 So met these two, and while they change a blow or twain,
   [two]
Our Romeus thrust him through the throat, and so is Tybalt
   slain. . . .

[The Prince Announces His Decree]

1045   The Prince doth pause, and then gives sentence in a while,
        That Romeus for slaying him should go into exile.

[6. The Friar Reproaches Romeo in His Cell]

1353   "Art thou," quoth he, "a man? Thy shape saith so thou art;
        Thy crying and thy weeping eyes denote a woman's heart. . . .

1449   Admit thou should'st abide [stay] abroad a year or twain,
        Should so short absence cause so long and eke [also] so
            grievous pain.
        Though thou ne [not] may'st thy friends here in Verona see,
        They are not banished Mantua, where safely thou may'st be. . . .

1463   He is too nice a weakling that shrinketh at a shower,
        And he unworthy of the sweet, that tasteth not the sour.

1465   Call now again to mind thy first consuming flame,
        How didst thou vainly burn in love of an unloving dame?
        Hadst thou not wellnigh wept quite out thy swelling eyne
            [eyes]?
        Did not thy parts, fordone with pain, languish away and pine
            [waste away]?
        Those griefs and others like were haply [by chance] overpast,

1470   And thou in height of Fortune's [Lady Fortune] wheel [the
            Wheel of Fortune] well placed at the last . . . ?"

[7. Romeo and Juliet's Leave-taking. Romeo Speaks.]

1678   "I will return to you, mine own, befall what may befall.
        And then by strength of friends, and with a mighty hand,
        From Verone will I carry thee into a foreign land,
        Not in man's weed [clothes] disguised, or as one scarcely
            known,
        But as my wife and only fere [peer], in garment of thine
            own. . . ."

[Juliet answers.]

1694   "One promise crave I at your hand, that grant me to fulfill;
        Fail not to let me have, at Friar Laurence' hand,
        The tidings of your health, and how your doubtful case shall
            stand. . . ."

1710   When Phoebus [sun god] from our hemisphere in western
            wave doth sink,
        What color then the heavens do show unto thine eyes,
        The same, or like, saw Romeus in farthest eastern skies.
        As yet he saw no day, ne [nor] could he call it night,
        With equal force decreasing dark fought with increasing light.

1715   Then Romeus in arms his lady 'gan to fold,

With friendly kiss, and ruthfully [sadly] she 'gan her knight
    behold.
With solemn oath they both their sorrowful leave do take. . . .

[8.   The Capulets Arrange Juliet's Marriage to Paris and Tell Her. Lady
       Capulet speaks to her husband.]

1842   "But now at length I have bethought me; and I do believe
      The only crop and root of all my daughter's pain
      Is grudging envy's faint disease: perhaps she doth disdain
1845   To see in wedlock yoke the most part of her feres [fellows],
      Whilst only she unmarried doth lose so many years.
      And more perchance she thinks you mind to keep her so. . . .
1851   Join her at once to some in link of marriage,
      That may be meet for our degree, and much about her
         age. . . ."

[Capulet Responds]

1857   "Oft have I thought, dear wife, of all these things ere [before]
        this,
      But evermore my mind me gave, it should not be amiss
      By farther leisure had a husband to provide;
1860   Scarce saw she yet full sixteen years: too young to be a
        bride. . . ."
1881   Among the rest was one inflamed with her desire,
      Who County Paris cleped [named] was; an earl he had to sire
        [father].
      Of all the suitors him the father liketh best. . . .

[Juliet Responds]

1899   When Juliet conceived her parents' whole intent,
      Whereto both love and reason's right forbode her to assent,
      Within herself she thought, rather than be forsworn [break her
        oath],
      With horses wild her tender parts asunder should be torn.
      Not now, with bashful brow, in wonted [accustomed] wise, she
        spake,
      But with unwonted boldness straight into these words she
        brake:
1905   "Madam, I marvel much that you so lavas [careless] are
      Of me your child, your jewel once, your only joy and care,
      As thus to yield me up at pleasure of another,
      Before you know if I do like or else mislike my lover.
      Do what you list [want], but yet of this assure you still,
1910   If you do as you say you will, I yield not there until [to it].
      For had I choice of twain [two], far rather would I choose

My part of all your goods and eke [also] my breath and life to
    lose

Than grant that he possess of me the smallest part;

First, weary of my painful life, my cares shall kill my heart,

1915   Else will I pierce my breast with sharp and bloody knife. . . ."

1945   The sire [father], whose swelling wrath [anger] her tears could
    not assuage [calm],

With fiery eyne [eyes], and scarlet cheeks, thus spake her in his
    rage,

Whilst ruthfully [sorrowfully] stood by the maiden's mother
    mild:

"Listen," quoth he, "Unthankful and thou disobedient child,

Hast thou so soon let slip out of thy mind the word

1950   That thou so oftentimes hast heard rehearsed at my board
    [dinnertable] . . . ?"

1985   For were it not that I to County Paris gave

My faith, which I must keep unfalsed, my honor so to save,

Ere [before] thou go hence, myself would see thee chastened
    so,

That thou should'st once for all be taught thy duty how to
    know;

And what revenge of old the angry sires did find

1990   Against their children that rebelled and showed themself
    unkind [unnatural]. . . .

[9. Juliet Appeals to the Friar for Help; He Introduces the Potion]

2015   But as she may, piecemeal she poureth in his lap

The marriage news, a mischief new, prepared by mishap [bad
    luck],

Her parents' promise erst [before] to County Paris past,

Her father's threats she telleth him, and thus concludes at last:

"Once was I wedded well, ne [nor] will I wed again;

2020   For since I know I may not be the wedded wife of twain [two],

For I am bound to have one God, one faith, one make [mate],

My purpose is as soon as I shall hence my journey take,

With these two hands, which joined unto the heavens I stretch,

The hasty death which I desire, unto myself to reach. . . ."

2062   With tender pity and with ruth [pity] his heart was won at last;

He thought he rather would in hazard [chance] set his fame,

Than suffer such adultery. Resolving on the same,

2065   Out of his closet straight he took a little glass,

And then with double haste returned where woeful Juliet was;

Whom he hath found wellnigh [almost] in trance, scarce
    drawing breath,

Attending still to hear the news of life or else of death.
Of whom he did enquire of the appointed day:
2070 "On Wednesday next," quod Juliet, "So doth my father say,
I must give my consent; but, as I do remember,
The solemn day of marriage is the tenth day of September."
"Dear daughter," quoth the friar, "Of good cheer see thou
be,
For lo, Saint Francis of his grace hath showed a way to me,
2075 By which I may both thee and Romeus together
Out of the bondage which you fear assuredly deliver. . . .
2127 Long since I did find out, and yet the way I know
Of certain roots and savory herbs to make a kind of dough,
Which baked hard, and beat into a powder fine,
2130 And drunk with conduit water [tap water], or with any kind of
wine,
It doth in half an hour astonne [knock out] the taker so,
And mast'reth all his senses, that he feeleth weal [health] nor
woe:
And so it burieth up the sprite [spirit] and living breath,
That even the skillful leech [doctor] would say, that he is slain
by death.
2135 One virtue more it hath, as marvellous as this;
The taker, by receiving it, at all not grieved is;
But painless as a man that thinketh nought [nothing] at all,
Into a sweet and quiet sleep immediately doth fall;
From which, according to the quantity he taketh,
2140 Longer or shorter is the time before the sleeper waketh;
And thence, th'effect once wrought [created], again it doth
restore
Him that received unto the state wherein he was before. . . .
2149 Receive this vial small and keep it as thine eye;
And on thy marriage day, before the sun do clear the sky,
Fill it with water full up to the very brim,
Then drink it off, and thou shalt feel throughout each vein and
limb
A pleasant slumber slide, and quite dispread [spread out] at
length
On all thy parts, from every part reave [take away] all thy
kindly [natural] strength. . . ."
2159 Thy corpse then will they bring to grave in this churchyard,
Where thy forefathers long ago a costly tomb prepared,
Both for themself and eke [also] for those that should come
after,

Both deep it is, and long and large, where thou shalt rest, my
    daughter,
Till I to Mantua send for Romeus, thy knight;
Out of the tomb both he and I will take thee forth that night.

2165   And when out of thy sleep thou shalt awake again,
Then may'st thou go with him from hence; and, healed of thy
    pain,
In Mantua lead with him unknown a pleasant life;
And yet perhaps in time to come, when cease shall all the
    strife,
And that the peace is made 'twixt Romeus and his foes,

2170   Myself may find so fit a time these secrets to disclose,
Both to my praise, and to thy tender parents' joy,
That dangerless, without reproach, thou shalt thy love
    enjoy. . . ."

[10. Juliet Takes the Potion and Produces False Death]

2383   And then when she again within herself had weighed
That quick [alive] she should be buried there, and by his side
    be laid,
All comfortless, for she shall living fere [fellow] have none,
But many a rotten carcass, and full many a naked bone;
Her dainty tender parts 'gan shiver all for dread,
Her golden hairs did stand upright upon her chillish [chilled]
    head. . . .

2399   As she had frantic been, in haste the glass she caught,
And up she drank the mixture quite, withouten [without]
    farther thought.
Then on her breast she crossed her arms long and small
    [narrow],
And so, her senses failing her, into a trance [coma] did fall.
    And when that Phoebus [sun god] bright heaved up his
    seemly [lovely] head,
And from the East in open skies his glist'ring [glistening] rays
    dispread [spread],

2405   The nurse unshut the door, for she the key did keep,
And doubting [fearing] she had slept too long, she thought to
    break her sleep;
First softly did she call, then louder thus did cry:
"Lady, you sleep too long; the earl will raise you by and by."
But, wellaway [an oath, like "Oh woe!"], in vain unto the deaf
    she calls,

2410   She thinks to speak to Juliet, but speaketh to the walls. . . .

2423   At last, with much ado, "Dead," quoth she, "is my child."
        "Now, out, alas," the mother cried, and as a tiger wild,
        Whose whelps, whilst she is gone out of her den to prey,
        The hunter greedy of his game doth kill or carry away;
        So raging forth she ran unto her Juliet's bed,
        And there she found her darling and her only comfort
            dead. . . .

            [Romeus with the Apothecary]

2567   An apothecary sat unbusied at his door,
        Whom by his heavy countenance he guessed to be poor.
        And in his shop he saw his boxes were but few,
        And in his window, of his wares [merchandise] there was so
            small a show;
2571   Wherefore our Romeus assuredly hath thought,
        What by no friendship could be got, with money should be
            bought;
        For needy lack is like the poor man to compel
        To sell that which the city's law forbiddeth him to sell.
2575   Then by the hand he drew the needy man apart,
        And with the sight of glitt'ring gold inflamed hath his heart:
        "Take fifty crowns of gold," quoth he, "I give them thee,
        So that, before I part from hence, thou straight deliver me
        Some poison strong, that may in less than half an hour
2580   Kill him whose wretched hap [fate] shall be the potion to
            devour.
        The wretch by covetise [greed] is won, and doth assent
        To sell the thing, whose sale ere [before] long, too late, he
            doth repent.
        In haste he poison sought, and closely he it bound,
        And then began with whispering voice thus in his ear to round
            [deliver]:
2585   "Fair sir," quoth he, "Be sure this is the speeding [quick] gear
            [stuff],
        And more there is than you shall need; for half of that is there
        Will serve, I undertake, in less than half an hour
        To kill the strongest man alive. Such is the poison's power."

            [11. The Double Suicide; Romeo in the Crypt]

2639   But when he could not find the signs of life he sought,
        Out of his cursed box he drew the poison that he bought;
        Whereof he greedily devoured the greater part. . . .
2655   Which little and little 'gan to overcome his heart,
        And whilst his busy eyne [eyes] he threw about to every part,

He saw, hard by the corse [body] of sleeping Juliet,
Bold Tybalt's carcass dead, which was not all consumed yet;
To whom, as having life, in this sort speaketh he:

2660   "Ah, cousin dear, Tybalt, whereso thy restless sprite [spirit] now be,
With stretched hands to thee for mercy now I cry,
For that before thy kindly [natural] hour I forced thee to die. . . ."

2709   But coming to herself she knew them, and said thus,
"What, Friar Laurence, is it you? Where is my Romeus?"
And then the ancient friar, that greatly stood in fear,
Lest, if they lingered over long they should be taken there,
In few plain words the whole that was betid [happened], he told,
And with his finger showed his corpse outstretched, stiff, and cold. . . .

2721   But lo, as soon as she had cast her ruthful [pitiful] eye
On Romeus' face, that pale and wan [gaunt] fast by her side did lie,
Straightway she did unstop the conduits [ducts] of her tears,
And out they gush—with cruel hand she tare [tore] her golden hairs. . . .

2761   And when our Juliet would continue still her moan,
The friar and the servant fled, and left her there alone;
For they a sudden noise fast [near] by the place did hear,
And lest they might be taken there, greatly they stood in fear. . . .

2772   With hasty hand she did draw out the dagger that he wore
"O welcome Death," quoth she, "End of unhappiness,
That also art beginning of assured happiness,
Fear not to dart me now, thy stripe [whipping] no longer stay,
Prolong no longer now my life, I hate this long delay. . . .

2787   That so our parted sprites [spirits] from light that we see here,
In place of endless light and bliss may ever live yfere [together]."
These said, her ruthless hand through-girt [cut through] her valiant heart:

2790   Ah, ladies, help with tears to wail the lady's deadly smart.
She groans, she stretcheth out her limbs, she shuts her eyes,
And from her corpse the sprite doth fly—what should I say— she dies. . . .

[The Friar's Tearful Confession of Error, Not Sin]

2889　For through mine age, whose hairs of long time since were
　　　　hoar [white],
　　　And credit great that I was in, with you, in time tofore,
　　　And eke [also] the sojourn [stay] short that I on earth must
　　　　make,
　　　That every day and hour do look my journey hence to take,
　　　My conscience inwardly should more torment me thrice,
　　　Than all the outward deadly pain that all you could devise.

[12. Prince Escalus' Distribution of Justice; the Reconciliation]

2971　Then Peter, not so much erst [before] as he was, dismayed;
　　　"My lords," quoth he, "Too true is all that Friar Laurence said.
　　　And when my master went into my mistress' grave,
　　　This letter that I offer you, unto me then he gave,
2975　Which he himself did write, as I do understand,
　　　And charged me to offer them unto his father's hand. . . ."
2985　The wiser sort, to council called by Escalus,
　　　Have given advice, and Escalus sagely decreeth [orders] thus:
　　　The nurse of Juliet is banished in her age,
　　　Because that from the parents she did hide the marriage,
　　　Which might have wrought [effected] much good had it in time
　　　　been known,
2990　Where now by her concealing it a mischief great is grown;
　　　And Peter, for he did obey his master's hest [request],
　　　In wonted [usual] freedom had good leave to lead his life in
　　　　rest,
　　　Th'apothecary [chemist] high is hanged by the throat,
　　　And for the pains he took with him the hangman had his coat
　　　　[In Brooke's day, hangmen in England were paid with the
　　　　clothing of the executed].
2995　But now what shall betide [happen to] of this grey-bearded
　　　　sire?
　　　Of Friar Laurence thus arraigned, that good barefooted friar?
　　　Because that many times he worthily did serve
　　　The commonwealth [nation], and in his life was never found to
　　　　swerve,
　　　He was discharged quite, and no mark of defame
3000　Did seem to blot or touch at all the honor of his name.
　　　But of himself he went into an hermitage,
　　　Two miles from Verone town, where he in prayers passed forth
　　　　his age,

Till that from earth to heaven his heavenly sprite [spirit] did fly,
Five years he lived an hermit and an hermit did he die.
3005   The strangeness of the chance, when tried was the truth,
The Montagues and Capulets hath moved so to ruth [pity],
That with their emptied tears their choler and their rage
Was emptied quite; and they, whose wrath [anger] no wisdom
        could assuage [calm],
Nor threat'ning of the prince, ne [nor] mind of murders done,
3010   At length, so mighty Jove it would, by pity they are won.
And lest that length of time might from our minds remove
The memory of so perfect, sound, and so approved love,
The bodies dead, removed from vault where they did die,
In stately tomb, on pillars great of marble, raise they high,
3015   On every side above were set, and eke [also] beneath,
Great store of cunning epitaphs, in honor of their death.
And even at this day the tomb is to be seen;
So that among the monuments that in Verona been,
There is no monument more worthy of the sight,
3020   Than is the tomb of Juliet and Romeus her knight.

NOTE

1. Brooke, according to his friend and fellow poet, George Turberville, died at a young age by drowning at sea.

STUDY QUESTIONS

1. After reading all of Shakespeare's play and the main source in Brooke, choose three "scenes" that Shakespeare changed—apparently to make them more dramatic. In these cases, how does Shakespeare's stagecraft differ from Brooke's narrative poetics? Would Shakespeare's scenes work well in Brooke's narrative? How? Where?

2. How does Shakespeare's Nurse differ from Brooke's Nurse? Is Juliet's breakup with the Nurse an important moment in Shakespeare's play? Why?

3. In a scene of your own devising, what would you do with Brooke's three-way meeting of Romeo, Juliet, and Mercutio? Where would you add this scene to Shakespeare's *Romeo and Juliet*?

4. Why do you suppose Brooke depicts Mucutio with cold hands and a reputation as a courtly lover? How could you use these qualities by adding them to Shakespeare's play?

5. What dramatic use might you make of (Brooke's) Friar Laurence's repentent speech at the end of the play? What would your final scene look like? Discuss.

6. Create an imaginary scene based on (Brooke's) Romeo's confrontation with Tybalt. Does Brooke's heroic sarcasm (the spoken irony between combatants) enhance your scene? Compare what you have created to Shakespeare's rendering.

7. Brooke suggests that envy lies at the heart of the struggle between the very similar families of Capulets and Montagues. Is there any suggestion of this envy in Shakespeare's play? Develop this idea.

8. Brooke's Capulet parents seem to agree that Juliet might be envious of other girls getting married. Is there any hint of this envy in Juliet's actions or words? Does she seem in a rush to marry, like her mother was? Develop this idea.

9. Brooke builds his narrative around the seasons suggested by the Christian calendar. Capulet's party takes place at Christmastide, the brawl occurs the day after Easter, the double suicide is in the fall, and so on. Is there any suggestion of the passing of the seasons in Shakespeare? Or is it all just a "midsummer day's madness"? Develop an argument on the subject, and present it to the class.

10. Brooke characterizes himself on line 961, and his audience of ladies on line 2790. Although Shakespeare's play is purely dramatic and thus mute about the author and the audience, does Shakespeare refer to himself in, for example, the Prologue and the second chorus, and is there any suggestion of the audience there, too? Develop by close reading of the prologue and the second chorus.

TOPICS FOR WRITTEN OR ORAL EXPLORATION

The comparative method provides the basic structure of argument papers. Most of the following proposed theses about Shakespeare and Brooke will require this approach.

1. Develop a paper on Shakespeare's use of Brooke's poetic descriptions of time, often using mythological figures such as Phoebus Apollo or Aurora. Why are these descriptions important to both poets? Be specific.

2. Develop an argument about Shakespeare's use of Brooke's descriptions of seafaring, mostly in the epic similes (extended comparisons). Do you suppose the fact that Brooke was a seafaring man who died of drowning in a shipwreck would have affected Shakespeare? Show how.

3. Develop a paper on the diatribe "To the Reader" at the beginning of Brooke's "tragedy." How does it relate to Shakespeare's play on the subject of Franciscan friars' supposed superstition?

5. How does Brooke's diatribe "To the Reader" relate to Shakespeare's play on the subject of sexual passion? Develop this idea in detail.

6. Create an argument on how two love complaints of Romeus and Juliet (in Brooke) might have affected Shakespeare's characterization of Romeo and Juliet. Quote and discuss. Be specific.

7. Do Brooke and Shakespeare seem to disagree about the value of sexual passion? Where? Be specific.

8. Compare Brooke's prefatory sonnet ("The Arguments") with Shakespeare's Prologue. What do you make of the difference? What do they add to each work?

9. Compare Friar Laurence's history as a "white magician," or creator of magical potions for the good, in Brooke with his gardening speech (2.3) in Shakespeare. Does Shakespeare suggest a similar past for his Friar? How? Develop this idea in detail.

10. Compare Juliet's fears as expressed in Brooke with those expressed in Shakespeare. Is Shakespeare's Juliet more courageous? Develop this idea in detail.

SUGGESTED READINGS

Bullough, Geoffrey. *Narrative and Dramatic Sources of Shakespeare.* London: Routledge and Kegan Paul, 1958.

Caso, Adolph, ed. *Romeo and Juliet: Original Text of: Masuccio Salernitano, Luigi Da Porto, Matteo Bandello, William Shakespeare.* Boston: Dante University of America Press, 1992.

Law, Robert Adger. "On Shakespeare's Changes of His Source Material in *Romeo and Juliet.*" *Studies in English* 9 (1929): 86–102.

Levenson, Jill. "Romeo and Juliet before Shakespeare." *Studies in Philology* 81, no.3 (1984): 325–347.

Muir, Kenneth. *Shakespeare's Sources: Comedies and Tragedies.* London: Methuen, 1957.

Munro, J. J. *Brooke's "Romeus and Juliet" Being the Original of Shakespeare's "Romeo and Juliet."* New York: Duffield, 1908.

4

The Lyrical Source of
Romeo and Juliet:
Sir Philip Sidney and the
Elizabethan Sonnet

INTRODUCTION

Although Arthur Brooke's *Tragedy of Romeus and Juliet* provides
the immediate narrative source for Shakespeare's *Romeo and
Juliet*, the play's force as a great poetic work comes largely from
the brilliant and playful English sonnet of the late sixteenth century. Indeed, the sonnet made Arthur Brooke's maneuvers as a
poet seem outdated and crude, or, as the English novelist and
essayist C. S. Lewis put it, "drab." The "golden" (also Lewis's
phrase) English sonnet has three related peculiarities. The first is
its unbalanced form; the second, its self-conscious wit and ambiguity based on the pun or double entendre; the third, its tendency
to provide topical compliments and covert advice to the Queen
herself.

As for its form, unlike the continental practice of Petrarch or
Ronsard who broke the fourteen-line sonnet into roughly equal
parts, what Shakespeare inherited from Sir Philip Sidney and others involves a long statement followed by the briefest possible
answer. For example, whereas Petrarch's stanzas of eight lines followed by six lines (or, less often, six followed by eight) allow for
a leisurely call and answer, the Elizabethan sonnet has three quatrains (four-line stanzas) crashing up like a tidal wave against a tiny
couplet that tries to sum up or answer the twelve preceding lines.

Complex ideas are answered in a few words that may resemble an aphorism, proverb, or jingle.

Many classically trained critics on the continent thought Shakespeare's plays were unbalanced with their sudden disasters or unions or accidents at the end, so they regarded the lopsided sonnet form to be far too violent in its outcome. Just as the Elizabethan sonnet's couplet "corks" things in a tragic, hilarious, or contradictory fashion, so Shakespeare's plays may seem corked with their funerals, multiple weddings (as in *A Midsummer Night's Dream*), or multiple-breakups (as in *Love's Labor's Lost*). All these events are part of recognition scenes at the end of the plays such as in the mourning and reconciliation of Montague and Capulet after the double suicide at the end of *Romeo and Juliet*.

The second identifying feature of the Elizabethan sonnet is its self-conscious wit in interior monologues or imagined dialogues. What happens if one reads the whole of Shakespeare's *Romeo and Juliet* as a celebration—and criticism—of the Elizabethan sonnet's form and content? One can see the sonnet used in significant scenes throughout the play, and its abrupt ending couplet reflected in the sudden, unexpected events at the play's end. The self-contradictory prologue (a sonnet) about free will and predestination, delivered by Chorus—probably as an old man, possibly played sometimes by Shakespeare himself—is a humorous monologue on the inscrutability of fate, or theology; at old man Capulet's party, Romeo and Juliet, in what may be the central moment of the play, trade a witty sonnet about sexual advances as religious pilgrimages (and their rejection as unholy) [passionate love as religion]; at the end of this scene, Chorus returns to mark Romeo's changing attention from Rosaline to Juliet (and her favorable response) in a breath-taking, understated sonnet [love—nature's creative impulse—as mutable, even dangerous]; the new soliloquies, speeches of various sorts, and witty exchanges, especially in the first balcony scene, all develop extended metaphors of the sonneteers [wit as erotic play]; Romeo and Friar Laurence trade lines that are rhymed or broken up, sonnet-like [moral philosophy]; then the double suicide and resulting peace between the families cap everything in an abrupt manner [the sacrificial corker]. The ending does away with most but not all the humor in a flash, as an Elizabethan sonnet's couplet might do.

The play's last two lines—a couplet, of course—seem to parody the pat endings of many Elizabethan sonnets:

For never was a story of more woe
Than this of Juliet and her Romeo.

These two lines perform the witty corking of a rather complex play. As soon as the audience hears "woe," it can expect a rhyme on "Romeo," reversing the sequence of—and thereby emphasizing—the names of the tragic principals, "Juliet and her Romeo." This couplet is more than a reminder of the importance of the heroine and hero. The audience recalls, among other things, that these willful and mismanaged teenage lovers died at their own hands, as Mercutio, Tybalt, Paris, and many citizens of both the Capulet and Montague clans—including Romeo's mother—did not. Furthermore, the play as a whole is about Verona and vendetta and contrariety and the dangers of the white magic of miracle drug and poison and rush, as well as about the love of Juliet and her Romeo. Thus, as in a good Elizabethan sonnet, the very ending leaves us scratching our heads in wonder. But the clue contained in the abrupt couplet is that Romeo and his Juliet brought about much of the good and, through their egoistic idealism, much of the havoc. The Elizabethan sonnet is always about such interesting characters. Like the Elizabethan drama, the play is largely about the fall of high-strung idealists, be they tragic or comic or somewhere in between.

Finally, as is evident in Mercutio's Queen Mab speech and the many addresses to the moon in the play and in all sonnet sequences of the period, *Romeo and Juliet* reminds us of the immediate circumstance of political poetry of the time. It consciously and wittily compliments the "Virgin Queen's" power as the fallible but virtuous Faerie Queene and protector of many peoples (the English, Welsh, Scottish, Irish, Manx [people from the Isle of Man], and Virginians) and of the arts. Moreover, though she was aging rapidly, it portrays the Queen as unapproachable love object and moon goddess of chastity, not to mention personification of justice in England's Golden Age.

SIR PHILIP SIDNEY AND *ROMEO AND JULIET*

The poetic revolution of sonneteering that lies behind *Romeo and Juliet* began and ended, in a sense, with Sir Philip Sidney, who had been dead for almost ten years when Shakespeare wrote his first love tragedy. Sidney, who was related to some of the ruling aristocracy in England, died young from a gangrenous thigh wound suffered from a bullet while fighting Spanish soldiers in the Netherlands in the War of the Spanish Succession. This action took place in 1586, two years before the defeat of the Spanish Armada in 1588. Shakespeare thus had to suffer an odd circumstance for a writer: Sidney was a senior contemporary (and something of a popular hero) who died at age thirty-one when Shakespeare was twenty-two; through the posthumous publication of his works, he became a sudden and significant influence on Shakespeare's work of 1595, when Shakespeare himself was thirty-one years old.

Notwithstanding the circulation of manuscripts of Sidney's poems (and Shakespeare did the same), *Romeo and Juliet* shows the sudden impact of Sidney's recently published verse. Especially significant was his sonnet sequence now called *Astrophil and Stella*, with its self-consciousness, its references to Elizabeth I and her court and other contemporary politics, and its gravitation toward the Gothic imagery of love melancholy at the end. Sidney had written more than some people had guessed. Four years after his death, in 1590, a revised fragment of his huge romance *Arcadia* that contains several sonnets appeared in print. His final group of *Certain Sonnets* did not appear until 1598—with many of his other works—when the vogue of such poems was on the wane, a full twelve years after his death.

In the interim, *Astrophil and Stella* appeared twice in 1591 and, in its first complete edition, in 1598. Shakespeare took up many of Sidney's typical poetic moves: the use of conceits such as the hunt image as a double-edged metaphor for love, the pet bird, or the book; procedural concepts such as the body catalogue, poetic description of time, personification of nature, or the examination of poetry itself; even evocation of the Gothic or horror world—the underbelly of existence—to denote psychic disorder in poet-lovers.

CONCEITS, OR EXTENDED METAPHORS IN LYRIC, IN *ROMEO AND JULIET*

Two of the leading extended metaphors in love sonnets have to do with human beings' basic animality: the love-as-hunt image, and the pet bird image. Sidney asks the moon in one sonnet if Cupid is allowed to shoot his piercing golden arrows to make one fall into passionate love, even in heaven. In a typical forceful enjambment (one line running into the next) he says, "What, may it be that even in heavenly place/That busy archer his sharp arrows tries?" (31.1). According to Olympian myth, Cupid hunts the people who fall in and out of love, but the lover also hunts the beloved by stalking and gazing and, indeed, writing witty poems. The hunt image is central to both Ovid's *Metamorphoses* and Petrarch's *Rime*. In fact, the English language allows for extensive punning on love as hunting animals, especially deer-hunting. Thus "venery" (deer-hunting: deer meat is venison) is seen as "venery" (venereal—from Venus—or sexual activity). The "hart" (deer, usually male) is a "heart" to hunt. One can "pray" to one's "prey." The "deer" becomes the familiar "dear." But he or she who is "chased" may well be "chaste."

As if Shakespeare wanted to write the history of the English sonnet in *Romeo and Juliet*, in the first scene of the play he depicts Romeo's distraught condition through the Petrarchan hunt image, as both Cupid's chase and the lover's. First we hear that Benvolio had sighted Romeo stealing "into the covert of the wood" (1.1.125). Then he "hounds" him until Romeo admits to suffering lost love. He specifies, "I do love a woman" (1.1.204). Benvolio responds, "I aimed so near when I supposed you loved," partly for the laugh he would share for recognizing Romeo's heterosexuality. As always, Romeo ably answers his friend:

> A right good marksman! And she's fair I love.
>
> BENVOLIO: A right fair mark, fair coz, is soonest hit.

Benvolio wittily shifts the meaning of "fair" from beautiful to highly visible or lighted up like a target to his "fair" (gentle) cousin. "Hit" is another pun implying both shot (as with Cupid's arrow) and seduced. Romeo corks this exchange with a couplet: "Well, in that hit you miss. She'll not be hit / With Cupid's arrow. She hath Dian's wit." But Benvolio, on a poetic roll, cannot resist adding that Rosaline must be "chaste/chased" (1.1.217). Indeed, she is both. Rosaline is still celibate and still sought after. However, the reference to Diana, the moon goddess of the hunt, contains one more compliment to Queen Elizabeth, who supposedly had the wit not to be hit (used sexually).

Sidney—as the distraught lover Astrophil—produces a sonnet of envy of his Stella's pet bird. His exasperated persona says, "I bare (with envy) yet I bare your song / When in her neck you did love ditties peep" (83.5), but finally he decides to warn his little namesake, "Leave that, Sir Phip, lest off your neck be wrung" (83.14). The conceit that pets (especially songbirds) have better access to beloved mistresses than lover-poets do harks back for Sidney and Shakespeare to Catullus' Poems 2 and 3 from Republican Rome and John Skelton's lecherous "Philip Sparrow" from Henry VIII's court, but we need go no further than Sidney's Astrophil of comic sonnet 83.

Returning to *Romeo and Juliet*, note how Romeo laments his exile from Juliet, again for about fourteen lines, to the Friar in his cell. He opens with the conceit that "every cat and dog / And little mouse, every unworthy thing, / Live here in heaven and may look on her, / But Romeo may not" (3.3.30). Then he sees those dangerous "carrion flies" that "may seize / On the white wonder of dear Juliet's hand / And steal immortal blessing from her lips"— as Stella's songbird does, drinking "nectar from that tongue" (83.13). Romeo's final line of this poetic development produces another pun: "Flies may do this but I from this must fly" (3.3.41). Romeo may fly (rush) and fly (flee) from Juliet and Verona, but he will never stop longing to be a fly buzzing around his beloved, nor will he disengage himself from the Elizabethan sonnet tradition.

Sidney's joke in Astrophil's final line about wringing the neck of a lovebird named "Sir Phip" alludes to the babytalk that Elizabeth I was known to encourage in conversation with and among her courtiers. Elizabeth's version included pretending that she could not enunciate the "l" sound when it was called for, only when she had to pronounce the "r" sound. Thus her lover "Robin" (Robert) Dudley (Sidney's uncle) became "Lobbin," but Walter Raleigh became "Water" (hence his famous lost poem to her, "Ocean to Cynthia"). Philip Sidney became "Phip" or "Pip" as in Charles Dickens' own allusion in *Great Expectations* (Sidney's ironic phrase) to Pip (and his Estella). Astrophil offers to kill his double and rival songbird, who bears the first name and nickname of his Elizabethan courtier creator and alter ego. But were Romeo and Juliet any less self-consciously witty? After all sonneteering is the language of love.

Recall the dialogue between Romeo and Juliet after their night of meeting in the Capulet mansion:

JULIET: 'Tis almost morning. I would have thee gone
And yet no farther than a wanton's [spoiled
    child's] bird,
That lets it hop a little from his hand,
Like a poor prisoner in his twisted gyves [rope
    bonds],
And with a silken thread plucks it back again,
So loving-jealous of his liberty.

ROMEO: I would I were thy bird.

JULIET: Sweet, so would I,
Yet I should kill thee with much cherishing.
(2.2.177)

Here, Romeo's alter ego and songbird would not require having his neck wrung. He would die, apparently, of the suffocation attendant on too much love and handling.

Sidney's Astrophil offers to read his beloved as a book and thus avoid desire: "Who will in fairest book of Nature know / How virtue may best lodged in beauty be, / Let him but learn of love to read in thee, / Stella, those fair lines which true goodness show" (71.1). In his final moment, however—so reminiscent of Romeo's outburst near the end of the first balcony scene, "O wilt thou leave me so unsatisfied?" (2.2.25)—Astrophil reverts to begging for sexual favors: " 'But, ah,' Desire still cries, 'give me some food' " (71.14).

Reading the beloved as a book reappears in Juliet's nameless young mother's instructions on observing Paris, to which Juliet gives her famous prim reply, "I'll look to like if looking liking move" (1.3.98). Juliet's mother instructs her to

Read o'er the volume of young Paris' face,
And find delight writ there with beauty's pen;
Examine every married lineament,
And see how one another lends content;
And what obscured in the fair volume lies
Find written in the margent [margin] of his eyes.
This precious book of love, this unbound lover,
To beautify him, only lacks a cover.   (1.3.82)

Perhaps modern readers can relate to images of hunting and pet animals better than to those of books. However, the printed book was a new product of technology during the Renaissance, and thus a world of wonder accompanies its image. Here the fact that Juliet's body is being compared to a cover for Paris' book reminds readers of the sexual expectations that her nurse and real mother instill in her. Overall, the continuous application of words such as "volumes," "content" (probably both happiness and contained meaning), "margins," "bindings," and "covers" as metaphors for the coupling of love and marriage produces a carefully constructed conceit.

THE BLAZON, OR BODY CATALOGUE, IN *ROMEO AND JULIET*

The poetic move of comparing a sequence of the beloved's body parts with precious gems, metals, or mythological attributes is the oldest and most original kind of poetry in three senses. First, the oldest recorded poetry from Mesopotamia and Egypt describes icons of the goddess Astarte or Isis, and the Bible offers the blazons of the Song of Solomon. Second, children first discover the effects of poetry ridiculing artificiality as they tend to make fun of all manifestations of love and sex. Thus children may giggle over "Your ears are flowers, cauliflowers; your eyes are pools, cesspools; etc." Third, the body catalogue is such an obvious poetic maneuver that nearly every imaginative person has given it an original spin, creating variations such as the vegetarian "Your hair is wheat germ, your eyes wild blueberries," and so forth.

One of Sidney's novel spins on the blazon occurs in his Sonnet 9, where he uses it to describe a palace. He opens with a compliment to Elizabeth I: "Queen Virtue's court, which some call Stella's face, / Prepared by Nature's choicest furniture, / Hath his front built of alablaster [alabaster] pure; / Gold is the covering of that stately place" [place and palace] (9.1). In this variation, the front of the palace and Stella's forehead (front) are both white, translucent alabaster; the roof and her hair, gold. Thereafter he describes the door (lips) of reddish purple porphyry, locks (teeth) of pearl, and windows (eyes) of the black stone known as touch. Through these images the reader learns that Stella was a rare dark-eyed natural blond. Furthermore, the word "touch" implies an incendiary device used to strike fires (e.g., flint) and also has a tactile and emotional meaning: I touch her arm and I am touched by her.[1]

Although the conventional Nordic ideal is overturned by Stella's black eyes, the whole set of comparisons, like gold and rock and gems, contradicts female softness and suggests monetary value.

In *Romeo and Juliet*, Mercutio satirizes any blazons that Romeo might deliver at the opening of the balcony scene. He offers a body catalogue of Rosaline as a conjuration (a chant-like calling on the devils) leading in a bawdy direction to shake up his best friend, the lover-poet Romeo, who he guesses is within earshot:

> I conjure thee by Rosaline's bright eyes,
> By her high forehead and her scarlet lip,
> By her fine foot, straight leg, and quivering thigh,
> And in the demesnes [domains] that there adjacent lie.   (2.1.18)

For this wicked reduction of love imagery to sexual suggestiveness, Benvolio remarks "thou wilt anger him" (i.e., Romeo). Romeo, angered, opens the following scene muttering, "He jests at scars that never felt a wound" (2.2.1).

CHRONOGRAPHIA, OR POETIC TELLING OF TIME, IN *ROMEO AND JULIET*

In Sidney's sonnet 31 Astrophil addresses the moon, but the concept of the poem (its conceit) merely tells the reader what time it is. It is moonrise. Thus he opens, "With how sad steps, O Moon, thou climbest the skies, / How silently, and with how wan a face" (31.1). The poem's poetic structure is chronographia. The lover cannot sleep and is addressing the moon.

We have seen how poetic telling of time marks every turn in *Romeo and Juliet*. Mysteriously, after the first balcony scene, the best version of the play (called Quarto 2, 1599) gives a number of the same lines to both Romeo (accidentally listed as Juliet) at the end of one scene and Friar Laurence at the beginning of the next. They are:

> The grey-eyed morn smiles on the frowning night,
> Check'ring the Eastern clouds with streaks of light,
> And fleckled darkness like a drunkard reels
> From forth day's path and Titan's fiery wheels.   (2.2.191ff. and
>   2.3.1)

Do these lines sound more like Romeo or Friar Laurence? Most editors attribute them only to the Friar. My suggestion, however, with all the emphasis on rush and the wheels of fire of the sun god cranking along, is to leave the text alone and have Romeo and Friar Laurence separately deliver the same lines. This will fore-shadow Juliet's sonnet-like soliloquy about the end of day; she begins with "Gallop apace, you fiery-footed steeds, / Towards Phoebus' lodging!" (3.2.1) when she wants to bring in her wed-ding night on the second evening of knowing Romeo. Whereas Sidney's moon of sonnet 31 moves slowly, causing reflection and self-analysis and self-conscious mistaking, the sonnet-like chrono-graphia of the principals of *Romeo and Juliet* seems to rush along, obliterating all thought.

PATHETIC, OR AMOROUS, FALLACY: PERSONIFICATION OF NATURE IN *ROMEO AND JULIET*

The art critic John Ruskin coined the term "pathetic fallacy" in Book Five of his *Modern Painters* in 1860. It implies that some poets falsify aspects of nature for cheap sentimental effect—for example, when buttercups are represented as crying after a child has died, when in fact the beads of water in the buttercup are merely the product of condensation. Today, however, the negative term "fallacy" (error) has a largely neutral meaning—in this case, pathetic fallacy as personification of nature. It implies everything that the great poets do in spiritualizing nature to show the effects of grief and love; it is especially evident in the works of Shake-speare, Dante, Homer (who Ruskin argued did not employ it), and Ovid.

When Stella is sick, Astrophil has the famous English mist ap-pear, thus delivering a weather report of meteorological conditions that imitate her perspiring in bed: "Nature with care sweats for her darling's sake, / Knowing worlds pass ere she enough can find / Of such heaven stuff, to clothe so heavenly a mind" (101.12). Mother Nature gives Stella the best compliment; imitation. Simi-larly, just after Romeo sees Juliet at the window in the first balcony scene, he says Moon looks pale because Juliet

That art her maid art far more fair than she.
Be not her maid, since she is envious.   (2.2.26)

Her vestal livery [clothing] is but sick and green
And none but fools do wear it. Cast it off.   (2.2.8)

Here the lover-poet Romeo depicts a moon responding with the sickness of envy of Juliet's beauty. But he is not only telling Juliet not to be chaste like Rosaline—do not be a vestal virgin of any goddess of chastity—he is also hoping to undress her with his words, saying only "fools" wear such clothing; "Cast it off." He is also referring to the supposed virginity of England's moon goddess, Queen Elizabeth.

EKPHRASIS, OR POETRY ABOUT POETRY AND ART, IN *ROMEO AND JULIET*

The leading art form of the Renaissance was painting, which explains why the dominant critical terms from that era are *line, composition, perspective*, and *illumination*. In the music-dominated nineteenth century, one hears of literary *rhythm, motif*, and *theme*. In the architecture-dominated twentieth century, one often hears of *stress, tension*, and *structure* in literary works. For sculpture-dominated fifth century Hellas, *plastic, form*, and *shape* became the crucial terminology. The great painters in Renaissance Italy often lived double artistic lives, painting (like Botticelli) chaste Virgin Marys for the church and sensual Ovidian subjects for the aristocracy, sometimes even using the same models. In mentioning "good poetry about bad poetry" in sonnet 6, Sidney has Astrophil condemn convention-bound poets as if they were the painters of the aristocracy. He says, "Some one his song in Jove, and Jove's strange tales, attires, / Bordered with bulls and swans, powdered with golden rain" (6.5). These lines refer to the Ovidian subjects of Jupiter's rapes of Europa, Leda, and Danae (see illustration) whose offspring help explain genius in the world. Predictably, Astrophil ends the poem by emphasizing his own sincerity, "When trembling voice brings forth that I do Stella love."

This poem is an ekphrasis, a poem about art (in this case, about other poems, but also about paintings) that wittily develops the idea that other poets are convention-bound plagiarists yet the present poet is simple and sincere.[2] Astrophil suggests that other poets must be limited to their hackneyed references to Olympian myth, such as to Muses who improbably inspire poets and the "strange"

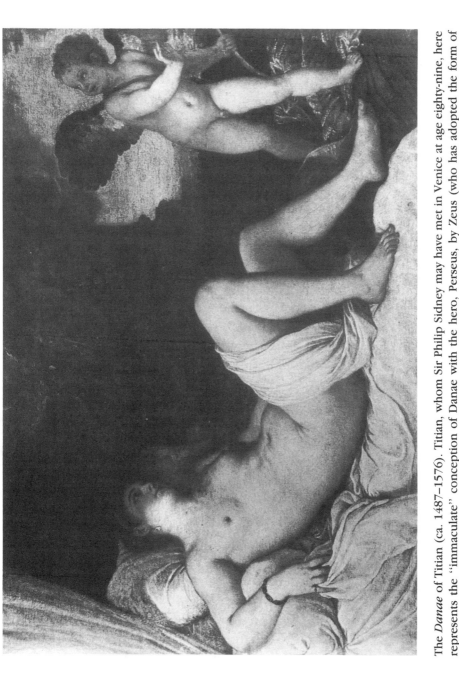

The *Danae* of Titian (ca. 1487–1576). Titian, whom Sir Philip Sidney may have met in Venice at age eighty-nine, here represents the "immaculate" conception of Danae with the hero, Perseus, by Zeus (who has adopted the form of golden rain). From the Museo e Galleria Nazionale di Capodimonte. Reproduced by permission of the Soprintendenza B.A.S. di Napoli Archivo Fotografico.

stories of Jupiter's (Jove's) rapes of humans in metamorphosed states—that is, in animal or inanimate (like golden rain) forms.

As in the wittiest of English sonnets, punning is very important. For example, in a hysterical moment Juliet plays all the changes she can on the homonyms of "I" (3.2.45ff.). Here the word "tale" (story) also suggests "tail" (both the bull's tail when Jupiter, metamorphosed into a bull, dashes into the Mediterranean Sea with Princess Europa on his back; and also his phallus). The picture of other lame poets trying to attach to themselves Jupiter's private parts is funny, but no more funny than Mercutio, who can be equally bawdy and even somewhat mad.

Mercutio faces off with Romeo in the streets of Verona before he encounters Juliet's nurse, still thinking his best friend is in love with Rosaline:

> How art thou fishified! Now he is for the numbers that Petrarch flowed in. Laura to his lady was but a kitchen wench—marry, she had a better love to berhyme her—Dido a dowdy, Cleopatra a gypsy, Helen and Hero hildings and harlots, Thisbe a gray eye or so, but not to the purpose. Signor Romeo, *bonjour!* (2.4.38)

Beyond addressing him in French to suggest Romeo's affectation, Mercutio here accomplishes several attacks on Romeo the lover-poet. First, Romeo is "fishified" (taken over by a woman's private parts) and thus feminized, a jibe that Romeo echoes when he is about to kill Tybalt: "O sweet Juliet, / Thy beauty hath made me effeminate" (3.1.113).[3] Second, he calls Romeo a conventional poet who uses negative comparisons (mostly to beautiful women from Olympian myth) to highlight his mistress's superiority. Thus he compares Rosaline favorably to Dido (the widow lover of Aeneas who is often connected to Queen Elizabeth, partly for her alternate name in Virgil's *Aeneid*: Elissa), Cleopatra, Helen of Troy, Hero (Leander's love), and Thisbe (the suicide lover of Pyramus in Ovid [see Chapter 2] and in the play-within-a-play in *A Midsummer Night's Dream*). Indeed, Juliet had suggested that Romeo kisses "by the book" (1.5.111) (as Tybalt, according to Mercutio, fights by the "book of arithmetic"; 3.1.101), suggesting for a second that he is a convention-bound lover, a true Romeo, working on a sequence of women by poetic rote.

One of the strangest moments in *Romeo and Juliet* occurs when

Romeo says to Benvolio that Rosaline would not "ope her lap to saint-seducing gold" (1.1.212). Although this is an elegant reference to Sidney's version of Jove impregnating Danae in an immaculate transformation "powdered with golden rain" (Sidney 6.6) [see illustration], Romeo seems to be allegorizing the myth as a reference to dealing money for sexual favors. Did he offer money to Rosaline, or is he simply carried away with his self-consciously witty sonneteering mode? I think the latter. He is inadvertently practicing ekphrasis, creating poetry out of art. In his mad poetic creation with Benvolio, he sees Rosaline as a version of the mother of Perseus fathered by Jupiter (and in the sexual fantasy, Romeo), and accidentally he creates a unique cynical moment for himself.[4]

Mercutio's unkindest cut of all suggests that Romeo is a plagiarist poet-lover and not a great one at that. Thus Romeo steals from the sonneteer Petrarch—as Astrophil had scoffed at poet-lovers rehearsing "Petrarch's long-deceased woes" (15.7)—but Petrarch's Laura had a better poet to praise her than Rosaline, or, for that matter, Juliet. This is a witty jibe even for Shakespeare, who gave Romeo words supposedly inferior to Petrarch's. Of course, all this witty complaining about convention is paradoxical because poetry is always created out of the fabric of archetypal myth and predictable rhetorical moves such as oxymorons and chronographia. As for the accusation of plagiarism, the American poet T. S. Eliot may have said it best: "Good poets borrow, great poets steal."

GOTHIC, OR HORROR, IMAGERY IN *ROMEO AND JULIET*

Lawrence Babb, in his study of Renaissance melancholy entitled *The Elizabethan Malady* (1951), puzzled over the inclusion of lycanthropy (wolfmanism), vampirism, and other forms of demonology as symptoms of the experience of lost love. However, Sidney makes the connection quite clear, especially in the final sonnets of *Astrophil and Stella* after his hero discovers he will never win Stella. So does Shakespeare early in *Romeo and Juliet* when Romeo feels certain he will not win Rosaline.

The frustrated lover, possessed by his or her absent beloved, hates his or her bed, especially at night, because it is a reminder of who is missing. He or she rises and travels through landscapes such as cemeteries and lonely woods. At daybreak he or she goes to sleep in the crypt of a darkened bedroom. The moon with all its pulls on the psyche becomes the central heavenly body (occasioning, of course, a compliment to the Queen as moon goddess). Pining and nausea causes the lover to appear bloodless, even ghoulish. His or her imagination dwells on the horrors connected with the demonology of lost things, to include haunted houses, rapid aging, dismemberment, living dead and other ghouls, and premature burial.

This Gothic excitement is part of the Elizabethan sonnet's tradition of exploring the effects, good and bad, of unrequited love. In the final poems of Sidney's sonnet sequence, Astrophil, now the fully rejected lover, pictures himself as a ghoul sleeping in a crypt (actually an artificially darkened room with a "tomb of lids" 99.12) during the day and experiencing all kinds of "black horrors of the silent night" (98.9), such as "ghastly [and ghostly]" "sprites [and spirits]" (96.10).

Compare old man Montague's poetic description of his son. The unrequited lover Romeo's only sleep comes from "artificial," or self-constructed, night during the day. Montague combines pathetic fallacy, chronographia, and a reference to the marriage in Olympian myth of Aurora (goddess of dawn, and her aging yet immortal husband, Tithonus) in fine sonnet-like tradition:

Many a morning hath he there been seen,
With tears augmenting the fresh morning's dew,
Adding to clouds more clouds with his deep sighs;
But all so soon as the all-cheering sun
Should in the farthest East begin to draw
The shading curtains from Aurora's bed,
Away from light steals home my heavy son
And private in his chamber pens himself,
Shuts up his windows, locks fair daylight out,
And makes himself an artificial night.
Black and portentous must this humor prove
Unless good counsel may the cause remove.   (1.1.131)

Punning on "sun/son," old man Montague produces a twelve-line sonnet about the fact that his son only sleeps when Aurora rises; he ends with a couplet describing Romeo's love melancholy and its diseased effects. Of course, Juliet, not "good counsel," will provide a cure for Romeo's Gothic insomnia. But it is not a complete one, as horror imagery comes to dominate the play's speeches and action right down to the visit of the principals to the Capulet tomb in the cemetery.

In this extended first scene of *Romeo and Juliet*, Montague sends Benvolio to find out about Romeo's disturbance by way of his "true shrift" (1.1.159), or confession.[5] Benvolio, after willingly losing Romeo in the sycamore woods because of his own unexplained grief, takes up the challenge. After a number of witty and sonnet-like evasions, Romeo admits to him that he loves a woman who has taken an oath of chastity by Diana's (the moon goddess's and, of course, Queen Elizabeth's) wit. Romeo says: "She hath forsworn to love, and in that vow / Do I live dead, that live to tell it now" (1.1.223). This is the "living death" that Astrophil scoffed at when poets declared to their beloveds that they suffered (6.4).

However, Romeo's imagination gravitates to similar tragic love-sonnet images, often (as illustrated in Chapter 1) by personifying Death as a horrific, all-devouring figure.[6] In the Friar's cell just before Juliet's arrival at their wedding, Romeo says, "Do thou but close our hands with holy words, / Then love-devouring Death do what he dare" (2.6.6 [capitals mine]). Thus Death becomes, in Romeo's imagination, his great competitor in love with Juliet. The Friar immediately rebels and compares the lovers to gunpowder about to explode and consume themselves, as, of course, they do. Whereas Astrophil's horror images reflect his well-deserved rejection—he boasted of his love and lied about it, as young men will—Romeo and Juliet's acceptance of mutual love seems to prime the pump of such sonnet-like horrific imaginings, especially in Juliet's mind. Is Shakespeare criticizing the effect of dark Elizabethan sonnets on an impressionable thirteen-year-old girl suffering the pangs of first love?

Any notion of marriage to Paris or of imminent separation or of death brings out horror in Juliet's words. But should it bring out the horrific high Gothic imagery of Sidney's last sonnets in Juliet's imagination, dwelling on burial alive, rotting corpses and their stench, and other forms of suffocation? Or is her imagination diseased? After all, she should have taken the practical option of eloping before she had any sexual contact with Romeo. At the mention of Paris' promised marriage, Juliet says to her mother, "make the bridal bed / In that dim monument where Tybalt lies" (3.5.202), where, of course, he is rotting. To the Friar she says, rather than marry her to Paris

                    bid me lurk
Where serpents are; chain me with roaring bears,
Or hide me nightly in a charnel [bone depository] house,
O'ercovered quite with dead men's rattling bones,
With reeky [stinking] shanks and yellow chapless [jawless] skulls;
Or bid me go into a new-made grave
And hide me with a dead man in his tomb
Things that, to hear them told, have made me tremble.   (4.1.79)

Is Juliet developing the conceit of death and night to create a sonnet-like excitation of horror?

On considering her fears about the sleep potion, Juliet says,

Or, if I live, is it not very like
The horrible conceit of death and night,
Together with the terror of the place—
As in a vault, an ancient receptacle,
Where for this many hundred years the bones
Of all my buried ancestors are packed;
Where bloody Tybalt, yet but green in earth [newly dead and
    buried],
Lies festering in his shroud [death sheet].   (4.3.36)

Juliet dwells on images of tombs and burial shrouds, putrefaction, and suffocation from the horrific smells of death. Where do Sidney and Shakespeare stand in all this? They probably marvel at the excitation of the thrill-seeking sonneteer's imagination, but they also see such poetry as a negative consequence of love melancholy. As Robert Scholes and Robert Kellogg long ago pointed out in their *Nature of Narrative* (1960), Elizabethan plays, like great Russian novels, are the product of a combination of traditional stories and empirical, very up-to-date psychology.

THE FIRST BALCONY SCENE OF *ROMEO AND JULIET*

One of the great poetic duets in history is the first balcony scene of *Romeo and Juliet*. It contains many jokes and mutually developed conceits: the concentration on Romeo's name, the mutual blazon, the borrowing of Cupid's wings, the elaborate worries about time and fidelity and safety. For example, in the last case, Juliet warns about her bloodthirsty relatives: "If they do see thee, they will murder thee" (2.2.70). Again Romeo turns to the sonneteering mode to describe the overwhelming power of Juliet's eyes, which create far greater danger of love (especially its gaze) than the martial danger a mob of other Capulets could effect: "Alack, there lies more peril in thine eye / Than twenty of their swords. Look thou but sweet, / And I am proof against their enmity."

As delightful and comic as this hyperbole is, there is a problem in the word "sweet" (one of Sidney's favorites in *Astrophil and Stella* and elsewhere). If Juliet has a perilous gaze, it should be unsweet and death-giving. But because enunciating "sweet" requires one to pucker, as in a kiss, the word gets some wonderful irrational mileage in Sidney and here. Consider, for example, Sidney's phrases from Astrophil: "Sweet swelling lip, well mayest thou swell in pride" and "Sweet lip, you teach my mouth with one sweet kiss" (80.1, 14). She will look sweet when she puckers her lips, but her looks may be death-dealing darts. Again Romeo also suggests that if Juliet gives him a sweet look, it will make him "proof," or impenetrable, to Capulet swords. Thus Romeo gets to reiterate the death wish of the young man in love.

There is an Oxford tradition that a 1623 First Folio, the expensive leather-bound first edition of Shakespeare's works, was attached by a chain to a desk at the Bodleian Library and only the pages of this balcony scene (and the second scene of the lovers' parting) were worn through from student perusal. Does this mean that *Romeo and Juliet* is for twenty-year-olds? The wearing through of the pages is a tribute to Shakespeare's distillation of the sonnet form into an otherwise perfectly naturalistic love scene between teenagers of different ages. It was loved so much because it was so funny, self-conscious, and fresh. And it best expressed the religion of love.

NOTES

1. Edgar Allan Poe borrowed Sidney's "architectural" move in the blazon of Madeline (and Roderick Usher?) in a song called "The Haunted Palace" at the center of "The Fall of the House of Usher."

2. The notion of just breathing out "I love you, Stella" or, conversely crying out her name here and elsewhere has a literary history that comes down to Tennessee Williams' Stanley Kowalski repeatedly shouting "Stella" up the stairwell in *A Streetcar Named Desire*. In fact, New Orleans has witnessed "Stella"-shouting contests that would have made Sidney howl with laughter.

3. Hamlet makes a similar thrust at Polonius' supposed selling of his daughter's parts in calling him a "fishmonger" (2.2.174) (in part, Elizabethan slang for pimp).

4. Much like the nameless poet in the Greek Anthology (the tenth-century collection of Greek short occasional poetry) did when he wrote, "Zeus gave to Danae gold, so I to thee— / More that a God's a man's gift may not be" (MacGregor 5).

5. Shakespeare uses this technique again, in *Hamlet*, when Claudius sends Rosencrantz and Guildenstern to investigate Hamlet's melancholy.

6. One that the great poet of the next generation, John Milton, took up at the end of Book Two of *Paradise Lost*.

STUDY QUESTIONS

1. In the spirit of the traded sonnet in the party scene, write your own Elizabethan sonnet in the form of the dialogue of two lovers called Romeo and Juliet. Explain its effects.

2. Explore the term "conceit" as extended metaphor in lyric, and analyze three conceits from three separate speeches in *Romeo and Juliet*—for example, the book, the rose, the moon, canker and cancer, gunpowder, stormy sea, or Death as a lover in the dance of death.

3. Create a sonnet for Paris about Juliet that is an original blazon (a body catalogue with a sequence of hyperbolic comparisons). Explain your choices.

4. Create a sonnet for Juliet that is a chronographia (poetic description of time), demanding haste in Romeo's arrival. Explain your mythological references.

5. Create a sonnet for Romeo that is pathetic fallacy (personification of nature) outlining his woes. Explain.

6. Create a humorous sonnet for Mercutio about Romeo's poetry that is an ekphrasis (a poetic description of art or poetry). Refer to specific passages, and explain their significance.

7. Watch a reputable horror film such as *Carrie*, *Wolf*, or *Nosferatu*, and recount how many of its Gothic themes or conventions—such as vampirism, rapid aging, visits to cemeteries—also appear in the poetry of *Romeo and Juliet*.

8. Identify four probable references to Queen Elizabeth in *Romeo and Juliet*. Describe how the Queen might have reacted.

9. With a friend, direct yourselves in a scene between Romeo and Juliet, Juliet and Paris, Juliet and Nurse, Romeo and Mercutio, Romeo and Benvolio, Benvolio and Mercutio, Capulet and Tybalt, or Capulet and Juliet. Enact it for the class, and then explain your choices and difficulties.

10. Study and discuss three of Shakespeare's puns in the play. Discuss their shock effect and probable meaning.

TOPICS FOR WRITTEN OR ORAL EXPLORATION

1. Look up and define "Petrarchism," and apply the term to the most anguished and self-lacerating love poetry in the play. Do you choose Romeo's or Juliet's? What is your conclusion?

2. Is Romeo more or less Petrarchan on the subject of Rosaline or Juliet? Take a position. Argue and exemplify and recapitulate.

3. Define anti-Petrarchism in the words of Mercutio. Is one of his central anti-Petrarchan puns on the word ''lie'' just before his Queen Mab speech? Develop an argument with a title and subtitle, such as ''Mercutio's Lies: Anti-Petrarchism in *Romeo and Juliet*.''

4. Insomnia—Romeo's, old man Capulet's, and, to some extent, Benvolio's—seems to be a theme in *Romeo and Juliet*. Compare the compulsions of the play's three sleepless characters, and develop a thesis about Shakespeare's use of this theme.

5. Friar Laurence's sleep potion and the Apothecary's poison seem to be magical drugs, one to give the appearance of death, the other to kill instantly. Are there any other signs of magic in the play? Develop a thesis about this issue in Shakespeare's *Romeo and Juliet*.

6. Modern society seems to worry more about youthful hyperactivity and gangs than about youthful sadness and melancholy. Elizabethan society seems to have been just the opposite. Show how the play condones youthful high spirits yet worries about low spirits, especially as evidenced in Montague's and Capulet's words.

7. Do you get the impression that Shakespeare finds sonneteering a way of expressing and therefore relieving melancholy? Give two examples from the play, and ''prove'' your point.

8. Find two instances when Romeo or Mercutio refers to other poetry. Do these examples give you the impression the play is about poetry? Develop an argument about this question, and show its validity.

9. Do the sonnets and other extended poetic speeches in the play sometimes give you the impression you are watching a play within a play? Develop an argument about Shakespeare's use of these conventional poetic monologues. Take a position and defend it.

10. Do some research on Queen Elizabeth, and explain why *Romeo and Juliet* might be welcome or unwelcome at her court.

11. Research the life of Philip Sidney, and try to solve some of the difficulties of interpreting his life. For example, analyze Queen Elizabeth's supposed remark that he threw away a gentleman's life with a soldier's death. Relate it to his sonnets described here.

12. Read Book Two of Milton's *Paradise Lost*, and compare the image of the character Death at the end of Milton's book to Romeo's image of death personified. Come to a conclusion about the nature of Shakespeare's influence on Milton—if that is what it is—and develop an argument based on your conclusions. Include quotations.

13. Read Edgar Allan Poe's *The Fall of the House of Usher* and the complete sonnet 9 from *Astrophil and Stella*. Then see if you do not detect the influence of Sidney and even some of Juliet's imaginings in *Romeo and Juliet*. Develop an argument based on your conclusions.

14. Do blazons in *Romeo and Juliet* suggest dismemberment of the love object, possibly to exclude parts not wanted? Or do they merely reflect the worship that goes with passionate love? Develop a paper on the poetic undercurrents of these poetic moments of body cataloguing.

SUGGESTED READINGS

Babb, Lawrence. *The Elizabethan Malady: A Study of Melancholia in English Literature from 1580 to 1642*. East Lansing: Michigan State College Press, 1951.

Bevington, David, ed. *The Complete Works of Shakespeare*, 4th ed. New York: HarperCollins, 1992.

Booth, Stephen, ed. *Shakespeare's Sonnets*. New Haven: Yale University Press, 1977.

Brooks-Davies, Douglas, ed. *Silver Poets of the Sixteenth Century: Wyatt, Surrey, Raleigh, Philip Sidney, Mary Sidney, Michael Drayton and Sir John Davies*. Everyman's Library. London and Rutland, VT: J. M. Dent & Sons and Charles E. Tuttle, 1992; orig. 1947.

Hager, Alan. *Dazzling Images: The Masks of Sir Philip Sidney*. Newark, DE, and London: University of Delaware Press and Associated University Presses, 1990.

Lewis, C. S. *English Literature in the Sixteenth Century Excluding Drama*. Oxford: Clarendon Press, 1954.

MacGregor, Major Robert Guthrie. *Greek Anthology with Notes Critical and Explanatory*. London: Nissen & Parker, [1864?].

Putzel, Max, ed. *Astrophil and Stella*. Garden City, NY: Anchor Books, 1967.

Ringler, William A., Jr., ed. *The Poems of Sir Philip Sidney*. Oxford: Clarendon Press, 1962.

Vance, Eugene. "Chaucer's *House of Fame* and the Poetics of Inflation." *Boundary* 7 (1979): 17–37.

Vickers, Nancy. " 'The blazon of sweet beauty's best': Shakespeare's *Lucrece*." In *Shakespeare and the Question of Theory*, eds. Patricia Parker and Geoffrey Hartman. New York: Methuen, 1985, pp. 95–118.

———. "Diana Described: Scattered Women and Scattered Rhyme." *Critical Inquiry* 8 (1981): 265–79.

5

The Performance History of *Romeo and Juliet*

INTRODUCTION

1564
: William Shakespeare is born in Stratford-on-Avon. Religious tensions in England between Puritans (anti-theatrical and otherwise largely middle class in sympathy) and Anglicans (pro-theater and otherwise largely aristocratic in sympathy) are growing.

1580–
1586
: Shakespeare probably attends the Mystery Plays (sections of the Bible told in dramatic form out of decorated wagons) in village squares in Stratford and elsewhere, sometimes with women playing female characters. Puritan authorities object to these plays, and they are suppressed by the end of the century.

Shakespeare probably also attended plays put on by the Earl of Leicester's Men, Lord Strange's Men, and Lord Essex's Men, performed at Stratford at the rate of approximately one a year.

1586
: Shakespeare probably departs for London.

1594
: Shakespeare's company of players and writers, with Richard Burbage and Shakespeare as leading members, officially becomes known as the Lord Chamberlain's (the Secretary of State's) Men. Such nominal protection is designed by court authority so that, by wearing state livery, actors can avoid arrest by Puritan sheriffs for vagrancy.

1595   *Romeo and Juliet* (and *A Midsummer Night's Dream*) are
            first performed in the outdoor theaters and probably at
            court. Through traditional propriety (going back to fifth
            century Hellas [Athens, Greece in the fourth century B.C.],
            boys play all women's parts.

1597   *Romeo and Juliet* appears in print in a so-called bad quarto
            (Q1) a pocketbook-size hardback, probably bootlegged,
            with many errors, in London.

1599   *Romeo and Juliet* appears in a so-called good quarto (Q2),
            longer and with many corrections of Q1, as if in answer to
            its errors.

1603   Queen Elizabeth I dies. Her nephew, the Scottish King
            James VI succeeds to the throne as James I of England. The
            Lord Chamberlain's Men become the King's Men.

1617   Shakespeare dies.

1623   The First Folio (a leather-bound, full page book) of thirty-
            six of Shakespeare's plays is published by Shakespeare's
            friends and associates in London. *Romeo and Juliet* in a
            further modified form appears in the Tragedy section.

1625   James I dies. His son Charles I succeeds to the throne.

1640   The English Civil Wars, essentially between religious parties,
            break out with many of the signs of revolution in its radical
            communes and levelling schemes and summary executions.
            A Puritan parliament renounces all hereditary rank.

1642   The Puritan Party closes the theaters in London.

1649   Charles I is beheaded in London.

1653–   Oliver Cromwell rules England as Lord Protector.
1657

1660   English royalty, traditional rank, and the Anglican Church
            are restored. Charles II, son of Charles I, is crowned in Lon-
            don. The theaters reopen with women playing female roles.
            In various altered forms, *Romeo and Juliet* reappears with
            "stars" installed in the lead roles.

The history of performance of *Romeo and Juliet* follows the pattern for all Shakespearean productions. First, the Grand Repertory
period (1595–1642) spanned contemporary productions in London and thereabouts at which Shakespeare was initially present.
During this period the portly Richard Burbage, who excelled at

appearing conflicted, usually played the male lead, Romeo; zany Will Kempe usually played Peter, the Nurse's man and clown; and a certain Robert Goffe probably played Juliet. This period was grand in many ways, especially for the developing British Empire, its culture, and its theater, which was already a worldwide tourist attraction.

Second, the Rise of the Star System (1660–1918) began with the restoration of royal rule after ten years and the coronation of Charles II and lasted through World War I. During this period *Romeo and Juliet* was altered to suit popular taste, was made a vehicle for stars, and finally was restored to its original form but with the star still in place. Third, the Multi-Media and Variable Expansion period (1919–present) encompasses contemporary world culture in which alteration of Shakespeare's plays in terms of types of presentation and textual change and media are widespread. These alterations are sometimes baffling yet always justified according to contemporary needs and an array of theories about unknown elements of the original context.

During the Grand Repertory period, Shakespeare at first acted different parts and no doubt explained and even directed *Romeo and Juliet*. He would have done this for both the Lord Chamberlain's Men from the mid-1590s and for the King's Men after 1603, when James I adopted the company of players in one of his first official acts as King. Why was such patronage needed for a money-making company of actors, writers, and managers? Wearing the livery of upper-echelon government figures saved the actors from being arrested for vagrancy on the streets of the city (as prostitutes were) in the chilly, anti-theatrical climate of London's statutes enforced by the Puritan city elders. Arresting a man wearing the livery of the Lord Chamberlain or Queen or King would invite a charge of high treason.

Government figures in high office, however, were also partisans if not fans of English drama. Theater has always been, in part, an aristocratic and courtly tradition in England, which may explain its anti-bourgeois bias. The original procedures and locations for production—at the Royal Court, at the great outdoor public theaters, at the indoor private theaters, and upcountry or on the continent or in Scotland—enjoyed continual changes until the closing of the theaters by the Puritans early during the Civil War in 1642. In fact, important but nonessential textual changes are evident in the play's script between the almost perfect second quarto (Q2) of 1599 and the very good First Folio of 1623.

This is considered a *repertory* period because even though there were many skillful actors (some better than others), the same ones were involved in each successive performance. There were no stars in the modern sense. In fact, the presence of an actor who thought he was a star would create conflicts that might break up a company. Shakespeare himself, possibly specializing in old men's parts, might play a large part (say, of Friar Laurence) one night, but the next time the play was presented (about three weeks later) he might play a figure with few lines (such as Chorus) or a walk-on with a spear in the Prince's retinue. Or he might replace another actor who was ill in some large or small role (such as Capulet or the Apothecary). Richard Burbage often got the lead in the play of the moment. The main clown was usually played by Will Kempe, but there were other skillful fellows with whom he could improvise. Likewise Robert Armin, who eventually replaced Kempe, excelled at improvising.

As in most earlier cultures, boys played girls' parts. Owing to the lack of effective boy actors for female parts—partly due to voices changing at puberty and the impossibility of projecting falsetto to a large outdoor audience—the number of women's parts in the plays was kept small. *Romeo and Juliet*, for example, has only four speaking roles for women as opposed to approximately thirty-eight for men. Apparently a sizeable number of plays (thirty, perhaps) were presented alternately by the Lord Chamberlain's Men. Thus *Romeo and Juliet, A Midsummer Night's Dream, Richard II*, and *Love's Labor's Lost* may have been presented on successive afternoons in 1595 with the same actors in similar roles.

Although to modern readers "repertory" suggests a standard group of performers, in Latin *reperire* means "discover" or "find," suggesting innovation. Indeed, there is evidence of a host of revisions of the text of *Romeo and Juliet* during this period of performances. Some were the product of censorship, but most were the result of a group improvisational atmosphere. Rehearsing was limited and intense. Suggestions were bountiful.

With the possible exception of the present-day rash of movie productions of *Romeo and Juliet* and other Shakespearean plays, the Grand Repertory period was the richest era of production of *Romeo and Juliet* and the rest of Shakespeare's works. There was little other large-scale outdoor or indoor entertainment in the booming London area of the 1590s, which was repopulating after the worst of the plague years of the previous two and a half centuries. The bars, the bear-baiting pits, and the playhouses—often barely outside the jurisdiction of the Puritan sheriff of London— were the places to go.

The staging of *Romeo and Juliet* by Shakespeare's repertory company, in fact, provided the combined equivalent of daytime soap opera, live entertainment, a high male and drag fashion show on the ramps, and Top Ten on the radio. After all, the songs and sonnets of the plays, often accompanied by instruments during this greatest age of English music, were staples of Shakespearean production. And distribution of sheet music among a large and musically literate populace followed the productions. The Lord Chamberlain's Men's staging of *Romeo and Juliet* at the Theater or the Globe in East Bankside (on the far side of the Thames River from London) might draw 2,000 men, women, and children on a weekday afternoon, and memorable new popular music—such as from Mercutio's band, from the music at the Capulet ball, or from the Musicians' scene (4.5.96–145)—would be one of the draws.

The second period of production, the Rise of the Star System (1660–1918), followed the Civil War and the period of Puritan rule and collapse known as the Interregnum ("between kings"). During this time the world's first fully recorded (or historical) revolution was followed by its sudden dissolution. Although it is hard to determine how long a break in production of *Romeo and Juliet* took place, performance was not continuous. Therefore it is impossible to recover the first period's performance style in its entirety. When the theaters in London reopened in 1660, there was a tremendous amount of revision in Shakespeare's play. This may have been the result of ignorance of traditional performance, or it may have reflected changing tastes in the so-called Age of Reason.

All of *Romeo and Juliet*, for example, might be presented in heroic couplets (rhymed pairs of lines of iambic pentameter). Shakespeare's original rhyme might be removed. The ending might be altered to meet the requirements of "poetic justice" (providential or "happy" endings in which evil was punished and virtue was rewarded). Juliet and Romeo might even revive together and live happily ever after. As if they had no thematic import, the songs of the Musicians' scene might be "modernized." There might be trends to remove unsavory comic elements from the words of Mercutio and Nurse, and to never mix princes and members of the lower classes on the stage; to curtail spread-out time structures; to reduce the play's action to the last day. A of these innovations were justified on the basis of the notion that Shakespeare's work was rough or chaotic or unmoral—the word used was "natural"—in an era that had been terrorized by the rough and chaotic immorality of the revolutionary experiment under the premise of a return to nature or, worse, grace.

The Rise of the Star System spans a considerable period during which a worldwide production endeavor developed. Female actresses first took the stage in *Romeo and Juliet* during the restoration of Stuart royalty and the coronation of King Charles II (1660). This was followed by the period of the actors David Garrick's and Spranger Barry's performances of Romeo and other roles during the age of Dr. Samuel Johnson (1735–1784). Then, in the early twentieth century, the actor and playwright Harley Granville-Barker and his students in and out of the universities attempted to reconstruct original Shakespearean production values.

By now there were major Shakespearean productions, and agents for the actors and actresses struggled over who would get what part in what repeated production of *Romeo and Juliet*. Productions tended to focus on one figure (such as Romeo, or Juliet, or Mercutio) played by a famous performer (a "star"), thereby unbalancing the original repertory sense of every part as equal in some sense. Because productions were repeated night after night until audiences flagged, spectacular production values and stage effects came into being, sometimes overpowering Shakespeare's words (which were always cut to some extent). Moreover, there were many alterations of the plays for commercial reasons and for the sake of realism and decorum.

The modern and contemporary era, the Multi-Media and Variable Expansion (1919–present) sees productions of Shakespeare in a wide variety of forms in an array of media—from stage to ballet to opera to movie to radio to video to CD-ROM. And there are all types of performances—in costumes ranging from ancient Greek to modern dress. *Romeo and Juliet* might be placed in political and cultural contexts, from ancient to contemporary, that would make an Elizabethan playgoer's head spin. And, of course, there are grass-roots attempts to duplicate the Theater or Elizabethan Court experience of 1595.

Sometimes highly innovative versions of *Romeo and Juliet* might seem to sacrifice Shakespeare's words and intentions, but just as often one is tempted to say that Shakespeare might have liked to be able to make use of the movie or television or CD-ROM industries. He was a popular artist, and innovation invariably comes with new media. Had he lived in the modern era, Shakespeare may well have initiated some of these innovations himself. In his own day, he probably altered *Romeo and Juliet* for upcountry performance before less sophisticated audiences, perhaps even in his home town of Stratford-on-Avon. There, for the country wives in the audience, Romeo might be the focus of the play rather than Mercutio or Juliet.

THE GRAND REPERTORY PERIOD (1595–1642)

There are certain commonly asked questions about production during the Grand Repertory period. Why were the play's words— be they prose or poetry—so difficult? What did the various stages look like? What kind of acting did the audience encounter? What kind of spectacle helped make the play so popular?

First, the London audience of 1595 was verbally more sophisticated than any audience we might encounter today. That original crowd must have understood better than we do the elements of ambiguity (double meanings), irony, and pathos, and how words can puzzle, cause laughter, and create sadness. Because rhetoric and grammar (analysis and re-creation of the language of witty and concise Latin poetical texts) were at the center of schooling in the era, audiences of men, women, and children were highly sophisticated linguistically.

Shakespeare, like any great author, wrote in part for his best audience. It likely constituted the law school dropouts and other members of the intelligentsia that became the great lyric and dramatic poets of the next generation—John Donne, Katherine Phillips, Ben Jonson, George Herbert, Thomas Carew, John Webster, John Middleton, Lady Mary Wroth, John Milton and others. They were quoting Shakespeare often before he was published; if everyone else in the audience did not catch his poetic moves and pith at a performance of *Romeo and Juliet* at the Globe, these individuals surely did. Besides, the audience always had time to catch up on what they missed in the poetry, because the productions would be restaged every three weeks or so. (Incidentally, relative comprehension was not a matter of class, but of education and intelligence. A member of the aristocracy could be well behind a down-and-out member of the so-called "rabble" in understanding *Romeo and Juliet*.) How many times can a person today watch with pleasure one episode of a well-written TV show? Three times? With Shakespeare's *Romeo and Juliet* the difficulty, complexity, and brilliance of the language allows people to see the work with pleasure many times. Furthermore, the words, the actors, and even the parts are always changing according to the improvisatory spirit that fits the play and constantly updates its topical references.

Second, Shakespeare's main stage for the vast majority of early performances of *Romeo and Juliet* was the public outdoor theater known as the Theatre (after 1599, the Globe) in East Bankside (see illustration). The audience in the pit, or floor, stood around a three-quarters jutting or lip stage; some sat in boxes above floor level on the sides and possibly in the back. The standing audience in the pit had a fair amount of room to move around, perhaps to follow closely a favorite actor, scene, or event. The stage lacked scenery but had a trap door, a balcony, a large rectangular front, and a curtained stage room to the rear. Because the shareholders of the company were all actors, apparently they wanted no competition from fancy scenery.

In its first year, *Romeo and Juliet* was probably performed six or seven times in rotation with contemporary plays such as *Richard II*, *The Taming of the Shrew*, *A Midsummer Night's Dream*, and *Love's Labor's Lost*. But during holiday seasons, especially Christmas through Twelfth Night (January 6), the same plays may have been performed for a much smaller audience of courtiers, nobility, royalty, and retainers at the royal court or in great country houses and palaces. These versions were probably acted out on an open stage without curtain for a seated audience that followed the protocol of rank. The Queen or King or Earl or Countess would be seated up front, almost part of the production.

After 1608, performances might have been held for an indoor audience at Blackfriars, a former monastery. These productions made use of lights and probably a curtain, and tickets were mod-

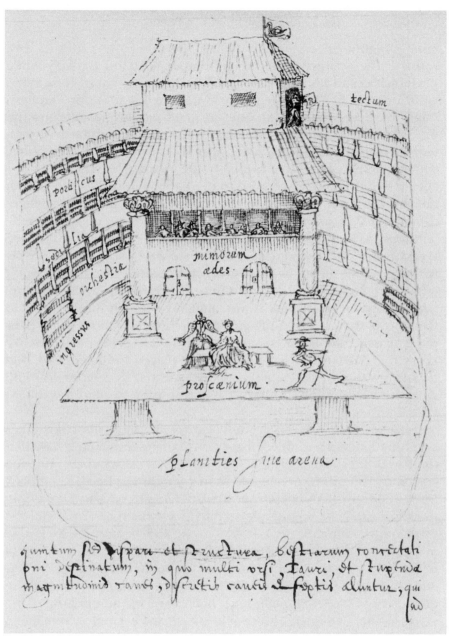

Diagram of the Swan Theatre by Van Buchell (ca. 1596) based on the observations of Johannes De Witt. This famous drawing of the Swan Theatre (similar to the Theatre, the Rose, and the Globe) is based on a description by a Dutch tourist (De Witt) in London around the time *Romeo and Juliet* was first performed. Notice how spread-out the crowd of two to three thousand in the pit (floor) could be; notice also certain special features of the stage such as the balcony behind the players, here manned by theater-goers (or more actors?). Reproduced by permission of the Universiteits Bibliotheek Utrecht.

erately highly priced. Finally, when the company made its rare tours of the country or the continent or Scotland (usually when performances in London were outlawed on account of censorship violations or epidemics such as bubonic plague), productions might have been staged indoors in great houses or outdoors on makeshift stages. These were used for the so-called miracle or mystery plays (Biblical stories acted out by various guilds) in public squares. Such plays were probably the dramatic staple of Shakespeare's youth, and he referred to them throughout his career with delight. But such sentimental tours were rare. London was where the money was, as well as the best audience, local and foreign.

Actors in Shakespeare's day started very young. Therefore the level of skill of the performers of *Romeo and Juliet* was probably very high, both in terms of gesture and ability to be heard over a large and sometimes noisy audience (contemporaries have remarked on the crunching of nut shells by shoes in the pit). There were no particular types of actors and "actresses" except perhaps the clowns in the Musicians' scene, who were true specialists. We know that Richard Burbage sometimes played the male lead, and it is likely that Shakespeare had Burbage's vast abilities in mind when he wrote Romeo's part. It is possible he wanted the role of Friar Laurence for himself.

Because there was no scenery except for fabricated box trees and rope ladders and other minor props, one might conclude that there was little spectacle on the Grand Repertory stage. But the costumes (often more valuable than everything else the company owned) and makeup were spectacular. The play was in part a fashion show, and the sound effects must have been as remarkable as those on the dramatic radio shows of the 1950s. How do we know? Shakespeare's company welcomed presenting storms as hints of magic or the presence of divinity that was essential to the tragedies and tragicomedies. Thus in the cemetery scene, for example, a great deal of creaking might have been used in the opening of the crypt of the Capulets. How such effects were created remains a mystery, but lead sheets must have been used for certain crashing cymbal effects. Also, when Romeo discovers the signs of battle in the first scene, lots of red dye (blood) must have been used. Sometimes gunfire and the use of candles and fire on the stage created spectacular effects like fireworks (if not in *Romeo and Juliet*, then in other productions).

THE RISE OF THE STAR SYSTEM (1660–1918)

During the English revolution, somewhere between 1642 and 1660, the continuity of Shakespearean production of *Romeo and Juliet* was lost. The theaters were closed in 1642, but there may have been performances at court or among exiles on the continent for another seven years. After the beheading of Charles I in 1649, the remaining Royal Party and its court either came to terms with the party of Oliver Cromwell (the Puritan Lord Protector of England, 1653–1658), or lived on the continent, mainly in the Netherlands and in Paris and Rome. At this time Shakespeare's *Romeo and Juliet* would have been rarely performed, if at all, for approximately a decade. That relatively small gap of time opened the door to significant innovation in later performance. If there had been perfect continuity we would know almost everything about the original production, and we could choose what we wanted to do with that knowledge.[1]

However, the gap in performance of *Romeo and Juliet* makes an accurate reconstruction of the original form of Shakespeare's play virtually impossible. The restoration of the monarchy and the coronation of Charles II in 1660 introduced the return of the theater in the "town" of London—that concentric royal neighborhood with its palaces, parks, coffee houses, and theaters surrounded by the "city," or commercial district. It also initiated the dismembering of Shakespeare's texts in the name of decorum.

Productions of Shakespeare's plays during this neoclassical age emulated French drama, in which the so-called Aristotelian unities were observed. It was thought that the action of *Romeo and Juliet* should take place in a single locale, reflecting unity of place. Its duration in stage time should be little more than twenty-four hours or one day, reflecting unity of time. And there should be only one plot, reflecting unity of action. The plot should not mix kings with commoners and vice versa, or comedy with tragedy and vice versa. Realism required action uncontaminated by the presence of supernatural elements. Exit all magic. And yet, somewhat contradictorily—in order to teach virtue, the plot should reward the good and punish the bad—there should be poetic justice at the final curtain. Puns were a bad idea; continual rhymed couplets were sometimes a good idea, or, when blank verse became preferred, sometimes an equally bad one. Remove Shakespeare's rhymes in couplet and sestet. With the advent of the rectangular theater with curtain, some of the lonely talk in aside and soliloquy began to appear awkward or unrealistic. So cut. And any domestic drama that was not a comedy of manners tended to have a bourgeois sentimental quality once women began to play the female roles, and sentiment was a virtue. Where does all this leave Shakespeare?

Although the first two quartos—bootleg quarter-page printed editions (half the size of a folio)—of 1597 and 1599 announce the popularity of Shakespeare's *The Most Excellent and Lamentable Tragedy of Romeo and Juliet*, the first recorded performance occurred in 1662. It was put on by the company of a man who pretended to be Shakespeare's son, Sir William Davenant, two years after the restoration of the monarchy. It was apparently a fiasco. Lines were not properly memorized, and some memorable mispronunciations caused laughter. For example, John Downes in his *Roscius Anglicanus* (1707) claims Lady Capulet mispronounced "O, my dear Count" as "O, my dear Cunt" to uproar in the theater. The famous diarist, libertine, and later secretary of the Admiralty, Samuel Pepys, present at the revival, was so irritated by the performance that he said *Romeo and Juliet* was "the worst that ever I heard in my life." Whatever his specific objections were, the alteration of Shakespeare's text was now set in motion. Downes recounts that in the interest of what he saw as poetic justice, James Howard wrote a happy ending "so that when the Tragedy was Reviv'd again it was Played Alternately, Tragical one Day, and Tragicomical another; for several Days together."

In 1679 the brilliant restoration playwright Thomas Otway redid the play as *The History and Fall of Caius Marius*. Now the most famous line in the play would read "O Marius, Marius, wherefore art thou Marius?" He displaced the play from Verona, Italy, in the early 1400s to Republican Rome in the era of the Civil War that was so appealing to a classically minded audience. The English had just suffered their own civil war during the Interregnum and were now identifying fully with a nation that was ruling an expanding empire through a senate and consuls, much like a fractious parliament, prime minister, and limited monarch. Although Otway added materials from Plutarch and Shakespeare's own *Coriolanus*, his most telling—and influential—alteration of the play was to have the youthful beloved of Romeo (Marius), Lavinia (Juliet), wake up before Marius dies. This opened the door to a tear-filled, tragicomical recognition scene between the lovers before Marius dies of poison and Lavinia stabs herself to death. Sentimentality and shock value of the ending are now enhanced, a tendency of most revivals of the work. When Otway's *History of the Fall of Caius Marius* finally gained success in the 1690s, it held the stage for forty years.

Theophilus Cibber—wayward son to the most famous adapter of Shakespeare, Colley Cibber—again altered the text in 1744. He borrowed freely from both Otway and Shakespeare's own earlier comedy placed in Verona, *Two Gentlemen of Verona* (1592?). Another version by the great Irish playwright Thomas Sheridan ran successfully in Dublin in 1746. But the greatest innovation during the Rise of the Star System was the version edited and rewritten, produced, directed, and acted by the great star David Garrick, in competition with Spranger Barry, at the end of the 1740s and the early 1750s at the Drury Lane Theater in the "town" of London.[2] Here is what a recent scholar, Jill Levenson, says about Garrick's era and its interpretation of *Romeo and Juliet*.

FROM JILL L. LEVENSON, *SHAKESPEARE PERFORMANCE: ROMEO AND JULIET*
(Manchester; Wolfeboro, NH: Manchester University Press, 1987, pp. 19–20. Spelling and punctuation Americanized by the editor.)

The Pathetic Romeo and Juliet

A gifted man of the theater, actor/manager Garrick rearranged Shakespeare's text to attract and entertain paying customers. Bardolatry [adoration of Shakespeare] curbed his entrepreneurial impulses so that he interfered as scrupulously as possible with the original play when he adapted it to mid-eighteenth-century theatrical conditions and taste. He had no need to tamper with the original conflation of romantic love and tragedy: his own age offered popular models for this blend in pathetic [sentimental] drama. Nevertheless, genre posed a problem; current notions of decorum insisted on separating tragedy from comedy. According to Branam in *Eighteenth-Century Adaptations of Shakespearean Tragedy* (1956), dramaturgy of this period countenanced neither tragicomedy nor comic relief in tragedy; and consequently Shakespearean adapters either cut or reformed comic figures (pp. 47–48). But Garrick did nothing so drastic. Although he trimmed comic passages, often removing their bawdy [sexual jokes], he did not cut Mercutio, the Nurse, or even the

Capulet servants from his version. And despite this pruning, Sampson and Gregory open the tragedy with their vulgar puns; the Nurse repeats that Juliet "wilt fall backward when thou hast more wit"; Mercutio conjures Romeo by a lady's anatomy and taunts the Nurse: "A bawd, a bawd, a bawd!" (Quotations are from the 1981 edition of Garrick's text done by Harry William Pedicord and Fredrick Louis Bergmann, *The Plays of David Garrick*, vol. III). All in all, Garrick—like Shakespeare—affronted the decorum of genre, allowing conventions of plot, character, and style from the comic mode to counterpoint a tragic narrative. Since his rendering of the text dominated the eighteenth-century stage, objections like the following (from a letter to *The General Evening Post*, I 1–13 August 1772) refer to Garrick's revival:

> In *Romeo and Juliet* there are many things unpardonable, particularly in the characters of Mercutio and the Nurse. There is no occasion whatever for speaking either Mercutio's conjuring speech or the ribaldries of the Nurse; yet, flagitiously impure as they are, we hear them constantly repeated, and they are even received with applause by the very audiences which consider the works of Congreve too scandalous for the theatre.

Initially Garrick meddled as little with plot as with genre. When his version first appeared in 1748, it included the twelve incidents from Shakespeare's *Romeo and Juliet* which the sixteenth century knew as the lovers' story. The only significant change occurred in the death-scene, where Garrick followed Otway and Cibber in having Juliet awake before Romeo expired. In addition, he created a seventy-five-line dialogue for the lovers—immediately after Romeo takes the poison—which intensified the pathos of their tragedy to the approval of eighteenth-century audiences. The trials of Garrick's protagonists bring both to the edge of madness: as she awakes, the disoriented Juliet mistakes Romeo for someone forcing her to marry Paris; as he fades, the distracted Romeo believes that enemies are bearing down on his heart and Juliet's:

> Capulet forbear! Paris loose your hold!
> Pull not our heartstrings thus; they crack, they break.
> O! Juliet! Juliet! (*Dies*).   (p. 144)

During the interim, Romeo's joy at Juliet's revival makes him forget that he has already swallowed poison; and they share a minute of blissful ignorance which heightens their poignancy as fate completes its design. This heightening effect accounted for the success of Garrick's alteration by eighteenth-century standards. According to an article by S. H. and A. K. in *The General Evening Post*, 17–19 October 1771, Shakespeare had neglected to fill his catastrophe with as much distress as it could hold;

Garrick's addition, with its sudden shift from rapture to despair, supplied the missing agonies as it deepened the passions of Romeo and Juliet.

Garrick also removed any reference to Rosaline and cut out the banter among the Montague men at the beginning of the play, all for the sake of decorum. The direct result of these transformations of Shakespeare's text and intentions was a split between the viewers of Shakespeare and his readers. The great minds of the early romantic era, such as Hazlitt, Wordsworth, Shelley, Keats, Lamb, and others, were happy to read, for example, Garrick's friend Samuel Johnson's editions of the individual plays with explanatory notes and notice of all emendations, rather than spend a fair amount of cash to see the Bard mangled. But one notable production with Romeo played by an American woman from Boston apparently caught everyone's attention.

The great event in production of *Romeo and Juliet* in the nineteenth century was Charlotte Cushman's mid-century portrayal of Romeo. This was a star production revolving around Cushman's romantic notion that the play was about the private life of a passionate young man, whom she played, often opposite her sister, Susan, from the late 1830s and in a notable run in London from 1845 to 1846. While no doubt part of Cushman's success came from the novelty of an American woman with a husky voice playing a man, reviews reveal that she did a remarkable job—in the midst of an otherwise mediocre performance—of impersonating her concept of Romeo rather than just delivering his lines. And although she decorously removed all "obscenity," she did begin the gradual effort of restoring elements of Shakespeare's play, both big and small, that had been discarded and "corrected" during the Restoration and throughout the eighteenth century.[3] For example, Cushman bolstered the play's structure by restoring the Rosaline plot in keeping with her concept of Romeo's erratic and passionate character. She also restored some of Shakespeare's supposedly earthly diction such as "dug" (breast), "knife," and "beast" that had been replaced with properly decorous "poetic diction."

The final restoration of a structurally sound and verbatim production of *Romeo and Juliet* (but not its repertory spirit) came in the early twentieth century under the leadership of Harley Granville-Barker. A close friend of George Bernard Shaw, Granville-Barker (1877–1946), like Shakespeare, was an actor, playwright, and director. He was also a producer. The best evidence today of his achievement is not so much contained in his productions of *Romeo and Juliet* and other plays, but in his *Prefaces to Shakespeare* (1927–1945), in which he explained himself and his procedures in terms of each of the Bard's plays. Each essay explores its play chronologically with an eye to the original production values with a brilliance unparalleled in academic criticism.

Granville-Barker is the consummate theater man with an eloquence that sometimes rivals that of his master. Consider his Shakespearean coining of the portmanteau word (a blend such as "smog" or "brunch") "stupent" to describe the young Capulet and Montague men's reaction to Romeo's riddling apology for not fighting Tybalt. Probably it means that Mercutio and Benvolio, Tybalt and others, were "stupendously stupified," but we can *see* a stupent response on the stage better that we can *articulate* it. That is the wizardly Granville-Barker's way.

If Granville-Barker reflects the Victorian age he was born into in his grumbling at Shakespeare's purported obscenity and at his supposedly "purple" (excessively elaborate) flourishes of rhetoric, he often gets closer to the heart of Shakespeare than anyone else does. In fact, he clearly shows his taste for Shakespeare's earthy mind and his conceits. And he always concentrates on the original stage effects, including a peculiar tendency of Shakespeare to shorten the time sequence, creating a double-time effect in *Romeo and Juliet* and *Othello* to emphasize headlong rush into passion.

One warning: Granville-Barker perpetuates a notion that *Romeo and Juliet* is an immature work. He even suggests at the close of his essay that the ending to *Romeo and Juliet* is somewhat weak, an often-repeated idea. For me, the play is as developed and finished as anything Shakespeare wrote. The ending merely has the deadpan ironic effect of the couplet of so many self-critical sonnets. But Granville-Barker subscribes to the idea that Shakespeare *developed*, and the code word for that system of belief is "mature." Here is what Granville-Barker says about Shakespeare's dramatic moves in the scene preceding the first balcony scene of *Romeo and Juliet*.

FROM HARLEY GRANVILLE-BARKER, *PREFACES TO ROMEO AND
JULIET, JULIUS CAESAR, AND LOVE'S LABOUR'S LOST* (1930)
(London: B. T. Batsford, 1958, pp. 315–316; orig. 1930. Author has
Americanized the spelling and punctuation, and removed the notes
on the principle that they generally refer to other *Prefaces* and/or
other plays.)

And now, with his finest stroke yet, all prepared and pending (the love
duet that is to be spoken from balcony to garden), Shakespeare pauses
to do still better by it; and at the same time fits Mercutio to his true place
in the character scheme. To appreciate the device we must first forget
the obliging editors—with their *Scene i, A lane by the wall of Capulet's
orchard. Enter Romeo. . . . He climbs the wall and leaps down within it.
. . . Scene ii, Capulet's orchard. Enter Romeo*—for all this has simply
obliterated the effect. The *Enter Romeo alone* of the Quartos and Folio
is the only authentic stage direction concerning him. What happens when
Mercutio and Benvolio arrive in pursuit? He hides somewhere about the
stage. He has, they say, "leapt this orchard wall"; but no wall is there,
and—more importantly—there is no break in the continuity of the scene,
now or later; it should be proof enough that to make one we must cut
a rhymed couplet in two. The confusion of whereabouts, such as it is,
that is involved, would not trouble the Elizabethans in the least; would
certainly not trouble an audience that later on was to see Juliet play half
a scene on the upper stage and half on the lower, with no particular
change of place implied. The effect, so carefully contrived, lies in Romeo's
being well within hearing of all the bawdry now to follow, which has no
other dramatic point; and that the chaff is about the chaste Rosaline
makes it doubly effective.

Dominating the stage with his lusty presence, vomiting his jolly inde-
cencies, we see the sensual man, Mercutio; while in the background lurks
Romeo, a-quiver at them, youth marked for tragedy. His heart's agonizing
after Rosaline had been real enough. He has forgotten that! But what
awaits him now, with another heart, passionate as his own, to encounter?
This is the eloquence of the picture, which is summed up in Romeo's
rhyming end to the whole dithyramb as he steals out, looking after the
two of them:

He jests at scars that never felt a wound.   (2.2.1)

The discord thus struck is perfect preparation for the harmony to
come; and Mercutio's ribaldry has hardly died from our ears before Juliet
is at her window.

THE MULTI-MEDIA AND VARIABLE EXPANSION ERA (1919–PRESENT)

The modern era presents *Romeo and Juliet* in a bewildering array of media. The following discussion explores modern productions in terms of the stage, the ballet and opera taken as one; and the movie, video, and recording taken as one.

The Stage

The staging of *Romeo and Juliet* during the Multi-Media and Variable Expansion era has been a highly innovative worldwide effort, but unlike the previous era, it has consistently attempted to recover Shakespeare's true intentions. By 1935, Sir John Gielgud, perhaps the premier English Shakespearean voice of his generation, saw himself as embodying the full-scale restoration of Shakespeare's purposes in the tradition of Granville-Barker and others. Oddly enough, because Gielgud's production grew out of college dramatics at Oxford, this *Romeo and Juliet* returned to the repertory concept of 1595. At first the male parts were played by undergraduates and the female ones, according to tradition, were played by professionals. For the original, professional Dame Peggy Ashcroft played Juliet and the outstanding Dame Edith Evans played the Nurse. But the amateur college actors must have exchanged parts as in Shakespeare's day, recreating the repertory spirit of exchanged roles and innovation of all the best amateur companies. Apparently Gielgud even demoted himself to old man Chorus on occasion, drawing a rave review from a young Sir Alec Guinness who thought he was witnessing a haunting version of Shakespeare's own voice for the space of those two sonnets.

When this production finally reached the Old Vic Theatre's London stage in 1935, Gielgud and Sir Laurence Olivier alternated the parts of Romeo and Mercutio, displaying a contrast in conception and acting styles perhaps unheard of in a significant London production since the Elizabethan era. The repertory spirit had, for a brief moment, returned to the professional stage. The number of figures in this *Romeo and Juliet* who were granted knighthoods and other exalted positions, mostly under Great Britain's second Queen Elizabeth, attests to their achievement of Shakespearean performance as a political act.

As Olivier had said, his style and Gielgud's were like two sides of a coin. Gielgud, in both roles, was all air and fire; Olivier, earth and water. Gielgud played a thoughtful Romeo stepping out of a romance and dominated by his poetic temperament. He delivered his lines with perfect cadence—with a slight pause at the end of the lines, however, that could interfere with perfect clarity in cases of Shakespeare's most severe enjambment (one line running into the next without pause). But his delivery always seemed to allow his thoughts to be read, in a sense, by a receptive and highly literate audience. Olivier apparently looked like he walked out of a novel with no such reverence for poetic qualities; he was a realistic figure, rather unhinged by his own poetic tendency. The scenes between Olivier and Ashcroft were said to be heated indeed. The same dual tendencies applied to the role of Mercutio; his racy jokes usually dominated Olivier's performance, but his wistful Queen Mab speech dominated Gielgud's.

In the 1960s and 1970s, the producer-director Peter Brook returned the appearance of the stage and its symbols to the stark, allegorical, Elizabethan look.[4] His *Romeo and Juliet* was no tribute to traditional versions of the lip stage but proved bare and allegorical like the Elizabethan, especially in the dueling scenes. Furthermore, he let Shakespeare's words do their own work without distraction. Even the clowns in the Musicians' scene were perfectly intelligible and suddenly intelligent. In an iconoclastic manner, Brook got very close to the original without the usual squawking cockney that the lower orders in Shakespearean production are required to use.

Franco Zeffirelli's production on commission from the Old Vic in 1960 was, however, the most surprising modern staging of *Romeo and Juliet*. And although it led to the famous movie, it deserves recognition as a stage production too, partly because it was in two ways a political act on Zeffirelli's part. First, he wanted to represent Romeo as a version of the Italian character in its supposedly sudden expression of emotion. This theory of Italian character (which arose in part from the works of the anthropologist Luigi Barzini) is open to question, but it allowed Zeffirelli, with assists from his musical score by Nino Rota and his set designers, to emphasize Romeo's supposedly Italian spontaneous emotions and the pathos of the losing hand Fate dealt him. Unfortunately much of Romeo's and Juliet's humor, which requires a sense of their witty overview on existence, was lost in the process.

Second, Zeffirelli wanted his production to help create a bond between Italy and England, whose relations were strained in the aftermath of World War II. What he produced was a highly successful Italian operatic musical and scenic version of the English play that led to the even more successful movie. In making the movie he gained complete control of the actors and their acting and of the scenery, thanks to the camera and a big budget. His most decisive move was to install teenagers in the lead roles. England seemed to enjoy Zeffirelli's Italian version; and even though the English critics complained about cutting and realistic design, Zeffirelli's political gestures were well appreciated.

Opera and Ballet

Although operatic and balletic versions of *Romeo and Juliet* date back to the early nineteenth century, the crowning adaptation was Leonard Bernstein's *West Side Story* of 1956, whose original staging is still largely available in the movie form. Since opera and ballet are, by definition, romantic art forms necessarily dominated by romantic music, it is not surprising that the vendetta plot—which Bernstein placed in a Latino West Side of Manhattan—suffers, as well as its paradox and emphasis on rush in comparison with the love plot. Thus opera and ballet, including *West Side Story*, use the plot of the lovers to glorify romantic concepts of love including the notion of Friar Laurence that human passion can be used for the purpose of peace-making. Besides Leonard Bernstein, the number of contributors of operatic and balletic versions of *Romeo and Juliet* reads like a French and Russian Romantic music hall of fame: Berlioz, Gounod, Tchaikovsky, and Prokofiev.

The greatest French Romantic composer, Louis Hector Berlioz (1803–1869), from southwestern France, may have experienced his greatest early success with his lyrical opera *Romeo and Juliet* as early as 1839, when he was thirty-five years old. His opera portrays the liberating experience of ideal love. The Parisian Charles Gounod (1818–1893), now best known for his opera *Faust* (1860) and his spiritual church music, scored his own first critical and popular success in 1867 with his opera *Romeo et Juliette*. His work overwhelms the audience with the spirituality of the young lovers, especially in the duets of the extended death scene. As in Thomas Otway's and David Garrick's plays and elsewhere, Gounod has Juliet awaken before Romeo dies.

In 1869, Peter Ilyich Tchaikovsky (1840–1893), perhaps the greatest Russian composer, produced a concert overture entitled *Romeo and Juliet*. Although it failed at first, after heavy revision in 1870 and again in 1880 it became, with *The Nutcracker* and *Swan Lake*, arguably the most popular of all his purely orchestral works. At the far end of the production of Romantic music, the Russian Sergei Prokofiev (1891–1953) produced a ballet of *Romeo and Juliet* in 1935 that gave equal emphasis to *pas de deux* (male and female balletic duets) of the lovers and to gaudy color-coded group scenes of the Capulet and Montague combatants.

But the greatest adaptation remains Leonard Bernstein's *West Side Story*. It replaces the solemn and sacrificial double suicide with the gunning down of Tony (Romeo), gang moll Maria's (Juliet's) lover. And it seems to combine the best of the previous romantic ballet and opera with some of America's greatest "classical" music.

All these works are available on CD and cassette. Some videos, such as those of Prokofiev's ballet starring Rudolph Nureyev, are available in stores as well as music and video libraries.

Film

The turn of the twentieth century introduced the world to two popular art forms, jazz and the movies. Forms of high art of earlier eras—even Elizabethan plays and certainly painting, sculpture, architecture, and earlier forms of music—depended to a certain extent on patronage, that is, support from people in positions of power and wealth. But in the twentieth century there has been an almost total dependence on popularity and commercial viability; thus there has been a great deal of bad jazz and bad movie-making. This is the product of formulaic duplication of successful models, mindless catering to lowbrow images of the mass audience, pure clumsiness, and misguided innovation in the name of progressivism in the arts. At the same time, however, we may be astounded at the achievements of jazz and its related genres of blues and rock, and by movies (silent, talkie, black-and-white, color, stereophonic, curved screen, and three-dimensional) as a magnificent storytelling and symbolistic form that often generates huge revenues entirely on its own. It could be said, of course, that a movie is only as good as its writers and actors; but film requires a great deal of creativity in the realm of visual effects and sound.

The problem of creating a film of *Romeo and Juliet* became apparent with the invention of the first motion picture camera near the end of the nineteenth century. One cannot make an effective film contained by a stage. Often one must go outdoors, where stunning scenery will come in conflict with the imagery of Shakespeare's language. Even though there were probably a dozen silent films of *Romeo and Juliet*—notably a version in 1916 with the star Theda Bara in the female lead—and at least three dozen films overall, debate over the conflict of visual scenery and verbal imagery in a movie did not erupt until 1936. The conflict arose over the American director George Cukor's film *Romeo and Juliet* starring the attractive (but severely overaged for teenager roles) English actors Leslie Howard (age forty-three) and Norma Shearer (age thirty-six). It presented hammy John Barrymore (age fifty-four) as Mercutio, Edna May Oliver as a fine Nurse, and a lot of cityscapes.

The principal combatants in the debate were Harley Granville-Barker and Alfred Hitchcock. Noting the rather stark German expressionist sets of Cukor's balcony, cell, or street scenes, Granville-Barker remarked that movie-making and theatrical production were "fatally opposed," with the pictorial and narrative always dominating an abbreviated poetical text. Let movies have Shakespeare without Shakespeare, he said. Just tell a pretty story. Hitchcock, a champion of German expressionism (he had learned his trade as a cameraman for silent films in the Weimar Republic), answered vehemently in favor of "realistic" locations as setpieces for Shakespeare's words in the face of what he saw as academic purism. Movies may be the best medium for Shakespeare, he said.

If Cukor's wonderful talkie raised a stir, however, the costly color productions of the Italian Franco Zeffirelli (1968)—with teenagers Leonard Whiting and Olivia Hussey in the leads, and with Michael York as Tybalt—and of the Australian director Baz Luhrmann (1996)—with teen idols Leonardo DiCaprio and Clare Danes—raised cyclones of debate. These were partly over the reduction of Shakespeare's text and partly over the dominance of purely cinematic images. Not just closeups of the beautiful kids but of striking outdoor shots.

There are four main exterior images in *Romeo and Juliet*: (1)

the hot and open city street covered with blood; (2) the sexual inner sanctum of Juliet's room and balcony and the rope ladder, Romeo's "highway"; (3) Friar Laurence's cell of yoked opposites—contemplation, marriage, and verbal encounters of various sorts; and (4) the crypt in the cemetery. These architectural locations are shown to some extent even from the beginning of Shakespearean production, but they are also extensively talked about in the play. A director with a brilliant pictorial sense like Franco Zeffirelli can easily make use of those images. In fact, his romantic movie production in 1968, dominated by Nino Rota's spectacular score, emphasized the open city square. To do this he chose to film a Hollywood version of the world's most remarkable open urban area, the *campo* (field) in the center of the great Tuscan city Siena. Michael York as Tybalt the street warrior dominated this production. Elsewhere Zeffirelli sought out spectacular on-site images from other great hill towns and landscapes of Tuscany and Umbria, far from Verona.

What kept the images—say, of Gothic horror among the lovers—from interfering with Zeffirelli's open streets was essentially the removal of those images from his text. Though he was always a fan of Shakespeare—especially of the play-within-a-play effect of Sir Laurence Olivier's movie *Henry V* (1948)—he was initially an opera producer. In opera one does not use the full *libro* of Shakespeare but a *libretto*, that is, an abbreviated text of highlights that can be sung and repeated. Zeffirelli's *Romeo and Juliet* contains about only a third of Shakespeare's original text. And there is little conflict of words and imagery in his shortened masterpiece.

Baz Luhrmann's production of 1996 with the popular young stars Leonardo DiCaprio and Claire Danes, again using about a third of the text, is another matter entirely. Whereas Zeffirelli removed the Rosaline part because it interfered with a romantic concept of the purity of Romeo's love, Luhrmann revived the notion that Romeo should not kill Paris and that Juliet, more properly age sixteen than thirteen, should wake up not just before Romeo dies of poison but in fact before he even takes it. Thus Luhrmann does one better than Otway and Garrick and Gounod. This change—as well as Romeo's overlooking a Priority Mail letter from the Friar delivered to his mobile home on Mantua Beach—makes Romeo seem rather oblivious and self-involved, even somewhat pathetic.

Thus the production of pathos, the great skill of world movie directors of the 1980s and 1990s, is intensified up to the moment of Juliet's blowing her brains out with a handgun.

Perhaps Luhrmann's biggest challenge was to make banishment from a noisy, traffic-ridden contemporary California Verona Beach—something like the rough neighborhoods of Venice, California—look like anything but relief. He solves the puzzle by representing Romeo's living quarters in Mantua as a depressing motor home perched at the head of a trash-strewn public beach.

However, although everything about Luhrmann's exciting production is new and extreme and aimed at a contemporary youth-cult audience, its dominant images—water and Christian iconography, such as the cross and the cathedral—come quite aptly from Shakespeare's words and not from any stage effects he could have created. The first image, of water, is easily traced to Arthur Brooke in *Romeus and Juliet*; he loved ocean and beach images, some of which Shakespeare echoed. Luhrmann uses a swimming pool in the Capulet mansion as a metaphor for baptism in love for the couple, which leads back again into Christian iconography.

The second image, of crucifixes and crosses and Madonnas and churches, partly owes its source to the Latino elements in Leonard Bernstein's *West Side Story*. These were essentially about Puerto Rican and Italian gang warfare, which raises the issue of an anachronistic stereotype that would have puzzled an Elizabethan. The fact that Shakespeare placed many of his plays in Italy was partly a recognition that Italy was the seat of a higher civilization than England's during the Renaissance. And Shakespeare always saw events in Italy as versions of events in England. In contrast, Luhrmann's portrayal of passionate Mediterranean or Latino Roman Catholic Americans suggests post–World War II stereotypes of hot-blooded gangs and mafia families, something that would be quite foreign to the Elizabethans. Yet Luhrmann's emphasis on Christianity to suggest a religion of love—as Romeo and Juliet do in their first meeting—is effective not only in his images (the Friar's cell essentially becomes a cathedral of love) but also in his use of Richard Wagner's overture to "Tristan and Isolde," perhaps the greatest musical expression of the religion of love, in the final moments of his movie.

All three movies—Cukor's of 1936, Zeffirelli's of 1968, and Luhrmann's of 1996—are available in the Blockbuster and other video catalogues. All three are significant productions of *Romeo and Juliet* available for group viewing. In this way, it might be argued that Shakespeare is best preserved, as Alfred Hitchcock suggested, for a mass audience not only through texts in the classroom but in film. All three directors are highly intelligent interpreters of the text, and some of their moves may cause viewers to pause and admire. For one, Zeffirelli and Luhrmann both suggest a relationship between Lady Capulet and Tybalt, which helps explain some of both Lady Capulet's praise of the dead Tybalt and Capulet's complaints about young wives. Moreover, there has been a recent tradition, culminating in the Baz Luhrmann movie of 1996, to present Mercutio as both black and, if not bisexual, at least as a humorous cross-dresser and female impersonator. The notion of a gay Mercutio is not directly contradicted by the play. He does make fun of sexual desire for women, but it seems Shakespeare's mercurial one is trying, through typical male taunting, to keep the gang of young men together by dissuading them from becoming involved with the opposite sex. Supposedly Mercutio has no scars whatsoever. That is, he seems mainly interested in bonding together a voluntary (and unstable) band of young men for purposes of friendship rather than honor (unlike the closely knit Capulet gang). Involvements and families would certainly negate Mercutio's "locker room" ideal.

Regarding the dark skin of Luhrmann's Mercutio, it allows directors to draw from the significant pool of black actors. Because it is sometimes hard to gauge how far back certain production traditions go, Luhrmann probably felt that it was best to continue traditions when the origins cannot be located. Thus when Tybalt says to Luhrmann's black, sexually ambiguous Mercutio, "thou *con*sortest with Romeo" (3.1.44 [italics mine]), for example, it may contain sexual innuendo based on wordplay on "con" or female private parts—which he repeats just before his death at Romeo's sword (3.1.128)—that is Shakespearean. Such wordplay having to do with sexual orientation—typical of high school insults—may be foreshadowed in the joke Mercutio lays on the Nurse when she says to Romeo, in a malapropism (an intentional verbal error), that she desires some "confidence" (2.4.120)—she means "conference"—with him. Mercutio shouts "a bawd, a bawd, a bawd" (a prostitute) as if she had delivered a proposition. Of course, Romeo's comment that Mercutio "never felt a pang" must mean he has never, apparently, been in love.[5]

In early 1999, Miramax pictures came out with *Shakespeare in Love* directed by John Madden and scripted by the fine satirical playwright Tom Stoppard out of Mark Norman's original. Shakespeare, played by Joseph Fiennes, is represented as struggling to write a play that will please Queen Elizabeth as much as *Two Gentlemen of Verona* had done, *Romeo and Something or Someone*. Meanwhile, the Bard and his upper-crust girlfriend, Viola De Lesseps (played by Gwyneth Paltrow), are actually living *Romeo and Juliet*, delivering the aubade-like lines of the balcony scenes, dealing with the nurse, and replacing suicidal gestures with sexual joy before the movie makes a right turn. If the stars do well, the Shakespeare lines are electrifying.

Not only are the three selected film versions of *Romeo and Juliet* available on videotape, but there is a quite presentable 1954 version with Lawrence Harvey as the male lead. See also Leonard Bernstein's *West Side Story* with Natalie Wood in the female lead, the Nureyev version of the Prokofiev ballet, and a complete BBC/Time-Life TV video of 1978 with Gielgud as Chorus. The complete play is also available in the Marlowe Society Recording.

NOTES

1. This continuity is evident in productions of works such as William Congreve's *Way of the World* (1700), Edmond Rostand's *Cyrano de Bergerac* (1897), or George Bernard Shaw's *Saint Joan* (1923).

2. Garrick was a friend of the literary dictator, Dr. Samuel Johnson, and a member of his coterie (his inner circle of friends) that included such artistic giants as Oliver Goldsmith, Fanny Burney, Edmund Burke, Joshua Reynolds, James Boswell, and Hannah More.

3. Cushman's removal of "obscenity" follows the tradition of Thomas Bowdler's censored *Family Shakespeare* (1818), which is the source of the word "bowdlerize" (to censor purportedly unseemly matter).

4. Brook was perhaps more successful with *Romeo and Juliet*'s twin, *A Midsummer Night's Dream*, which sometimes looked like it was being played on swings in a racquetball court with an open front.

5. As for Mercutio's sometime dark skin color: perhaps the most famous duke in northern Italy in the *quattrocento*—the time of the original

Veronese story's events in the fifteenth century—was Ludovico il Moro (Lodowick the Moor) of Lombardy and its capital, Milan, who originally hired Leonardo da Vinci as artist and inventor of military hardware. How dark-skinned this member of the Sforza family was is hard to say.

STUDY QUESTIONS

1. Rent the George Cukor film of 1936. Select your favorite scene, and decide how the director used his skill and knowledge to bring out its effectiveness.

2. Do the same with Zeffirelli's movie of 1968.

3. Do the same with Baz Luhrmann's film of 1996.

4. Find in the library two contemporary reviews of the movie version you choose—such as the *New York Times*—and evaluate and criticize the reviewers' comments. Keep in mind the probable editorial policy of the journal or newspaper in question.

5. Research Henry VIII's clown, Will Somers, and James I's clown, Archie Armstrong. Do a report on the Nurse's servant, Peter, and how he fits the bill of court jester or wise clown.

6. Research Will Kempe, Robert Armin, and other actors who portrayed Shakespeare's clowns. Decide how the Musicians' scene at the end of act 4, scene 5, works in the play as a whole.

7. Visit a library and take out Berlioz's operatic version of *Romeo and Juliet*. See what changes have been made to Shakespeare's work and how effective they are.

8. Do the same with Gounod's spiritual opera. Does Shakespeare seem to share Gounod's implied idea of love?

9. Research Tchaikovsky's life and do the same with Tchaikovsky's concert overture to *Romeo and Juliet* in reference to his life.

10. Do the same with Prokofiev's ballet. Compare it to his *Peter and the Wolf*.

TOPICS FOR WRITTEN OR ORAL EXPRESSION

1. Go to the library and read David Garrick's changes and additions to the crypt scene at the end of *Romeo and Juliet*. Argue how pathos (the creation of sadness) is developed positively or negatively in these changes. Develop a theory of pathos.

2. Research the restoration of the Globe Theater in London. Argue how a favorite scene of the play might best be performed in that theater space. Then act out the scene with a friend or two.

3. Rent the movie and do a report on Leonard Bernstein's *West Side Story*. What is entirely removed from the original? What is added to the original? Does relevance to the present—such as gang wars and

handguns—matter? How do you define "relevance"? Develop an essay on this issue.

4. Using your library resources, do a report on William Poel, the first man to try to reconstruct Shakespeare's productions at the end of the nineteenth century.

5. Do some research and give a report on Harley Granville-Barker and his famous relationship to a live white male, George Bernard Shaw, and a dead white male, Shakespeare. Do you suppose it was difficult to remain friendly to both? Develop an essay about this subject. Be limited and specific and argumentative.

6. Take out of your music library Prokofiev's ballet and the production with Rudolph Nureyev. What seems removed from the original? What seems added to the original? Consider the problem of color-coding the Montagues and Capulets (what does Mercutio wear?), and the erotic nature of dance as a fair way of expressing Romeo and Juliet's love. Do a comprehensive review with a title and a thesis.

7. Read a chapter, perhaps on opera, from Luigi Barzini's *The Italians* (1964). See how his theory of Italian behavior might be applied to the characterization of Romeo or Juliet in one of your favorite scenes. Compare it to Zeffirelli's version, and develop an argument paper on the subject.

8. Do a report on Samuel Johnson's circle. Try to decide how Garrick could have changed so much in the play when his friend Johnson was desperately trying to establish the original text and Shakespeare's full intentions in his edition of Shakespeare.

9. Read about Charlotte Cushman, the nineteenth-century American woman who played Romeo to her sister Susan's Juliet. Give a report on what happened in her London performances of 1845 and 1846.

10. Read Thomas Otway's *History and Fall of Caius Marius*. Give a report on how the departures from Shakespeare might reflect English taste during the Restoration era.

11. Read up on the anecdotes about Richard Burbage and his acting techniques. Give a report on your findings.

12. Read up on Shakespeare's last two companies, the Lord Chamberlain's Men and the King's Men. Give a report on a day in their lives.

13. Develop an argument about a possible relationship between Lady Capulet and Tybalt. Use quotations from the play.

SUGGESTED READINGS

Included are a number of recent collections of critical essays, all of which contain brief discussions of the performance history of *Romeo and Juliet*.

Andrews, John F., ed. *Romeo and Juliet: Critical Essays*. New York: Garland, 1993.

Ball, Robert Hamilton. *Shakespeare on Silent Film: A Strange Eventful History*. New York: Theater Arts Books, 1968.

Barzini, Luigi Georgio. *The Italians*. New York: Atheneum, 1964.

Black, James. "The Visual Artistry of *Romeo and Juliet*." *Studies in English Literature, 1500–1900* 15 (1975): 245–256.

Carpenter, Humphrey. *OUDS: A Centenary History of the Oxford University Drama Society, 1885–1985*. Oxford: Oxford University Press, 1985.

Cirillo, Albert R. "The Art of Franco Zeffirelli and Shakespeare's *Romeo and Juliet*." *TriQuarterly* 16 (1969): 68–93.

Cole, Douglas, ed. *Twentieth Century Interpretations of Romeo and Juliet: A Collection of Critical Essays*. Englewood Cliffs, NJ: Prentice-Hall, 1970.

Davies, Anthony, and Stanley Wells, eds. *Shakespeare and the Moving Image: The Plays on Film and Television*. Cambridge: Cambridge University Press, 1994.

Granville-Barker, Harley. "Alas, Poor Will." *Listener* (3 March 1936): 387–389, 425–426.

———. *Prefaces to Romeo and Juliet, Julius Caesar, and Love's Labor's Lost*. London: B. T. Batsford, 1958; orig. 1930.

Halio, Jay, ed. *Shakespeare's Romeo and Juliet: Texts, Contexts, and Interpretations*. Newark, DE: University of Delaware Press, 1995.

Hitchcock, Alfred. "Much Ado about Nothing? I." *Listener* (10 March 1936): 448–450.

Holderness, Graham, ed. *William Shakespeare's Romeo and Juliet*. New York: Penguin, 1990.

Holding, Peter. *Romeo and Juliet: Text and Performance*. Basingstoke: Macmillan, 1992.

Levenson, Jill L. *Shakespeare Performance: Romeo and Juliet*. Manchester; Wolfeboro, NH: Manchester University Press, 1987.

Porter, Joseph A. *Critical Essays on Shakespeare's Romeo and Juliet*. New York: G. K. Hall, 1997.

Puknat, Elisabeth M. "Romeo Was a Lady: Charlotte Cushman's London Triumph." *Theatre Annual* 9 (1951): 59–68.

Shakespeare, William. *Romeo and Juliet, by David Garrick, 1750*. London: Cornmarket Press, 1969.

Watts, Cedric Thomas. *Romeo and Juliet*. Boston: Twayne, 1991.

William Shakespeare's Romeo and Juliet: The Contemporary Film, The Classic Play. Bantam Doubleday Dell Books for Young Readers. New York: Bantam Doubleday Dell, 1996.

All the following items can be ordered on the Internet or at other major cassette, book, and video stores.

Cassettes

Romeo and Juliet, starring Claire Bloom and Albert Finney (2 cassettes). HarperCollins Publishers: February 1996.

Romeo and Juliet: BBC Radio Presents, vol. 3 (3 cassettes). Bantam Doubleday Dell Publishing Group: December 1993.

Audio CDs

Berlioz, Hector. *Roméo et Juliette* (selections) (2 discs). Conductor: André Cluytens, Carlo Maria Giulini. Performers: Ernest Blanc, Remy Corazza et al. Orchestra: Orchestra de la Societé du Conservatoire Paris, René Duclos Chorus et al. EMI Classics 685861. November 19, 1996.

Bernstein, Leonard. *West Side Story* (1 disc). Conductor: Leonard Bernstein. Orchestra: New York Philharmonic. SONY, UPC 074646072424. September 15, 1998.

Gounod, Charles. *Roméo et Juliette* (2 discs). Conductor: Charles Munch. Performers: Leslie Chaboy, Margaret Roggero et al. Orchestra: Boston Symphony Orchestra, Harvard Glee Club et al. BMG/RCA Victor 60681. April 14, 1992.

———. *Roméo et Juliette* (3 discs). Conductor: Michael Plasson. Performer: Roberto Alagna, Yann Beuron et al. Orchestra: Toulouse Capitole Chorus, Toulouse Capitole Orchestra. EMD/EMI Classics 56123. April 7, 1998.

Prokofiev, Sergei. *Romeo and Juliet* (2 discs). Conductor: André Previn. Orchestra: London Symphony Orchestra. EMD/EMI Classics 68607. May 21, 1996.

———. *Romeo and Juliet* (2 discs). Conductor: Lorin Maazel. Orchestra: Cleveland Orchestra. PGD/London Classics 452970. June 9, 1998.

Tchaikovski, Peter Ilyich. *Symphony no. 4, Romeo & Juliet/Barenboim* (1 disc). Conductor: Daniel Barenboim. Orchestra: Chicago Symphony Orchestra. WEA/Atlantic/Teldec 13698. October 31, 1998.

Videotapes (in chronological order of performance)

Romeo and Juliet (1936) (1 videotape). Director: George Cukor. Starring Leslie Howard and Norma Shearer. Black and White. Studio: MGM/UA. Run Time: 126 minutes.

West Side Story (1961) (1 videotape). Director: Robert Wise. Choreographer: Jerome Robbins. Script: Ernest Lehman from the play by Arthur Laurents. Score: Leonard Bernstein and Stephen Sondheim.

Starring Natalie Wood, Richard Beymer, Rita Moreno et al. Color. HiFi Sound. Studio: PGD/Deutsche Grammophon. Run Time: 151 minutes.

Romeo and Juliet (1966) (1 videotape). Director: Rudolf Nurevev. Performers: Rudolph Nurevev and the Royal Ballet. Score: Sergei Prokofiev. Color. HiFi Sound. Subtitles in Spanish. Studio: Kultur Video. Run Time: 124 minutes.

Romeo and Juliet (1968) (1 videotape). Director: Franco Zeffirelli. Starring Leonard Whiting, Olivia Hussey and Michael York et al. Narrator: Lawrence Olivier. Color. HiFi Sound. Studio: Paramount Studios. Run Time: 138 minutes.

William Shakespeare's Romeo + Juliet (1996) (1 videotape). Director: Baz Luhrmann. Starring Leonardo DiCaprio, Claire Danes et al. Color. Closed Captioned. HiFi Sound. Surround Sound. Digital Sound. Studio: Twentieth Century Fox. Run Time: 120 minutes.

6 ───────────────────────────────────

The Historical Context of
Romeo and Juliet

INTRODUCTION

Because *Romeo and Juliet* is based on a romance, its historical context lies mainly in the universe of ideas. There are, of course, connections with Verona in northeastern Italy and to Italy at large, including Sicily, in the early fifteenth century, but those connections were realized and developed well after the fact when Shakespeare's play became world-famous following the Romantic era (1770–1835) that glorified love, nature, and individualism. Thus the importance of *Romeo and Juliet* to Verona, most intensely felt today, will be discussed in Chapter 7, "*Romeo and Juliet* in the 1990s." Shakespeare's Verona is largely a place of the mind where love, vendetta, contrariety, and rush reign. The origin of ideas about these subjects lies in the misty past of human consciousness as suggested by the following key primary and secondary documents.

THE NATURE OF LOVE

All cultures have developed concepts of love between and among the sexes. Hindus in India developed both the reincarnated love of Rama and Sita and the notion of Tantrism—techniques and rituals concerning meditation and sexual practices, based in Hindu scripture—that is also reflected in Buddhist and Jainist theology sometimes far to the east of India. Partly through painted erotic art, the far eastern Japanese developed an aristocratic concept of sexual variety, while in the huge Moslem world Sufism developed a notion of the pure spiritualism of human love that takes its form not so much in theology but in some exceptional Arabic, Persian, Indian, and North African love poetry.

Shakespeare's concept of love derives from two major sources: Plato, Plotinus, and Platonism; and Provençal poetry (love lyric from the south of France) and the courtly love tradition that spread its gospel of love through Europe. Even as a practicing Anglican, Shakespeare would have heard from these two schools of thought on love in readings of the Church of England's *Book of Common Prayer*. The Anglican marriage liturgy, for example, asks one to worship the body of one's mate and see the ritual of human mating as providing a mystical glimpse of Jesus' marriage to the church, or of the soul with God. Its theology has one word, "love," for love of God, of one's children and parents, of humanity at large, and of one's mate. Both Platonism and the courtly love tradition have left their imprint on these words.

All these famous cultural approaches to love suggest a spark of divinity in human love—at least a psychic element—but there remain enduring questions: How important and/or lasting is human love? Is human love only a rung on a ladder that leads to religion? Is human love much more than that, a fellow to religion? Or does human love exist outside of desire for beauty and upward mobility? These questions cannot be answered with certainty no matter how many theologians, philosophers, and critics wrestle with them. When the Greeks represented their gods of love and death, Eros and Thanatos, with blindfolds over their eyes, they not only suggested these gods' random or accidental presence in human existence but also their enduring mystery. If the gods do not know, then mortals do not know; only the one god—or is it fate?—knows.

PLATO, PLOTINUS, AND PLATONISM

THE SYMPOSIUM OF PLATO (428–348 B.C.)

Philosopher Alfred North Whitehead once characterized all Western philosophy as "footnotes to Plato." Although Plato's own best student, Aristotle, consistently disagreed with what he understood to be his master's doctrine—and many readers have struggled with his ethical, metaphysical, and religious positions—his reputation remains rock solid. Part of Plato's acclaim results from the fact that (as Shakespeare's contemporary, Sir Philip Sidney, put it) he is the "most poetical" of philosophers. He never wrote "fixed dead words" (according to Plato himself in a devastating review of one of his own student's textbooks) good for filling up notebooks but not promoting creative, independent thought. He wrote stories that rely for excitement mainly on dialogue between very different men and women who rarely agree on difficult subjects. The reader must decide. Indeed, when his characters all agree it may be a dangerously collective occasion.

Plato not only wrote the large part of his philosophy in dramatic dialogues, but he constantly excites the mind by failing to resolve conflicts among his characters and even among the dialogues themselves. For example, some of his characters who appear in separate dialogues seem to change their opinions from one dialogue to the next, given a new context. For example, Plato's most famous dialogue, *The Republic*, with Plato's Socrates at its center, assumes as its theme the unquestionable importance of *ethos*, or the nature of man as a primarily political animal in a culture, group, society, city, or state. Politics is king. But a dialogue written at about the same time, *The Symposium*, again with Socrates at its center (here excerpted), assumes the universal importance of eros, or love, in the individual human and in the universe regardless of any social contract. In fact, the only theory of government we hear of is love of the beautiful in institutions. Love conquers all.

The Symposium—a banquet or drinking party in Greek—is a frame narrative probably told by Plato himself on the authority of a fanatic follower of Socrates known as Aristodemus. In the spring of 406 B.C., Aristodemus had attended a famous dinner party hosted by Agathon, the winner of the previous day's contest in tragedy. The party included some of the greatest minds of fifth-century Greece. Partly in deference to Bacchus (or Dionysus), the god of tragedy, of all collective activity, and of wine, and partly by inclination, everyone has drunk excessively. The narrative delivers a sequence of speeches, as agreed upon by the participants, in praise of the Greek god of love, Eros.

In the first major skirmish of the dialogue, Plato's version of the great comic playwright, Aristophanes, who satirized Plato's idol Socrates in *The Clouds* (423 B.C.), gets to deliver the following hilarious myth about the nature of man and love. According to Aristophanes, humankind was once made up of double beings with double organs. Because its members—double male, double female, and male-female (hermaphrodite)—committed the tragic mistake of impiously racing on their eight limbs up to Mount Olympus to take over heaven from the gods, they were cut in half, leaving only man's present form. Thus humans are always doomed to long for and seek their other half. This is love.

One of the many jokes implied by Aristophanes' tale lies in the fact that the gods themselves must have been cut in half too, because they are not double and have navels and tell-tale creases in their bellies, and they fall in love too—that is their history in Greek mythology. But those inconsistencies are just part of the great comedian's rather serious joke. Aristophanes has produced a creation myth that is in part a cautionary tale designed for the atheistic doctor Eryximachus, who has just reduced the Greek god of love, Eros, to little more than the scientific principle of orderliness in the universe and good digestion in man. But Aristophanes also suggests the mystery that only high poetry and art—not science—can help explain love relationships. They are written by a higher being, the one god.

Aristophanes, whose moment to speak had originally been delayed because of a case of hiccups caused by his hangover from celebrating the dramatic victories, says not only that the nature of eros, or love, is a divine mystery but that love invests human beings with the power of longing for and achieving a dynamic combination, such as Romeo and Juliet often evoke in their poetic statements. Like formerly halved humans, Romeo and Juliet always sing of their fatal contact and union and their absolute devotion to their soulmate in ways a smiling Aristophanes could have predicted. The disgruntled doctor Eryximachus opens the first excerpt.

FROM PLATO'S *SYMPOSIUM* (385 B.C.?)
(From *The Symposium*, translated by Michael Joyce, in *Five
Dialogues of Plato*, London: J. M. Dent, 1938, page numbers in the
text.)

First Selection

"It is for you, Aristophanes, to make good my deficiencies, that is un-less you're thinking of some other kind of eulogy. But in any case, let us hear what you have to say—now you've recovered from your hiccups."

To which, Aristodemus went on to tell me, Aristophanes replied, "Yes, I'm better now, thank you; but not before I'd had recourse to sneezing which made me wonder, Eryximachus, how your orderly principle of the body could possibly have called for such an appalling union of noise and irritation: yet there's no denying that the hiccups stopped immediately I sneezed."

"Now, Aristophanes, take care," retorted Eryximachus, "and don't try to raise a laugh before you've even started. You'll only have yourself to thank if I'm waiting to pounce on your silly jokes, instead of giving your speech a proper hearing." (37)

"First of all I must explain the real nature of man and the change which it has undergone—for in the beginning we were nothing like we are now. For one thing, the race was divided into three; that is to say, besides the two sexes, male and female, which we have at present, there was a third which partook of the nature of both and for which we still have a name though the creature itself is forgotten. For though 'hermaphrodite' is only used nowadays as a term of contempt, there really was a man-woman in those days, a being which was half male and half female.

"And secondly, gentlemen, each of these beings was globular in shape, with rounded back and sides, four arms and four legs, and two faces, both the same, on a cylindrical neck and one head, with one face one side and one the other, and four ears and two lots of privates and all the other parts to match. They walked erect, as we do ourselves, backwards or forwards whichever they pleased, but when they broke into a run they simply stuck their legs straight out and went whirling round and round like a clown turning cartwheels. And since they had eight legs, if you count their arms as well, you can imagine that they went bowling along at a pretty good speed.

"The three sexes, I may say, arose as follows: the males were descended from the sun, the females from the earth, and the hermaphrodites from the moon, which partakes of either sex; and they were round and they *went* round, because they took after their parents. And such, gentlemen, was their strength and energy, and such their arrogance, that they actually tried—like Ephialtes and Otus in Homer [giants who sought to storm Mount Olympus]—to scale the heights of heaven and set upon the gods.

"At this Zeus took counsel with the other gods as to what was to be done. They found themselves in rather an awkward position; they didn't want to blast them out of existence with thunderbolts as they did the giants, because that would be saying good-bye to all their offerings and devotions; but at the same time they couldn't let them get altogether out of hand. At last, however, after racking his brains, Zeus offered a solution.

"I think I can see my way, he said, to put an end to this disturbance by weakening these people without destroying them. What I propose to do is to cut them all in half thus killing two birds with one stone; for each one will be only half as strong, and there'll be twice as many of them, which will suit us very nicely. They can walk about, upright, on their two legs; and if, said Zeus, I have any more trouble with them, I shall split them up again, and they'll have to hop about on one.

"So saying, he cut them all in half just as you or I might chop up sorb-apples for pickling, or slice an egg with a hair. And as each half was ready he told Apollo to turn its face, with the half-neck that was left, towards the side that was cut away—thinking that the sight of such a gash might frighten it into keeping quiet—and then to heal the whole thing up. So Apollo turned their faces back to front, and, pulling in the skin all the way around, he stretched it over what we now call the belly—like those bags you pull together with a string—and tied up the one remaining opening so as to form what we call the navel. As for the creases that were left, he smoothed most of them away, finishing off the chest with the sort of tool a cobbler uses to smooth down the leather on the last, but he left a few puckers round about the belly and the navel, to remind us of what we suffered long ago.

"Now, when the work of bisection was complete it left each half with a desperate yearning for the other; and they ran together and flung their arms around each other's necks, and asked for nothing better than to be rolled into one." (38–40)

"Now, supposing Hephaestus were to come and stand over them with his tool-bag as they lay there side by side; and suppose he were to ask:
  'Tell me, my dear creatures; what do you really want with one another?'
"And suppose they didn't know what to say, and he went on:

'How would you like to be rolled into one, so that you could always be together, day and night, and never be parted again? Because if that's what you want, I can easily weld you together; and then you can live your two lives in one, and, when the time comes, you can die a common death and still be two in one in the lower world. Now, what do you say? Is that what you'd like me to do? And would you be happy if I did?'

"We may be sure, gentlemen, that no lover on earth would dream of refusing such an offer." (41–42)

Plato's Socrates, who delivers The Symposium's *final formal speech in praise of Love—learned, he says, from the priestess Diotima—, emphasizes Love's divinity as lacking and longing for the good and the beautiful that eventually encompasses all religion and understanding of the universe. If one begins with sexual longing for the beautiful object, one ends with trascendental meditation on the ideals of Good and Beautiful and True. Socrates' exposition of the so-called ladder of love— often connected in the Renaissance with Jacob's dream of the ladder to heaven (Genesis 28:10–22)—lends to Socrates' finish a crescendo effect that leads to uproarious applause from the participants that is curiously interrupted. At this moment a beautiful young and drunken aristocrat, Alcibiades—disguised as Dionysus, the god of wine, of tragedy, and of all collective loss of identity—crashes Agathon's party to deliver a drunken speech (he says "In vino veritas") in praise of Socrates' absolute individualism, sobriety, and self-control in the face of sensual temptation or even panic and deprivation on the battlefield. The handsome young man, dressed as the god of wine, praises in the form of Socrates the rational and individualistic elements that are the opposite of his godly domain, all in the name of Eros.*

Socrates opens his speech by countering—through typical Socratic question and answer—the host's idea that love is best characterized as a beautiful and good boy. Then Socrates shows himself the victim of just such argument and answer with Diotima on the same subject. Note that Diotima's best example of the lover is the poet (also meaning "creator" in Greek). In The Republic, *Socrates had proposed that the ideal communist state should expel all poets who did not restrictively praise athletes and politicians. Note also that somewhat ironically, the priestess Diotima's most praised love between humans is, as in Aristophanes' fable, that between an older and a younger man. In this case a woman, Drotina, has the last word. Socrates is speaking:*

Second Selection

"No, no, dear Agathon: it's the truth you find unanswerable, not Socrates. And now I'm going to leave you in peace, because I want to talk about some lessons I was given, once upon a time, by a Mantinean woman called Diotima; a woman who was deeply versed in this and many other fields of knowledge. It was she who brought about a ten years' postponement of the great plague of Athens on the occasion of a certain sacrifice; and it was she who taught me the philosophy of Love." (53)

'Well then,' she began, 'the candidate for this initiation cannot, if his efforts are to be rewarded, begin too early to devote himself to the beauties of the body. First of all, if his preceptor instructs him as he should, he will fall in love with the beauty of one individual body, so that his passion may give life to noble discourse. Next he must consider how nearly related the beauty of any one body is to the beauty of any other, when he will see that if he is to devote himself to loveliness of form it will be absurd to deny that the beauty of each and every body is the same. Having reached this point, he must set himself to be the lover of every lovely body, and bring his passion for the one into due proportion by deeming it of little or of no importance.

'Next he must grasp that the beauties of the body are as nothing to the beauties of the soul; so that wherever he meets with spiritual loveliness, even in the husk of an unlovely body, he will find it beautiful enough to fall in love with and to cherish, and beautiful enough to quicken in his heart a longing for such discourse as tends towards the building of a noble nature. And from this he will be led to contemplate the beauty of laws and institutions; and when he discovers how nearly every kind of beauty is akin to every other he will conclude that the beauty of the body is not, after all, of so great moment.'

'And next, his attention should be diverted from institutions to the sciences, so that he may know the beauty of every kind of knowledge; and thus, by scanning beauty's wide horizon, he will be saved from a slavish and illiberal devotion to the individual loveliness of a single boy, a single man, or a single institution; and, turning his eyes towards the open sea of beauty, he will find in such contemplation the seed of the most fruitful discourse and the loftiest thought, and reap a golden harvest of philosophy; until, confirmed and strengthened, he will come upon one single form of knowledge, the knowledge of the beauty I am about to speak of. And here,' she said, 'you must follow me as closely as you can.

'Whoever has been initiated so far in the mysteries of Love and has viewed all these aspects of the beautiful in due succession, is at last drawing near the final revelation. And now, Socrates, there bursts upon him that wondrous vision which is the very soul of the beauty he has toiled so long for. It is an everlasting loveliness which neither comes nor goes, which neither flowers nor fades; for such beauty is the same on every hand, the same then as now, here as there, this way as that way, the same to every worshipper as it is to every other.

'Nor will his vision of the beautiful take the form of a face, or of bands, or of anything that is of the flesh; it will be neither words, nor knowledge, nor a something that exists in something else such as a living creature or the earth, or the heavens, or anything that is subsisting of itself and by itself in an eternal oneness; while every lovely thing partakes of it in such sort that, however much the parts may wax and wane, it will be neither more nor less, but still the same inviolable whole.' (64–66)

"This, Phaedrus—this, gentlemen—was the doctrine of Diotima. I was convinced, and in that conviction I try to bring others to the same creed, and to convince them that, if we are to make this gift our own, Love will help our mortal nature more than all the world. And this is why I say that every man of us should worship the god of Love; and this is why I cultivate and worship all the elements of Love myself, and bid others do the same; and all my life I shall pay the power and the might of Love such homage as I can. So you may call this my eulogy of Love, Phaedrus, if you choose; if not, well, call it what you like."

Socrates took his seat amid applause from every one but Aristophanes, who was just going to take up the reference Socrates had made to his own theories, when suddenly there came a knocking at the outer door, followed by the notes of a flute and the sound of festive brawling in the street.

"Go and see who it is," said Agathon to the servants. "If it's one of our particular friends you can ask him in, but if not, you'd better say the party's over and there's nothing left to drink."

Well, it wasn't long before they could hear Alcibiades shouting in the courtyard, evidently very drunk, and demanding where Agathon was, because he must see Agathon at once. So the flute-girl and some of his other followers helped him stagger in, and there he stood in the doorway, with a mass of ribbons and an enormous wreath of ivy and violets sprouting on his head, and addressed the company. (67)

PLOTINUS (205–270 A.D.)

Aside from Aristotle, and perhaps Cicero and Plutarch, Plato's best student in the classical world was Plotinus, an Egyptian who lived in Rome in the third century A.D. His philosophy written between the ages of forty-nine and sixty-five was collected by his student, Porphyry (233–304 A.D.), and organized into the *Enneads*, or tracts with nine parts. Porphyry also delivers Plotinus' biography.

The following is one of his many tracts on love that had profound influence on the philosophical school that he founded, now called Neoplatonism. In it, there is always an implied ladder of love in one's travels from earth to spirit. Although the following passage may seem to be a mere commentary on Plato's *Symposium*, it is clear that Plotinus disagreed with Plato on the importance of the material world, which Plotinus sees as entirely spiritualized—even the inanimate world. This emphasis on the importance of the physical and mortal could (and did) lead to a notion of the religion of earthly love as found in some of Romeo and Juliet's speeches and elsewhere in mystical love poetry that is Neoplatonic in spirit (such as John Donne's).

Plotinus' Greek, like Aristotle's at times, gives the translator problems because of its jagged and unpolished quality, as if drawn from seminar notes. Furthermore, Plotinus depends on abstractions like *nous* (spirit or intelligence) or *eros* (love) that are perhaps best capitalized as in the following text.

FROM PLOTINUS' *SIX ENNEADS* (AFTER 253 A.D.)
(From Grace H. Turnbull, ed., *The Essence of Plotinus*. Based on
the translation of Stephen Mackenna. Oxford and New York:
Oxford University Press, 1948, pp. 93–94.)

Love (50) [3.5.1]

Everyone recognizes that the emotional state for which we make love responsible rises in souls aspiring to be knit in the closest union with some beautiful object; and it is sound, I think, to find the primal source of love in a tendency of the soul towards pure beauty, in a recognition of it and a kinship with it. The ugly is in clash, at once, with nature and with God, for nature produces by looking to the Good, and towards order which has its being in the consistent total of the good; and nature itself clearly springs from the Divine Realm, from Good and Beauty.

Now when anything brings delight and a sense of kinship, its very image attracts. Those that desire earthly procreation are satisfied with the beauty found on earth; it is because they are strangers to that Archetype, source of the very attraction they feel towards what is lovely here. There are souls to whom earthly beauty is a reminder of that in the Higher Realm and these love the earthly as an image (of the Other); those that have not attained to this memory do not understand what is happening within them, and take the image for the reality.

Pure love seeks the beauty alone, whether there is reminiscence or not; but there are those that feel also a desire of such immortality as lies within mortal reach; and these are seeking beauty in their demand for perpetuity, the desire of the eternal; they are conscious of insufficiency, and, wishing to produce beauty, nature teaches them to sow the seed and to beget in beauty, to sow towards eternity, but in beauty through their own kinship with the beautiful. And indeed the eternal is of the one stock with the beautiful, the Eternal Nature is the first shaping of beauty and makes beautiful all that rises from it.

And there are those that, loving beauty of person without physical desire, love for beauty's sake. They venerate the beauty of the Other World while they still have no contempt for this in which they recognize a last outgrowth, an attenuation of the higher. They are innocent frequenters of beauty, but there are others to whom it becomes an occasion of fall into the ugly. These last have not mastered the right use of the images of beauty; they know not what the authentic Beauty is.

PROVENÇAL POETRY AND COURTLY LOVE

THE POEMS OF ARNAUT DANIEL (CA. 1190)

From about the middle of the twelfth century A.D. itinerant poets and musicians called troubadours, *jongleurs*, or *trouvères*, wandering among towns in southwestern France, developed elaborate love psychology in their songs about unrequited love, all in a now-extinct language in the areas of Toulouse and Languedoc. The original language of the southern region was called Languedoc, or the "language of hoc," because of its use of the Latin *hoc* ("that") to say "yes." This language, also known as Provençal, differed from the northern French "langue d'hui," which survives as modern French.

Languedoc or Provençal culture was cruelly suppressed during the so-called Albigensian Crusade, a church-approved military expedition (1208–ca. 1333), which also gave rise to the Inquisition, the dreaded church courts of heresy. Pope Innocent III called on his followers in the north of France to crush various supposed heresies generated by Provençal culture. One "heresy" was the love cult connected with some of the poetry; another was a belief in the equally balanced struggle between good and evil in the world (that is, between spirit and body). However, the true object of this crusade remains a mystery even in the words of one of its cruelest perpetrators, the mystical author and theologian St. Bernard of Clairvaux. As a result of the crusade, most of the official records of Provençal culture were destroyed. The crusade was a memorable atrocity committed by French against French.

Starting in 1233 the infamous Inquisition—originating in southwestern France—began to use all its resources, ranging from interrogation to book-burning to torture and execution, to obliterate theological "errors" born of this refined medieval culture and its language. But the Italian poets Dante and Petrarch, and the English poets Chaucer and Shakespeare, never forgot it.[1] Even though Romeo and Juliet seem happy in their love, they speak the language of the analytic love psychology of the Provençal love complaint, that is, the unrequited lover determined to obtain a poetic release from suffering.

The following poems by the aristocratic troubadour, or *jongleur*, Arnaut Daniel provide an impression of this love poetry.[2] It is a representation of the world of courtly love in which the female love object (distant, almost always married) reigns in her perfection, while the male poet tries to make sense of his living death in poetry, the product of the "explosion" of split-up love. Note the emphasis on secrecy in a courtly world of would-be spies. What the lover so often gets is one kiss and the immortality of his poetic output. Arnaut appears in Dante's *Divine Comedy* speaking in his native tongue from purgatory, where his relatively forgivable sins of the religion of love are being burned away. He also appears in a humorous anecdote in the *Vidas* (thirteenth-and fourteenth-century biographies of the troubadours in Provençal). In this anecdote, while suffering from a case of writer's cramp he plagiarizes a competitor who had audibly sung his own newly composed song in an adjoining cell. Called to perform, Arnaut sings his borrowed song to his amazed competitor and his judge, the King of England, (Richard the Lion-Hearted), who was also a Provençal poet of considerable skill. When he explains his writer's cramp and his ruse, the amused king rewards both Arnaut and his competitor.

This tale suggests that Arnaut wrote with difficulty (only eighteen of his poems remain), but we know he generally wrote difficult poems filled with allusion and coined words. He used some of the most complex poetic forms in existence, notably the sestina, a six-stanza poem that reuses in sequential change the same end words, which are brought together in the coda.

FROM *TROBADOR POETS: SELECTIONS FROM THE POEMS OF
EIGHT TROBADORS*
(Barbara Smythe, ed. and trans., London: Chatto & Windus, 1929,
pp. 110–113.)

I

When the leaves fall from the highest tree-tops and the cold grows proud, so that the wild vine and the osier [willow] are withered, I see that the wood no longer echoes with the sweet refrains, but I am eminent in love, whoever tears himself from it.

All things freeze, but I cannot grow cold, for a new love makes my heart grow verdant again; I ought not to shiver, for love covers and hides me and makes me keep my value and leads me.

A good thing is life if joy sustains it, for some cry out against it who are by no means so fortunate. I cannot complain of anything in my lot, for by my faith my portion is of the best.

I cannot blame anything with regard to love, for the nobility of others I regard as worthless. I cannot compare my lady with her equal, for there is no one who is not second to her.

I do not wish that my heart should turn to another love, so that I rob myself of it and she turns her head elsewhere; I do not fear that ever he of Pontremoli [probably the aristocratic Italian troubadour, Marguis Albert of Maldopina] has a fairer one than her, or one who resembles her.

She whose friend I am is by no means cruel; a fairer one does not live this side of Savoy; she pleases me so well that I have more joy in her than Paris, the Trojan, had in Helen.

She who keeps me joyful seems so fair, that her lovely face conquers thirty of the fairest. Indeed, then it is right that she should hear my song, for she is so noble and well dowered with great honour.

Go, song, present thyself before her, for were it not for her, Arnaut would not have troubled to write thee.

II

> To this tune that sounds so gaily
> Words I fashion of the rarest;
> True and certain will they be
> When my file has shaped them neatly;
> Love makes smooth and gilds full fairly
> This my song, inspired by one
> Who is noble altogether.
>
> Better, purer grow I daily,
> Seeing her who is the fairest,
> This I tell you openly.
> Head to foot I'm hers completely
> And though cold winds blow not rarely,
> My heart's love, like summer sun,
> Keeps me warm in wintry weather.
>
> Thousand masses I've attended,
> Lights of wax and oil I'm burning,
> That God may to pity move
> Her 'gainst whom I can't protect me;
> When I see her golden tresses

And her figure fair and slim,
Nought on earth so much I treasure.

My heart's love on her's expended
And I ever fear her spurning,
So that love my loss may prove.
In a flood of love she's wrecked me
Which, ne'er ebbing, still me blesses,
I obey her every whim,
Write her songs in bounteous measure.

Emperor I would not make me,
Nor the Papacy desire,
If from her I had to part
For whose sake my heart is breaking.
If to kiss me soon she pleases
Not, 'twill kill me, I declare,
And her soul to hell deliver.

Ne'er from loving will I take me
Though I suffer torment dire,
And she never cheers my heart.
When a lover toils at making
Verse, all other toil mere ease is.
He of Monclin did not care
More for his belov'd a stiver [a nickel, nothing].

I'm Arnaut who hoards the breezes,
With the ox I hunt the hare,
Swim against the rising river.

GOTTFRIED VON STRASSBURG'S *TRISTAN AND ISOLDE* (1210 A.D.)

Among the many narrative poems that celebrated courtly love
following the fall of Languedoc, perhaps the most famous evocation of the religion of love was Gottfried von Strassburg's *Tristan
and Isolde*. Most memorable is the following scene in which the
recently exiled lovers are viewed by a huntsman and then by
Isolde's husband—and Tristan's uncle—King Mark of Cornwall in
a love nest in the woods ("The Grotto of Love"). They are sleeping,
lying naked, turned away from each other, with Tristan's sword
between them on the bed. At the end of this scene the king decides

they are innocent. He then invites them back, reinstated as Knight Protector and Queen Consort to the Cornish court.

Gottfried treats the religion of love (an inexorable force called *Minne* in New High German) without reference to Christianity or other forms of spirituality except the Norse spirits and their magic potions and giants. Earlier in the story Tristan and Isolde fall in love after accidentally drinking a love potion on shipboard headed for King Mark's capital. Their love seems to inspire them with shrewd trickiness—as in their use of the naked sword in bed. A clerk, not an aristocrat, Gottfried wrote in remarkably subtle tetrameter couplets composed of rhyming pairs of four-beat lines, imitated ably by translator Edwin Zeydel. The excerpt opens with an unnamed huntsman speaking to King Mark.

FROM *THE "TRISTAN AND ISOLDE" OF GOTTFRIED VON STRASSBURG* (1210)
(Trans. Edwin H. Zeydel. Princeton: Princeton University Press for the University of Cincinnati, 1948, pp. 167–169, lines [of the original] 17468–17535.)

"I've found a secret lovers' cave."
"I prithee, where and how? Confess!"
"O sire, in yonder wilderness."
"In yon fierce wilderness?" "O yea!"
"Are living beings in it, pray?"
"Yea, sire, and in the cave I'll shew
a man and eke a goddess, too:
them lying in a bed I found
and sleeping peacefully and sound.
The man is just like any man;
but doubt I must, as doubt I can,
if she with him, unless I'm blind,
a woman is of human kind:
more lovely than a fairy she,
such flesh and bone I ne'er did see
or dream upon this earth, I swear,
where'er I've tarried, anywhere.
I know not what it signifies:
between the two a great sword lies,
'tis gleaming, beautiful, and bare."
The king now spake: "O take me there!"
    The huntsman bold, he did not fail

to lead the king adown his trail,
to where he'd tied his hunting steed.
The king dismounted in grass and weed,
proceeding now upon his way.
The hunter at his post did stay,
and Marke reached the door instead.
He left the door and went ahead,
but at the very top
King Marke made a stop;
the region all he now inspected
just as the hunter had directed.
He found a little window, too,
and lost no time in spying through,
for joy or deep despair,
and there he saw the pair
asleep, in bed reclining,
a bed with crystals shining,
as once the hunter had discerned:
they lay from one another turned,
he this way, she the other way,
between the two the bare sword lay.
He recognized Isôt and him;
his heart and eke his every limb
with grief supreme grew cold,
no less with love now old.
The way in which they lay apart
brought grief and gladness o'er his heart.
His joy from this conviction came
that innocent they were of shame;
but grief by constant doubt was bred;
within his secret heart he said:
"O gracious God, reveal to me,
what may the situation be?
If anything 'twixt them's occurred
that my suspicions have inferred,
o why lie they like this?
A woman should in bliss
in lover's arms abide,
reclining by his side:
o why are they, if lovers, sundered?"
But then again he mused and wondered:
"Are these suspicions false or founded,
is't guilt, or is my fear unfounded?"

Again his doubts were wide awake.
"Is't guilt? Forsooth, it is," he spake.
"Is't guilt? Forsooth, 'tis not," he said.

DENIS DE ROUGEMONT'S *LOVE IN THE WESTERN WORLD*

Swiss editor, academic, and political thinker Denis de Rougemont was a great analyst of the school of love in Western culture in the twentieth century. His masterwork, *L'Amour et l'Occident* (1939), called in this country *Love in the Western World* and in Great Britain *Passion and Society*, sees human love as essentially psychic and upward bound.[3] The work is based on the myth of Tristan and Isolde that culminates for de Rougemont in the opera of the same name by Richard Wagner in the mid-nineteenth century, but what de Rougemont had to say about love often applies equally to the words of Romeo and Juliet (except for their anxiety to marry), and he discusses them briefly.

What is eye-opening about de Rougemont's argument is his radical position: he sees the great love poets of medieval southern France as high priests delivering yet hiding in their apparent love poetry a dualistic religion in which good and evil are equal. Whether or not one accepts this argument (and de Rougemont backed off somewhat in a revision of this very work in 1956), one must marvel at his ability to account for so many peculiarities of this great poetry that was influential on *Romeo and Juliet*. For example, he handles the issue of the tortured conceits (for secrecy), the self-flagellating poses (asceticism), the notion of the religion of love (on the ladder to Christian love), the emphasis on secrecy (priestly care) that helps get Romeo and Juliet into such trouble, and the emphasis on the first kiss (*consolamentum*) and on suicide (denial of the body), and on death.

The following is an excerpt from the first version of de Rougemont's masterpiece describing the peculiar development in late medieval southern France of the troubadours and their songs.

FROM "COURTLY LOVE: TROUBADOURS AND CATHARS," IN
DENIS DE ROUGEMONT'S *LOVE IN THE WESTERN WORLD*
(Trans. Montgomery Belgion, New York: Harcourt Brace, 1940,
pp. 83–85.)

This one-in-three love, this feminine principle ("amor" in Provençal is
of the feminine gender), which Dante presently found "moving the sky
and all the stars," seems indeed to be the Divinity-in-itself of the great
heterodox mystics, the God of before the Trinity mentioned both in the
Gnosis and by Master Eckhart. Nothing else could produce that uncertainty, that sense of equivocation, which it is impossible to throw off as
we read the love poems of the troubadours. The poems are always about
a real woman. But so is the Song of Songs, and there too the tone is truly
mystical.

I come to a song by Peire de Rogiers.

Bitter, bitter my distress must be,
And never, never must my heart give up
Its great and overwhelming grief for her,
Nor I be granted e'en a passing hope
Of joy however sweet however good.
Great joy could acts of prowess bring to me.
I'll do none; all I know to want is SHE.

And here is Bernart de Ventadour:

She has taken my heart, she has taken my self, she has taken from
me the world, and then she has eluded me, leaving me with only
my desire and my parched heart.

And next two verses by Arnaut Daniel—a nobleman who turned wandering jongleur and whose poems, according to authorities on the Romance languages, are "devoid of thought"—seem to me to display the
unmistakable demeanor of negative mysticism hovering over its strictly
unvaried metaphors.

I love and seek her so eagerly that I believe the very violence of my
desire of her would deprive me of all desire whatsoever could one
lose aught by loving well. For her heart drowns mine in a never-
diminishing flood. . . .

I want neither the Roman empire nor to be named its pope, if I
am not to be brought back to her for whom my heart is ablaze and
cleft in twain. But if she has not solaced my anguish with a kiss
[*consolamentum*] before the New Year, she will destroy me and I
shall be damned.

At the end of the poem a touch of Southern petulance screens the grave import of what he is doing—namely, setting up two Churches in opposition to one another.

> I am Arnaut who piles up the wind, who courses hares with a bullock; I swim against the tide!

It will be recalled that when Arnaut Daniel appears in the *Purgatorio*, he utters his name to Dante, his disciple, in a verse of purest Provençal:

> Ieu sui Arnaut, que plor e vau cantan. . . .

URBAN VENDETTA

Urban vendetta and gang warfare over "territorial rights" and collective action by crowds on the streets have to some degree plagued every city known to humankind. Shakespeare himself got to witness enough civil disturbance in Elizabethan London to justify his use of it as a central theme in many of his plays (notably *Henry VI, Part Three*; *Romeo and Juliet*; *Julius Caesar*; *Troilus and Cressida*; and *Coriolanus*). Modern culture often associates gang warfare and family face-offs with the Great Smoky Mountains region or beyond, but we know such activity is actually close to home. Even the terms "lynch," "lynch mob," and "feud" seem to come from a rural South, although in fact lynching and feuds of various sorts are encountered on city streets in Houston, Chicago, Los Angeles, and New York. Feuds are ominously present in institutions and, of course, in every school play yard.

Today, for complex reasons, Italy—and especially Sicily—has provided many of the terms commonly used to describe the kind of urban civil disorder that escalates into destruction of all parties. *Vendetta* ("feuding"), *cosa nostra* ("family thing"), *padrone* ("master," "godfather"), *capo* ("head man"), and, to a lesser degree, *la mano nera* ("the black hand"—the instrument of reprisal) all come from Sicily. This is a remote—and island—extension of Europe, supposedly unpoliced or barely policed like Shakespeare's streets of Verona.

Does the use of these foreign terms in English suggest racial and national bias?[4] It may be comforting to stigmatize a common problem by placing its evil securely in a distant culture or a racial minority. Such use of language hints at prejudice that might have been entirely foreign to Shakespeare but present in subsequent criticism and interpretation of *Romeo and Juliet*. How else might Leonard Bernstein's musical, *West Side Story*, place Shakespeare's feud among Verona's finest families—"alike in dignity" in their grand public squares—in poverty-stricken Hispanic neighborhoods on the west side of New York? How else might Baz Luhrmann place his 1996 movie version of *Romeo and Juliet* in a fictional Verona Beach (portrayed as a rough area of urban Southern California) rife with ethnic gang and mafia drug activity?

Interpreters of *Romeo and Juliet* have often looked for a reason behind the feud between the Montagues and Capulets. Sometimes the Capulets are presented as nouveau riche and the Montagues old aristocratic, but there is no textual support for such a distinction. Shakespeare merely presents two very rich and powerful (and powerfully similar) families in a mysterious feud that is beginning to wane, but dangerously so. For example, Capulet I is lenient about "enemy" party crashers but nearly produces a bloodbath in the process. Shakespeare's text even fails to support the popular color-coding of the retainers of the two houses to reflect the historical—initially medieval—Italian feud between Ghibellines (the "whites," aristocratic supporters of the Holy Roman Emperor) and Guelphs (the "blacks," popular supporters of the Pope). Shakespeare is emphatically and peculiarly quiet on this point, but his vagueness may have a purpose. After all, Italy and England (especially Sicily and England) at the time could both be regarded as improperly policed islands on the edge of Europe, reflecting powerful similarities. Shakespeare might have had such feelings about Sicily.

Sicily and England of Shakespeare's day had a lot in common. They were both made representative kingdoms at about the same time following Norman invasions. They had identical treasury systems, probably of Sicilian origin. Bonds were created through intermarriage of royalty and extended visits between rulers and dignitaries. For example, Richard the Lion-Hearted and Thomas a Beckett, archbishop of Canterbury, visited Sicily, and expatriates such as Walter of England, archbishop of Palermo, spent time there. In Shakespeare's day, after Venetian liberties were curbed, the English and Sicilians were proud to boast the only effective constitutional parliaments in the world; both were peculiar in that they ruled (or barely ruled) under two monarchs at war, Queen Elizabeth and Philip II of Spain. Perhaps Europe allowed considerable liberty to the two largest islands set off from the continent by the Strait of Messina and the English Channel, but one of the products of that freedom was the licence of civil disturbance like the kind Shakespeare presents in Verona. Nonetheless, such insurrections were probable given human nature in general, not geographic location.

In other words, if Shakespeare remains quiet on why the Capulets and Montagues feud, he may have had special reason for doing so. Feuds, like fits of jealousy, often have no good reason—they thrive on trivial irritations like imagined insults (as with Tybalt) and lost handkerchiefs (as with Othello). They grow into serious conflicts most quickly among likes, twins, similar races, or families, and they follow alike among aristocratic and middle-class and poverty-stricken families. They often resolve themselves, tragically, only when there is a colossal sacrifice, a real or imagined collective murder on everyone's part, such as the human sacrifice of Romeo and Juliet implied at the end of Shakespeare's play. Nowhere is their death at their owns hands seen as the mortal Christian sin of suicide, but as a ritual human sacrifice.

If such collective human destruction is not unanimous there will still be bad blood, but if the blood is on everyone's hands (Montague and Capulet, Prince and family alike), the conflagration will be contained. All this inevitable feuding and scapegoating in the play suggests a depressing view of human nature.[5] Shakespeare knew that Romeo and Juliet were perfect candidates for sacrifice. After all, not only were they the highly visible and only living children of two feuding houses, but they represented a distinctive blend of Capulet and Montague given their secret marriage. They represented the kind of mix or contamination that would threaten and enrage a stubborn adherent of one family's faction, like Tybalt.

Although there were Italy-haters in Elizabethan England (such as the Queen's own tutor, Roger Ascham), it is apparent that Shakespeare saw Italy as a superior civilization. Perhaps he even noted that the Italians had a refreshing way of exposing and analyzing their urban problems. The Italians always loved to tell and retell, even in Verdi's operatic form, the story of civil disturbance that gets out of hand. Similarly, Shakespeare often tells the story of the mob violence that sometimes plagues England's relative political freedom.

GAY TALESE'S NOVEL *UNTO THE SONS*

Journalist and novelist Gay Talese, of Calabrian Italian descent, writes about Palermo's most famous eruption of feuding, which may have helped found the mafia for which the city is (perhaps unfairly) world famous. It also set in motion the war of the whites

(Ghibellines) and the blacks (Guelphs) that Shakespeare chose to ignore in favor of his ahistorical study of human nature in *Romeo and Juliet*.

Recalling how Saint Francis of Paola—a fifteenth-century mystic—supposedly flew over the seas by a magic carpet from the toe of Italy to Sicily over the Strait of Messina, Talese writes the following, a section of *Unto the Sons* known as "the Sicilian Vespers."

FROM GAY TALESE, *UNTO THE SONS*
(New York: Knopf; distributed by Random House, 1992, pp. 22–24.)

Brother of the devout King Louis IX of France (later canonized as Saint Louis), Charles d'Anjou came to Italy with pious credentials, which are exemplified in the large heroic painting of him that my father as a boy saw hanging in the Maida church where the Talese family worshipped. In the portrait, Charles is presented as a benign figure, almost enshrined in heavenly sunlight, being blessed by the Pope. According to my father, however, Charles d'Anjou's thirteenth-century invasion and conquest of Frederick II's dominions in southern Italy and Sicily was—quite apart from Charles's building many splendid churches that pacified the papacy—more accurately characterized by the activities of his soldiers, who burned the crops of farmers, extorted money from men whom they later murdered, and abducted and raped women.

Several years of such behavior finally led to a people's rebellion, an eruption of such magnitude that it culminated in the death of two thousand French soldiers of occupation and quickly diminished the size and influence of Charles d'Anjou's dynasty in the Kingdom of Southern Italy.

The spark of the insurrection was ignited in Sicily during a quiet afternoon in a park on the outskirts of Palermo. The year was 1282. It was Easter Monday, a sultry day on which many Sicilian men, women, and children wore holiday clothes and strolled or relaxed on the grass surrounded by baskets filled with fruit, cheese, and wine.

French soldiers were also in the park, patrolling the area in pairs, and they would occasionally join the picnickers without being invited and help themselves to the wine and make personal comments that, while embarrassing to the women, the Sicilian men tried to ignore.

But as the drinking continued and the soldiers' remarks became more bold and crude, some Sicilians began to express their resentment. When two men stood up to address the soldiers more directly, a drunken French officer appeared on the scene and ordered his soldiers to search the men to determine whether they carried knives or other dangerous objects. When nothing was discovered, the officer demanded that the search be extended to include the women in the area; as this was being done, the officer saw walking along a path a beautiful young woman, accompanied by the man she had married earlier that morning.

Pointing to the woman, the officer announced that he would search her himself, and as her husband was held back by soldiers, the officer proceeded to move his hands up under her skirts and then into her blouse, where he fondled her breasts, causing her to faint. Her anguished husband was provoked to yell out to the crowd: "Death to all the French!"

Suddenly from behind trees and bushes came Sicilians armed with knives which they thrust into the backs of the officer and his soldiers. After confiscating the dead Frenchmen's weapons, they formed a mob armed mostly with knives, sticks, and stones, and rushed out of the park in a rampageous spirit exacerbated as they were joined by hundreds of other Sicilians who were eager to attack and kill every Frenchman they could find.

By sheer numbers they overwhelmed the French garrisons on the island, killing not only soldiers but also French women and children— anyone who was French faced the likelihood of a brutal death. The method the mob used to identify the French occupants of Sicily was to force them at knifepoint to pronounce one word: *ciceri*. This is the name for a small vegetable, a beige bean about the size of a pea, and its proper pronunciation (*chi*-che-ri) was so beyond the mastery of the French tongue that its mere mispronunciation provided the mob with ample evidence for a throat-slashing death sentence. When news of this massacre reached Charles d'Anjou, who was then traveling near Rome, he immediately dispatched one hundred thirty armed ships toward Sicily, while he himself led the charge of five thousand cavalry officers down the coast through the Maida valley toward the seething southernmost tip of Italy.

But before Charles d'Anjou could fight his way across the Strait of Messina to reconquer Sicily, the rebels had gained the support of the Spanish king, Peter of Aragon, who sailed with ten thousand soldiers from his African campaign against the Moors toward the western shore of Sicily. From there he crossed the island and contributed to the destruction of the French cavalry and fleet.

In addition to King Peter's army, many of the noble families of Sicily and southern Italy supported the cause of the mob, which had meanwhile organized itself into secret groups led by underground chieftains who, according to my father, were the first "godfathers" of the Mafia.

CONTRARIETY

Contrariety conceptualizes the world according to the principle of paired antinomies or yoked opposites.[6] Contraries in the universe may be mind and matter, body and soul, harmony and discord, light and dark, health and sickness, and so on. Existing alongside these sometimes rationalized notions lies something like a mystical religion of contrariety. It tells us that to fully understand the universe we must simultaneously apprehend the yoked opposites suggested by those pairs of dualities.

Like the doctrine of love that Shakespeare links to contrariety, this simultaneous comprehension of opposites finds its best expression in a Zen Buddhist aphorism or Zoan, such as "We know the sound of two hands clapping / But what is the sound of one hand clapping?" and in other forms of mystical poetry including Shakespeare's. Walt Whitman in "Crossing Brooklyn Ferry" asks the reader to "knit the knot of contrariety" and see both the seagull rotating in a "gyre" in the blue sky over the East River and the belching furnaces of the Brooklyn Navy Yard as two visual extremes of nature in action. Plato suggests in several places that the Olympian gods may be messengers of contrariety, as in the notion of Apollo as god of health yet also of contagious disease, or Hera (Juno) as goddess of marital concord yet also of bitchiness. But to find poetic expositions of harmony of discord or discord of harmony one need not go beyond Shakespeare and his fellow poets, Sir Philip Sidney and Edmund Spenser.

Shakespeare's obvious fondness for staging, analyzing, and even poking fun at the mystical doctrine of contrariety has puzzled critics far and wide. Norman Rabkin, in an analysis of Shakespeare's yoking of opposite positions in his plays, *Shakespeare and the Common Understanding* (1967), once saw "complementarity" (a concept borrowed from the theories of modern physics) as a parallel. Other authors, such as Edgar Wind and Robert Grudin (excerpted later in this chapter), have looked for the source in the Renaissance thought that grew out of the rediscovery of mystical doctrines from classical times of the harmony of discords (*discordia concors*). These thinkers deal with the fusion and synthesis of the theory of contrariety with Christian mysticism—not only among artists such as Botticelli, Veronese, and Shakespeare; philosophers such as Giordano Bruno, Baldassare Castiglione, and Francis Bacon; but among scientists familiar to Shakespeare such as Paracelsus, William Gilbert, and Bacon.

PARACELSUS (1493–1541)

Born Philippus Aureolus Theophrastus Bombastus von Hohenheim, Paracelsus—a *nom de plume* meaning "beyond Celsus," an ancient medical encyclopedist—was perhaps the greatest physician of his era. He had, among many others, Erasmus as his patient. But he was also the founder of modern chemistry (a word he coined) and a promoter of the mystery of contraries in the universe. The son of a physician in Zurich, Switzerland, Paracelsus was apprenticed to the nearby Fueger mines, where he became fascinated by metallurgy and miner's diseases, and eventually by the most complex human disease then known, syphilis, for which he developed new uses of mercury as a "friendly" antidote. He fully understood the modern medical axiom that if you knew syphilis, you knew internal medicine.

Like many geniuses, Paracelsus was a difficult man, given to mood swings and arrogance and eccentricity. Yet he always had powerful friends. Here, in formulating the principles of modern homeopathic medicine—such as the use of zinc to counter the effects of the common cold—he wrote the following discussion of poison and chemical cures in terms of natural contrariety, a probable source for some of Friar Laurence's philosophy of herbs. His two leading Latin terms, *mysterium* and *arcanum*, mean essentially the same thing: "a hidden fact about nature."

FROM *PARACELSUS: SELECTED WRITINGS*
(Ed. Jolande Jacobi, Trans. Norbert Guterman, Bollingen Series 28,
New York: Pantheon, 1951, pp. 95–96)

Is not a mystery of nature concealed even in poison? . . . What has God created that He did not bless with some great gift for the benefit of man? Why then should poison be rejected and despised, if we consider not the poison but its curative virtue? . . . And who has composed the prescriptions of nature? Was it not God? In His hand there abides all wisdom, and He alone knows what He put into each *mysterium*. Why then should

I be surprised and why should I let myself be frightened? Should I, because one part of a remedy contains poison, also include the other part in my contempt? Each thing should be used for its proper purpose, and we should use it without fear, for God Himself is the true physician and the true medicine. . . . He who despises poison does not know what is hidden in it; for the arcanum that is contained in the poison is so blessed that the poison can neither detract from it nor harm it.

In all things there is a poison, and there is nothing without a poison. It depends only upon the dose whether a poison is poison or not . . . I separate that which does not belong to the arcanum from that which is effective as the arcanum, and I prescribe it in the right dose . . . then the recipe is correctly made. . . . That which redounds to the benefit of man is not poison; only that which is not of service to him, but which injures him, is poison.

When a medicine is found in accordance with the star, when hot is applied against hot, and cold against cold, all this accords with the arcanum. For in administering medicine we must always set entity against entity so that each becomes in a sense the wife or husband of the other.

BALDASSARE CASTIGLIONE'S *COURTIER* (1528)

The great Renaissance student of courtly manners and human nature, Baldassare Castiglione (1478–1529), discusses in the following selection how wit itself grows out of contraries. A soldier and diplomat from Casatico, near Mantua, Castiglione gained a reputation as a youth for his love poetry and eclogues (pastoral narratives in poetic form). But *Il libro del cortegiano* (*The Book of the Courtier*), a dialogue in four books, is his masterpiece. In the following passage his character, Bernardo da Bibbiena, himself author of a comedy, explains the contrary nature of humor. To be complete, human beings need laughter, and laughter comes from the opposite of ourselves. Thus a complete human being is in himself—or herself—a yoked opposite in itself. And a potentially hilarious one.

FROM *THE BOOK OF THE COURTIER* BY BALDASSARE
CASTIGLIONE
(Leonard Eckstein Opdyke, trans. and ed. N. p.: Immortal Classics,
1929, p. 150)

"Nor is there less laughter when we reply to something that our interlocutor has not said, or pretend to believe he has done something that he has not but ought to have done. As when Andrea Coscia, having gone to visit a gentleman who rudely kept his seat and left his guest to stand, said: 'Since your Lordship commands me, I will sit down to obey you,' and so sat down.

". . . We laugh also when a man accuses himself of some fault humorously. As when I told my lord Duke's chaplain the other day that my lord Cardinal had a chaplain who said mass faster than he, he answered me: 'It is not possible,' and coming close to my ear, he said; 'You must know, I do not recite a third of the silent prayers.'

"Again, a priest at Milan having died, Biagino Crivello begged his benefice of the Duke, who however was minded to give it to someone else. At last Biagino saw that further argument was of no avail, and said: 'What! After I have had the priest killed, why will you not give me his benefice?' "

THE HEROIC FRENZIES OF GIORDANO BRUNO (1548–1600)

Giordano Bruno, the great Renaissance philosopher of contraries, had a profound influence on Western thinkers, from physicists and astronomers to the great twentieth-century Irish authors James Joyce and William Butler Yeats. Initially a Dominican cleric, Bruno traveled widely in Europe. He even journeyed to England in a mysterious long visit in the company of the French ambassador, Michel de Castelnau. His major statements on contrariety were published in Italian in London in the mid-1580s and dedicated to Sir Philip Sidney. For his doctrines such as that of the infinite size of the universe (a complement to Copernican theory), and his acquaintances, such as the English Protestants, the Inquisition in Rome had him burned at the stake in Campo dei Fiori in Rome on February 17, 1600. To this day, fish vendors burn boxes below his statue in this square, which faces—some say with accusation and regret— St. Peter's Dome in the Vatican on the other side of the Tiber River. The following selection is a statement of the doctrine of contrariety in human nature in Bruno's most complex dialogue, *De gli eroici furori (The Heroic Frenzies)* (1585).

FROM *GIORDANO BRUNO'S THE HEROIC FRENZIES* (1585)
(Paul Eugene Memmo Jr., ed. and trans., Chapel Hill: University of North Carolina Press, 1964, p. 187.)

It is by these enticements, then, that nature's power and skill cause one to be consumed by the pleasure of what destroys him, bringing him content in the midst of torment and torment in the midst of every contentment, for nothing results from an absolutely uncontested principle, but everything results from contrary principles through the triumph and conquest of one of the contraries. There is not pleasure of generation on the one hand without the displeasure of corruption on the other; and where things which are generated and destroyed are found to be conjoined and as though composed in the same subject the feeling of delight and sadness is found at the same time; but more readily it is called delectation rather than sadness, if it happens that delectation predominates and solicits the sensibility of the subject with greater impact.

EDGAR WIND'S *PAGAN MYSTERIES IN THE RENAISSANCE*

The following is a selection from the groundbreaking work of iconology (study of the meaning of images in painting and sculpture), entitled *Pagan Mysteries in the Renaissance* (1958), by German art historian Edgar Wind. He talks of the wierd currency of the esoteric doctrine of contrariety that actually found its way into popular art by a contrariety all its own.

FROM "RIPENESS IS ALL," IN EDGAR WIND, *PAGAN MYSTERIES IN THE RENAISSANCE*
(Revised edition; New York: W. W. Norton, 1968 [orig. 1958],
pp. 98–99, 107–108. Text Americanized by editor.)

As Erasmus explained in the *Adagia*, σπεῦδε βραδέως or *festina lente* ("make haste slowly") became the most widely cherished Renaissance maxim; and those who chose it as a device made a sport of expressing the same idea by an unlimited variety of images. A dolphin around an anchor [see Illustration in Chapter 1], a tortoise carrying a sail, a dolphin tied to a tortoise, a sail attached to a column, a butterfly on a crab, a falcon holding the weights of a clock in its beak, a remora twisting around an arrow, an eagle and a lamb, a blindfolded lynx—these and innumerable other emblematic combinations were adopted to signify the rule of life that ripeness is achieved by a growth of strength in which quickness and steadiness are equally developed. . . .

An excellent travesty of this inexhaustible subject is to be found in *Love's Labors Lost* (3.1), where a dialogue between Armado and Moth, introduced by the phrase "Bring him festinately hither," ends as follows:

MOTH:	As swift as lead, sir.
ARMADO:	Thy meaning, pretty ingenious? Is not lead a metal heavy, dull, and slow?
MOTH:	*Minime* [hardly] honest master; or rather, master, no.
ARMADO:	I say, lead is slow.
MOTH:	You are too swift, sir, to say so. Is that lead slow which is fired from a gun?
ARMADO:	Sweet smoke of rhetoric! He reputes me a cannon. . . .

The cannon-ball that so aptly exploded at the climax of Shakespeare's quip was not a new conceit for *festina lente*; it was conventional, and that increased the satirical force of the image.

ROBERT GRUDIN'S *MIGHTY OPPOSITES: SHAKESPEARE AND RENAISSANCE CONTRARIETY*

The Renaissance scholar, essayist, and novelist Robert Grudin provides an analysis of complementarity and contrariety specifically in Shakespeare's sources and in *Romeo and Juliet*. Although his position on the relative immaturity of Shakespeare's use of the theme of contrariety in *Romeo and Juliet* is debatable, he does precisely what a fine critic must do: bring the reader closer to the text by gradually fitting the evidence to the argument. At first he mentions generally the great Renaissance philosopher of contraries, Giordano Bruno; then he discusses the great master of the literary dialogue structure, Baldessare Castiglione, author of *The Book of the Courtier* (1528). Then he examines the great scientist of contraries, the founder of chemistry, Paracelsus; finally he focuses on Shakespeare's *Romeo and Juliet*.

Grudin opens with the probable importance of the thought of the medical doctor and scientist, Paracelsus, to Friar Laurence's versions of contrariety.

FROM "THE INFANT RIND," IN ROBERT GRUDIN, *MIGHTY OPPOSITES: SHAKESPEARE AND RENAISSANCE CONTRARIETY*
(Berkeley: University of California Press, 1980, p. 39.)

[T]o suggest a method of interpretation alternative to the popular theory of the Prologue, Shakespeare has given us the speech of Friar Laurence.

Laurence's philosophy has nothing to do with the stars or fate. It suggests a free causality in which elements of health and disease, virtue and vice, are inherent in the individual, and entrusted to his control. Grace itself (line 28) is not predestined or dependent on divinity but is rather (as in Paracelsus) inborn. Shakespeare's phrase, "Revolts from true birth, stumbling on abuse" (line 20), recalls the idea of the Fall; but the implication is that here the Fall is not a single event governing all mankind so much as a disaster latent in each individual. Laurence emphasizes the moral implications of his Paracelsian source when he repeats the word "virtue," intending it the second time not as a physical endowment but as a moral attribute: "Virtue itself turns vice, being misapplied, / And vice sometime by action dignified." (lines 21–22). Not man's inherent properties alone, but these properties in conjunction with his own self-direction, make him good or evil. Without measure and wisdom the healthiest and finest things—a flower or a pair of noble lovers—are prey to the canker death. Such a philosophy of coexistent destiny and freedom was, as we have seen, made explicit by Paracelsus himself.

NOTES

1. The legacy of the Provençal poets can be seen in mystical authors from William Blake to Herman Melville, and in the poetry of Walt Whitman, T. S. Eliot, and the Beat poets.

2. The first poem, a *trobar leou*, is repetitive and easy; the second is a *trobar clus*, which is rather more difficult.

3. *L'Amour et l'Occident* is, in part, a Christian existentialist answer to Marx and Freud on the material aspects of love such as rank or money, or mating impulse and pure sexual attraction.

4. An example of this would be the term "paparazzo" (an obnoxious tabloid photographer), taken from a figure in Fellini's film *La Dolce Vita*.

5. Thomas Hobbes, an English philosopher some twenty years younger than Shakespeare, was known for his view of the mechanical nature of urban strife and conflict.

6. Concepts of dualism, and its mystical fellow contrariety, in the universe go back far beyond the supposed Manicheism of our Provençal authors. We have the Taoist concepts of yin and yang (eleventh century A.D.); early Christian Manicheism (third century A.D.); Neoplatonic and Judaic sources; Pythagoreanism; Buddhism (sixth century B.C.); and Persian and Medean Zoroastrianism (seventh century B.C.), which paints a world controlled by the equipoise of light (Ahura Mazda) and dark (Ahriman) until the final victory of the good.

STUDY QUESTIONS

1. In Plato, how does Aristophanes' idea of the two halves separated and rejoined apply to some of Romeo and Juliet's words and actions? Do they show no uncertainty, as if they were actually rejoined parts of a whole? Find evidence in the text, and document it.

2. In Plato, Socrates' discussion of love's ever yearning for higher and more refined objects seems to lead to a kind of transcendental meditation. Do you see any of this extreme religious yearning in Romeo? In Juliet? In Friar Laurence? Explain in detail.

3. Plotinus seems to see divine love in the here-and-now real world and directed at "physical" objects. Do Romeo and Juliet share this idea about their love? Does the resulting idealism about this world and about sex itself seem dangerous to you? Exemplify, discuss, and show.

4. What would Mercutio say to Plotinus about the spiritual in the real world? What does he say about Romeo's love? About the Nurse? Discuss.

5. Do you remain puzzled by the difficulty of any particular passages in *Romeo and Juliet*? Choose two and lead a discussion of them. Do you think the problem lies in Shakespeare's distance from the modern age? Or does he seem to be trying to confuse the reader? What is your conclusion?

6. Does Romeo ever hide his thoughts with tricky expressions? With Mercutio? With Tybalt? Discuss and show evidence.

7. Does secrecy play a role in Romeo and Juliet's love? How? Would de Rougemont say it was another symptom of the influence of Provençal lyric on Shakespeare? Discuss.

8. De Rougemont suggests that great poetry of love grows out of the pangs of lost love. Select a passage from Romeo on this subject and discuss. Do the same with Juliet. Does their love ever seem lost to you, or do they just seem to be exaggerating?

9. Gay Talese describes an urban slaughter that results from an insult to a woman. Could Tybalt's challenges and various slaughters after Capulet's party be seen in the same way? Discuss and show evidence.

10. Could the Friar's first speech be seen as a popularization of the notion of contrariety that produces maturity or "ripeness," as Edgar Wind says? Discuss and show evidence.

11. Look up Giordano Bruno in several encyclopedias. Discuss whether they bear out what Grudin has to say about Bruno's love of contra-

riety. Does it seem possible that Bruno would not have great influence in England? And on Shakespeare? Why? Explain.

TOPICS FOR WRITTEN OR ORAL EXPLORATION

1. Plato's Aristophanes introduces several absurdities, such as the evidence of separation in the creases around the belly button, in his discussion of the halved humans who experience love. What other parts of Aristophanes' tale seem absurd to you? Does their absurdity suggest profound thought or mere gags? Be specific and discuss.

2. Plato's Socrates says he learned all he knows of love from a woman, Diotima. Are Rosaline, Juliet, and the Nurse the experts on love in *Romeo and Juliet*? Do they ever seem, like Diotima, to suggest a higher love? Where? Discuss and show evidence.

3. Plotinus suggests that love begins as a search for the beautiful. How does this ideal search appear in Romeo's words? Develop a point-of-view argument paper on this subject, and follow your thesis carefully.

4. De Rougemont introduces the reader to several poets, including Dante's favorite, Arnaut Daniel. Develop a paper on the similarity between Arnaut and what he says and Romeo and what he says. Where does their "negative" idealism come into play?

5. Romeo and Juliet develop a sonnet together in the party scene that uses religion as its conceit. Could this sonnet be evidence for de Rougemont's theory that a religion of contrary forces lies behind Shakespeare's poetry? Or are Romeo and Juliet just flirting? Develop a theory of your own on this subject, and write a closely argued paper taking a narrow position.

6. De Rougemont shows that Romeo, in the cemetery scene, has an obsession with death and even the figure of the grim reaper as a possible religious symbol. Do you agree? Does Romeo seem to have an unorthodox religion in which death plays a role? Develop an argument paper on this subject called "Romeo's Religion." Explain the evidence.

7. Develop a paper on vendetta and scapegoating in *Romeo and Juliet*, referring to descriptions of the actual events of urban slaughter in Gay Talese's *Unto the Sons*. What are the differences between fact and Shakespeare's fiction? Argue closely.

8. Edgar Wind shows that Shakespeare is joking at the expense of the learned use of contrariety in the "festinate" passage of *Love's Labor's Lost* between the boy Moth and Armado. Where does Shakespeare make fun of the idea of contrariety in *Romeo and Juliet*? Choose a

passage (perhaps of Romeo's oxymorons in the first scene) and show how wit and humor on the subject reign. Be specific and do a close reading of the text in question.

9. Look up Francis Bacon in several sources such as dictionaries and encyclopedias. Discuss his approach to contrariety. At one time many people, such as Sigmund Freud, thought Bacon had written the works of Shakespeare. How do your findings fit with what you understand of Shakespeare based on your reading of *Romeo and Juliet?* Discuss in detail.

10. Look up Paracelsus in several sources and do a report on contrariety and the founding of modern chemistry.

11. Look up Castiglione in several encyclopedias and prepare a report on his interest in contrariety. Compare it to Shakespeare's.

12. Choose to disagree with Robert Grudin about the "immaturity" of Shakespeare's use of contrariety, and develop a personal argument on the use of yoked opposites in *Romeo and Juliet.* Develop the evidence; that is, place the quote naturally, quote it, paraphrase it, and show how it fits your argument.

SUGGESTED READINGS

Grudin, Robert. *Mighty Opposites: Shakespeare and Renaissance Contrariety*. Berkeley, Los Angeles, and London: University of California Press, 1980.

Nystrom, Anders. *Agape and Eros*. Philadelphia: Westminster Press, 1953.

Paracelsus. *The Hermetic and Alchemical Writings of Aureolus Philippus Theophrastus Bombast, of Hohenheim, called Paracelsus the Great*. New Hyde Park, NY: University Books, 1967.

———. *Selected Writings*, 2nd ed. Ed. with an introduction by Jolande Jacobi; trans. Norbert Guterman. Bollingen Series no. 28. New York: Pantheon Books, 1958.

Plato. *The Symposium*, trans. Michael Joyce, in *Five Dialogues of Plato*. London: J. M. Dent, 1938.

Plotinus. *The Essence of Plotinus: Extracts from the Six Enneads and Porphyry's Life of Plotinus*. Based on the translation by Stephen Mackenna. Compiled by Grace H. Turnbull. New York: Oxford University Press, 1934.

Rabkin, Norman. *Shakespeare and the Common Understanding*. New York: Free Press, 1967.

Rougemont, Denis de. *Love in the Western World*, trans. Montgomery Belgion. New York: Harcourt Brace, 1940; revised 1956.

Talese, Gay. *Unto the Sons*. New York: Knopf, distributed by Random House, 1992.

Wind, Edgar. *Pagan Mysteries in the Renaissance*, rev. ed. New York: W. W. Norton, 1968; orig. 1958.

7 ─────────────────────────

Romeo and Juliet in the 1990s

INTRODUCTION

By 1990, general knowledge of Shakespeare's *Romeo and Juliet* had become almost universal. Popular culture indicated that it was one of the world's favorite stories. In the age of international English, a "romeo" had become a common term meaning "serial lover." Rock and roll songs in many languages proclaimed Romeo and Juliet's love; video and other versions—sometimes satirical—made millions of dollars; and newspaper headlines and editorials regularly referred to the vendetta and the love in the play as common knowledge. Romeo and Juliet became the symbols for the letters "r" and "j" in the new international alphabetic code (required in airline piloting and control); and in Italy one of the world's great car makers played again and again on the names of the play's principals, labeling its models Alfa Romeo, Giulietta, Super Giulia, and so on. The play itself was used in a number of controversial suicide-education courses in school districts around the country. Ironically, partly because Shakespeare was subjected to unusual censure among New Historical researchers (contemporary marxian ideological critics largely on the West Coast of this country and in England), suddenly there was an explosion of Shakespeare production on stage and in film.

Selling Romeo and Juliet became a cottage industry in the ancient city of Verona (this was somewhat ironic, because the original romance was placed in Siena and in the Tuscan countryside). And the Australian director Baz Luhrmann's 1996 movie of the play helped fuel the present Shakespeare explosion in world cinema. Why had this play won a war for the most bandied about of Shakespeare's plays, becoming even more popular than *Hamlet*?[1]

Probably, in part, a worldwide emphasis on early youth culture, based on the demographics of the population explosion following World War II, helped make the play so popular. But the fashion world of the 1980s and 1990s also made it look like everyone wanted to be a teenager. And anyone who did not want to become a teenager wanted to criticize one. Emphasis on the so-called sexual revolution, youthful suicide, and gang warfare caused schools in the United States to assign the play as the first Shakespeare reading in the curriculum of many seventh, eighth, and ninth grade classes. The play's emphasis also led to worries about its possible influence in the dual realms of sex and violence, but in the process the play became part of the very language of analysis.

THE WERTHER SYNDROME

In 1774, the early romantic German poet and novelist Johann Wolf-gang von Goethe—now generally considered the German national poet, as Shakespeare is generally considered the English national poet—at the young age of twenty-five published an epistolary novel (that is, a work of fiction written in the form of exchanged letters) called *The Sorrows of Young Werther* (*Die Leiden des jungen Werther*). In it, a charming and fanciful young painter, writer, and clerk falls in love with a young woman, Lotte (short for Charlotte), who is betrothed to another man. When the hero realizes that his passion for Lotte is not requited, he commits suicide with a pistol shot to the head.

For good reasons, in 1774 *The Sorrows of Young Werther* became a worldwide literary sensation—on a par with, for example, J. D. Salinger's *The Catcher in the Rye* in 1951. Both novels portrayed the life of the imagination of a talented and sensitive young man opposed to society's norms. But just as social critics noted a supposed rise in runaway teenagers in 1951 and following, so in 1774 and following they recorded a supposed increase in youthful suicide. The suicidal *Wertherfieber*, or Werther fever, even became the subject of clinical examinations of "brain fever," or encephalitis, in young patients. Of course, *Romeo and Juliet* was often a leading referent.

The case of a work of art supposedly tempting a young person to suicide became known as the Werther effect, or syndrome. As social critics debated whether a purely fictive work of art could actually draw members of a young audience to a suicide like Werther's or Romeo's or Juliet's, much larger issues suddenly appeared on the horizon. In the mid-1980s the Werther syndrome became the subject of a rather high-level scientific debate, ostensibly over the impact of two series of fictive TV shows representing youthful suicide. (I say "ostensibly" because the stakes in such a debate are large and often go beyond the questions at hand.) Radical positions in such an argument could lead to censorship and could influence the outcome of lawsuits and criminal proceedings, such as the John W. Hinckley Jr. trial.

In April 1981 John Hinckley had attempted to assassinate President Ronald Reagan out of a morbid obsession with the ending of Martin Scorsese's classic film, *Taxi Driver* (1976). The courts saw Hinckley's imitation of a film character as insane; but some people believe that one does not need to be insane to imitate the actions of a charismatic figure like the violent crime buster—and would-be protector of a thirteen-year-old hooker, played by Jodie Foster—played by Robert De Niro in Scorsese's film.

ARISTOTLE'S *POETICS* (330 B.C.?)

The question of imitation of, and identification with, dramatic figures goes back at least as far as Aristotle's fragmentary *Poetics* on the nature of tragedy (ca. 330 B.C.). Whether he is prescribing rules of tragedy, as the neoclassical authors suggest, or merely describing tragedy as he knew it, Aristotle notes that the hero or heroine of tragedy is only slightly above average. He suggests that such a hero or heroine can be a vehicle for audience identification, which he thought was impossible in the case of narrative poems about superheroes or supervillains. And he wanted this identification with an ultimately maimed or killed tragic protagonist—a version of the god Dionysus or Bacchus—to produce a catharsis of pity and fear through the extremes of self-pity and fear for the self that are experienced when one feels one is being dismembered and/or killed outright. Why purge pity and fear? Because pity and fear are neutralizing and distancing emotions. These were useless in Aristotle's view of the polity, the city of Athens.

According to Aristotle, the absence of pity and fear would lead to compassion and civic virtue in humankind's greatest achievement as a political animal, the city. Thus, as one leaves the amphitheatre on the outskirts of Athens—and has just been dismembered, so to speak—one is now ready to try to handle difficult problems in the city. By purging pity and fear at the amphitheater, a person would become a true citizen of the city, capable of fearless compassion. Thus tragedy—humankind's greatest poetic achievement in Aristotle's view—was specifically designed for identification on the part of man, the imitative animal and citizen or city-dweller.

FROM *THE POETICS* IN *ARISTOTLE'S THEORY OF POETRY AND FINE ART*

(Trans. S. H. Butcher. London: Macmillan, 1907, p. 45)

[Tragedy] should . . . imitate actions which excite pity and fear, this being the distinctive mark of tragic imitation. It follows plainly, in the first place, that the change of fortune presented must not be the spectacle of a virtuous man brought from prosperity to adversity: for this moves neither pity nor fear; it merely shocks us. Nor, again, that of a bad man passing from adversity to prosperity: for nothing can be more alien to the spirit of Tragedy; it possesses no single tragic quality; it neither satisfies the moral sense nor calls forth pity or fear. Nor, again, should the downfall of the utter villain be exhibited. A plot of this kind would, doubtless, satisfy the moral sense, but it would inspire neither pity nor fear; for pity is aroused by unmerited misfortune, fear by the misfortune of a man like ourselves. Such an event, therefore, will be neither pitiful nor terrible. There remains, then, the character between these two extremes—that of a man who is not eminently good and just, yet whose misfortune is brought about not by vice or depravity, but by some error or frailty.

RECENT ANALOGUES

In the context of theories of identification, it might be worthwhile to ask how many times one has witnessed people altering their own habits and, for example, lighting up a cigarette after watching a heroic Humphrey Bogart vehicle such as *The Maltese Falcon, The Big Sleep*, or *Casablanca*. The hero, with whom the new-found smoker had identified, had been smoking cigarettes throughout the film, and the imitation of his actions in this case may not be an entirely conscious action. That smoking might be harmful, but by analogy could imitative behavior in a sane person go as far as suicide? Doubtful. It is possible that an insane girl or woman could stab herself to death in imitation of Juliet at the end of the cemetery scene in *Romeo and Juliet*, but such a person could just as likely find her model in anything else—an article in the *New York Times* noting the details of a recent suicide, or a sociological thesis in the *New England Journal of Medicine* that mentioned the means of suicide, or even a casual remark like "hang me." Need we worry about unconscious effects in a pathologically sound audience?

Obviously such a discussion opens the door to attempts to define the unconscious element of people's reception of subliminal messages and much more. Do we ever outgrow identification? Or can imitative behavior be located and quarantined in adolescence? Modern psychologists, often influenced by Sigmund Freud and Erik Erikson—especially on the violent and self-violent aspects of teenagers in various societies—think they know. So do modern sociologists, often influenced by statistical studies of suicide patterns inspired by the French sociologist Emile Durkheim in 1897. But do they? In *Childhood and Society* (1950), Erikson developed a theory of the life cycle in which adolescence is taken to be the central problematic stage, fraught with identity crises and other hyperactive and ultrapassive difficulties. But does one developmental stage deserve such denigration? Or do they all? Are we not always in danger of losing our sense of identity? I think Shakespeare, with his old Capulets and King Lears, and his middle-aged Lady Capulets and Lady Macbeths, would say "Yes."

The following excerpt is a typical newspaper account with predictable statistics of a double suicide of teenage lovers in Miami. It expresses the special concern of the 1980s and 1990s about adolescent "copycat" behavior—perhaps inspired by this very account in *USA Today* itself, but perhaps more powerfully delivered in a story like *Romeo and Juliet*. Note that given their separate suicide notes, it is fairly certain that this was a double suicide. In other words, it was probably not a case of one lover taking the other lover with him or her; rather, they both wanted equally to die.[2] Note in this article the breathless jounalistic paragraphing (one- or two-sentence paragraphs that act almost like headlines).

FROM STEVE MARSHALL, "FORBIDDEN LOVE LEADS TO
SUICIDE OF 8TH GRADERS"
(*USA Today*, Thursday, November 9, 1995, p. 4A)

Forbidden from continuing their romance, two Miami teen-agers took what they thought was the only choice—being together in death.

Medical examiners determined Wednesday that eighth-graders Christian Davila, 14, and Maryling Flores, 13, drowned when they jumped into a canal. Neither could swim.

The teens were found Tuesday two days after sneaking out into the darkness, leaving behind heart-rending suicide notes to family and friends.

"I can't go on living. I've lost Maryling," Christian said in a note his parents found Sunday morning. "I'm escaping from the realm of reality to the darkness the unknown. Because reality is, I can't be with Maryling . . ."

One of Maryling's notes to "Mom and Dad" said: "You'll never be able to understand the love between me and Christian. You don't let me see him in this world, so we're going to another place. Please don't cry for me, this is what I want. I want to feel happy because I'm going to a place where I can be with Christian."

Maryling's fear, one shared with her mother, was that she was pregnant. But that wasn't true, according to the autopsy.

The events leading to the deaths began Saturday, when Maryling's parents told her she could no longer date Christian, partly because of their ages.

"Love can be such a driving force that you start messing with it only at high risk for everybody involved," says psychiatrist Paul Steinberg, associate director of Georgetown University's counseling service. "You may be worried that your kid may go off the deep end if they stay with this lover, but they can go off the deep end without the lover."

Crisis counselors were at Ruben Dario Middle School in West Dade, where both teens were honor students.

One danger, says Steinberg and other mental health experts, is that teen suicides inspire copycats.

Miami psychologist David Lustig wonders, "Didn't anyone in their lives know how upset they were? Usually people send out some pretty clear signals when they're feeling that bad. It's almost unimaginable they didn't tip off anyone at all.

"If other kids were going to learn from this, there would almost be a positive aspect to the tragedy, but unfortunately it's not likely to have that effect."

There were 2,151 suicides by youngsters ages 10 to 19 in 1992, the last year for which statistics are available, said the Centers for Disease Control and Prevention. Only 304 of those were younger than 15.

"A 13-year-old doesn't know there are other ways of coping. It's sort of like the end of the world," says Steinberg. "They don't have the larger perspective that even a 20-year-old might have."

ROMEO AND JULIET TEACHING ABOUT SUICIDE

The following excerpt is a piece of the inconclusive debate about art teaching suicide—or art teaching about suicide—laced with assorted quotes (and one misquote) from Shakespeare's *Romeo and Juliet*. It also contains some statistics taken from surveys that are hard to gauge. One of a reader's questions might be (as with all sex surveys): How many people are likely to tell the truth about their feelings about such an intimate subject as suicide? Especially on call in a survey.

FROM AN UNATTRIBUTED *NEWSVIEW* ON "TEENAGERS"
(*USA Today* (Magazine) 118 [December 1989]: 15.)

Romeo and Juliet and . . . Suicide

Suicide is second only to accidents as the leading cause of death among young people aged 13–21, and teen suicides are growing in number. It has been estimated that between 5,050 and 7,000 teens kill themselves each year in the U.S.

The National Adolescent Student Health Survey, conducted by the Centers for Disease Control in Atlanta, polled 11,000 students in 20 states on subjects including sex, alcohol, and violence. Respondents revealed that 25% of the boys and 42% of the girls had thought seriously about killing themselves and that 15% had gone as far as trying to inflict potentially fatal injuries.

Ed Beckham, assistant professor of psychiatry and behavioral sciences at the University of Oklahoma Health Sciences Center, feels there are lessons to be learned from examining the thoughts of two of literature's most star-crossed lovers—Romeo and Juliet—about "ending it all." Each of the following quotes from the play's characters is followed by his analysis.

"Past hope, past cure, past help!" Most parents believe that teenagers think everything is a life-or-death issue, but such statements as "there's no hope" could be a special message. "While depression is correlated with suicide, hopelessness has an even stronger association with taking one's own life. People who see no hope at all for the future are at highest risk. Because [teenagers have] had less experience than adults, they may not understand that life often presents major obstacles which are, by and large, overcome with the passage of time."

"How oft when men are at the point of death have they been merry?" The idea that death finally brings bliss may tell teenagers that suicide will "end" their troubles. Reports describing a "feeling of peace" by those who claim to have died and come back to life may appeal greatly to some teens. "It has been observed that some suicides are very calm after they make their decision to kill themselves. Thus, if a family is concerned about a suicidal family member, a sudden calmness is not necessarily a good sign."

"For never was a story of more woe, than this of Juliet and Romeo" [*sic*]. The feeling that teens are alone in their troubles and that no one else in the world could be feeling what they are feeling or be as sad as they are feeling often seems to serve as the perfect ticket to suicide. What is the answer? "It is important for adults not to discount the intensity of teenagers' feelings. We need not only to understand how they are feeling, but also to communicate our desire to understand. This can help reduce feelings of aloneness and alienation."

"O Romeo, Romeo, wherefore art thou, Romeo? Deny thy father, and refuse thy name." So much of the trouble of "starcrossed lovers" stems from conflicts between their parents and their lover's families. What is the answer when teens sometimes must choose between family and love—or death? "It is sometimes futile for parents to attempt to stop teenage romances. Rather than attempt to halt certain relationships altogether, which may lead to rebelliousness or hopelessess, parents can try to guide and put limits on dating patterns."

ON ART TEACHING SUICIDE, AND *THE NEW ENGLAND JOURNAL OF MEDICINE*

The following is part of a debate in what may be the world's premier medical journal, *The New England Journal of Medicine*. The authors, beyond their dazzling use of mathematics and statistics with some very uncertain data, are concerned that a fictive TV show can cause adolescent suicide, perhaps even among a population that is not suicidal to start with. Here, with very little open reference, the old debate about the Werther syndrome rears its head. It raises once again the two central questions: Are adolescents especially susceptible to copycat behavior? Can any representation of something as extreme and intimate as suicide actually cause a sane person to imitate it? Note, however, the remarkably scrupulous argumentation and self-examination contained in this medical thesis. (Reference number 24 of the full article, incidentally, refers to the British poet and critic Stephen Spender's 1962 translation of Goethe's novel, *The Sorrows of Young Werther*, mentioned nowhere in the text.)

FROM MADELYN S. GOULD, PH.D., M.P.H., AND DAVID
SHAFFER, M.D., "THE IMPACT OF SUICIDE IN TELEVISION
MOVIES: EVIDENCE OF IMITATION"
(*The New England Journal of Medicine* 315 (1986): 690–694.

Abstract

Increasing evidence suggests that imitative behavior may have a role in suicide among teenagers. We studied the variation in the numbers of suicides and attempted suicides by teenagers in the greater New York area two weeks before and two weeks after four fictional films were broadcast on television in the fall and winter of 1984–1985. The mean number of attempts in the two week periods after the broadcasts (22) was significantly greater than the mean number of attempts before the broadcasts (14; $P < 0.05$), and a significant excess in completed suicides, when compared with the number predicted, was found after three of the broadcasts ($P < 0.05$).

We conclude that the results are consistent with the hypothesis that some teenage suicides are imitative and that alternative explanations for the findings, such as increased referrals to hospitals or increased sensitivity to adolescent suicidal behavior on the part of medical examiners or hospital personnel, are unlikely to account for the increase in attempted and completed suicides.

THE RESPONSE

The article that followed this abstract led to an international cat-fight among sociologists, psychiatrists, medical doctors, psychologists, and—through extensive media coverage—the public at large, some of whom attacked the methods and the purported results in the article by Gould and Shaffer. In general, they questioned the thesis that fictive shows can cause increased suicide rates. Perhaps the most insidious attack was contained in a separate article by David P. Phillips and Daniel J. Paight published in the *The New England Journal of Medicine* in 1987 that proposed to replicate the evidence and conclusions of Gould and Shaffer but failed in a rather spectacular fashion. Here is a brief flurry of letters on the subject of the experiment and the various conclusions that appeared in the journal a full year and a half later. Professor Tanner from the University of Wisconsin, while questioning controls on who actually saw the shows, ironically suggests that the announcement of upcoming situation-tragedies involving suicide on TV might actually cause the suicide rate to decrease.

Perhaps one should conclude that science sometimes rushes in where only art and literature can point the way. These articles and letters create a stir in the press to this day, as does congressional funding of an attempt by researchers at the University of Wisconsin to decide why people fall in love and with whom. All this controversy may prove that current understanding of sex and violence (or of love and death, as English professors like to say) is the precious preserve of the arts, not science. Perhaps it helps explain why the Olympian gods of love and death are portrayed as blinded. Perhaps Eros and Thanatos are blind (blindfolded) because no mortal knows who will die or fall in love next, and no science can help. But keeping science from studying suicidology, as it is called, if it could be done, would be as dangerous a form of censorship as to censor Shakespeare. If anything, this particular controversy encouraged schools to adopt *Romeo and Juliet* as an English text, because it dealt with important aspects of anyone's everyday reality, which is no one's special preserve.

FROM "LETTERS TO THE EDITOR," IN *THE NEW ENGLAND JOURNAL OF MEDICINE*
(318 [1988]: 707–708. Copyright © 1988 Massachusetts Medical Society. All rights reserved.)

The Impact of Televised Movies about Suicide

To the Editor: To the casual reader, the inability of Phillips and Paight (Sept. 24, 1987, issue)[1] to replicate the results of Gould and Shaffer (Sept. 11, 1986, issue)[2] comes as no surprise. The extensive confounding of the variable of interest with numerous extraneous variables, as well the inability to determine who actually watched the movies, would seem to cast doubt on the reliability of the results of the Gould and Shaffer paper. The more observant reader may have expected that the results would not be reproduced, given the peculiar patterns of the data reported by Gould and Shaffer. In their study, the number of both attempted and completed suicides that preceded the televised movies was significantly lower than would have been expected by chance. Does this statistical result imply that the anticipation of a movie depicting suicide decreases the rates of both attempted and completed suicides? Judging from the work of Phillips and Paight, we may be safe in answering no, though I would prefer to wait until this observation is tested in a larger population and in a study that is not handicapped by severe confounding and by an inability to determine who received the "treatment."

Martin A. Tanner
University of Wisconsin
Clinical Cancer Center
Madison, WI 53706

1. Phillips DP, Paight DJ. The impact of televised movies about suicide: a replicative study. *N Engl J Med* 1987; 317:809–11.
2. Gould MS, Shaffer D. The impact of suicide in television movies: evidence of imitation. *N Engl J Med* 1986; 315: 690–4.

[Joseph A. Murray from Dublin, Ireland, also wonders how many adolescents actually saw the shows. How can we know?   ed.]

To the Editor: I believe that before one can compare the supposed effect or lack of effect on suicide rates among young people of televising fictional stories about suicide, one must take into account the probable audience actually watching such films. Phillips and Paight do not make any references to the time the films were shown either in Pennsylvania or California. It is possible that the lack of effect on these states may have been due to differences in the numbers of young people viewing the movies. It is important that all studies of this type take into account the television ratings for the particular movies studied in the various locations.

Joseph A Murray, M.B., M.R.C.P.I.
St. Laurence's Hospital
Dublin 7, Ireland

VERONA AND *ROMEO AND JULIET*

IN SEARCH OF JULIET'S VERONA

As the following humorous travelogue mentions, the story of Romeo and Juliet may have been originally placed in the countryside of Lombardia (that state of northern Italy controlled for 200 years by Teutonic invaders, the Lombards), and not the Tuscany of Siena or the Veneto of Verona. By placing it in the streets of Verona, the developers of the story (notably Shakespeare) opened the door for a Veronese cottage industry selling everything from apocryphal stories about houses and tombs of Juliet, to trinkets and crystal renderings of the lovers, and even a burgeoning nonprofit business in advice to the lovelorn.

A club, made up in part of international graduate students, will answer mail in many languages addressed to "Juliet" (Capulet or Montague or neither)—or even "Romeo"—"Verona, Italy." The writer Barbara Ascher fluently weaves into her description of the sights and some of the joys of Verona the gradual movement of the principals to a glorious outdoor performance of Verdi's opera *Aida*, which climaxes with the duet of the dying lovers, Radames and the noble Aida, who, like Juliet, chooses to join her man in death and echoes her own lamentation.

FROM BARBARA LAZEAR ASCHER, "TRYING TO AVOID ROMEO AND JULIET: IN VERONA FOR THE OPERA, A VISITOR FINDS THERE IS NO ESCAPING THE CITY'S MOST FAMOUS COUPLE" (*New York Times*, Sunday, May 12, 1996, pp. 11–12.)

ROMEO E GUILIETTA! Tomba di Giulietta. Casa Giulietta. Albergo Giulietta Romeo. Romeo e Glulietta Flamenco to be performed tonight by Luisillo's Spanish Dance Theater . . . The advertisements and signs start appearing in the outskirts of Verona, where modern apartment buildings, car showrooms and cinder block hotels could make us forget that we are approaching what the guidebooks tell us is the "city of love"—a city where, they promise, the atmosphere of that ancient romance will enliven our own.

Are we jaded, aging and churlish? Neither my husband nor I is feeling

the least bit romantic on this cold, rainy day in late August. We're disgruntled and decidedly lost as we search for a way inside the city walls
surrounding the medieval center they once protected. The "Centro"
signs seem to be sending us in circles and we begin to wonder if that's
what "centro" really means. Verona has spent centuries keeping foreign-
ers out. The Romans built the walls; in 312 Constantine laid siege to
them. The Goths were next, in 402, and their leader, Theodoric, plun-
dered stones from the Roman arena to build new walls. The Lombards,
whose power lasted two centuries, from 568 to 774, were followed by
the Scaligers, or Della Scala dynasty, referred to by Ruskin as the central
light of Italian chivalry. During the 13th and 14th centuries they reforti-
fied and maintained the red brick crenelated walls, watch towers and
battlements that keep us out today. Penetrating the city remains a battle
of wits.

We stop at Juliet's Cafe to ask directions. Nobody speaks English. My
spotty Italian falters as I struggle to explain my destination. The waiter
shakes his head sadly. He summons his co-workers, who make sympa-
thetic clucking sounds as they huddle over my crumpled map. After much
discussion and head-shaking among themselves, a young cook who has
wandered out of the kitchen suggests brightly in Italian, "But you're very
close to Juliet's tomb."

Said sweetly, to soothe a tourist's growing distress, to urge her gently
toward this particular Veronese enthusiasm. I'm the wrong tourist. I was
told before I left the States that Juliet's tomb is probably nothing more
than an old horse trough. That even the city fathers know this, but it
makes people happy. Nobody complains. I don't want romance: I want
a hot bath. Sorry, they shrug and hold up their arms in a gesture of
helplessness.

After six more stops for directions we cross a stone bridge spanning
the Adige River, which, unlike us, knows exactly where it's going as it
flows greenly from Alps to Adriatic. We make smaller and smaller circles
through increasingly dark, car-width streets until we come to a halt in
Piazza Sant'Anastasia. There is the looming Gothic brick facade of
Sant'Anastasia, and there on the adjacent corner is the Due Torri Hotel.
We've arrived.

As we go through the doors I begin to resign myself to the fact that
there is no escaping this city's romantic clutches. The lobby, once the
courtyard of a 14th-century Scaliger guesthouse, is a frescoed, tiled,
gilded and columned fantasy. Our room is furnished in mid-19th-century
mahogany extravagance, the moldings are gold leaf, and the tub in the
pink marble bathroom has a Jacuzzi. There is a basket of fruit tied with
pretty ribbons placed on a small table next to a settee designed for sug-

gestive reclining. Unfortunately I failed to pack the requisite Jean Harlowe negligee.

You can measure a city's soul by how it takes you in out of the rain. Following our concierge's directions and accepting the loan of his umbrellas, we head for Caffe Dante and a late lunch. We wander down streets so narrow that as a young woman approaches from the opposite direction we all fold up our umbrellas in order to pass. Within 10 minutes we are at the Piazza dei Signori. There is something about a cool, gray day in a medieval square that makes you believe you are there not as a tourist but as a citizen in the time before the rush of light that was the Renaissance. The sense of dark enclosure is especially keen as we are surrounded by the somber 12th-and 13th-century buildings in which the Scaligers, or Scalas, lived and governed from 1262 until 1390, overseeing a period of flourishing art and chivalry.

Two gentlemen of Verona, Catullus and Pliny the Younger, perch on top of the Palazzo del Consiglio, and a statue of Dante, exile from Florence and frequent house guest of Cangrande della Scala, appears out of the mist. In 1865 the sculptor Ugo Zannoni captured the poet for all eternity in the pose favored by 20th-century authors—hand beneath chin conveying deep thought. He won't be interrupted today. The square spreads before him empty and silent. Then there is a moment when I am certain I hear a hushed "Nel mezzo del cammin di nostra vita . . ." ("In the middle of the journey of our life . . ."). I glance at my husband to see if he's heard it, but he's already heading for the refuge of a warm cafe.

We shake our umbrellas, stamp our boots and leave the damp gloom behind as we open a heavy, varnished oak door and enter what was early in the century Verona's favorite reading room. It maintains that ambiance although it is now a restaurant. Patrons sit on brocade chairs or curl up on green banquettes softened with fringed, pink pillows. They read their newspapers, opera librettos and novels by the light of crystal sconces and chandeliers. Frescoed Piedmont kings and heroic soldiers stare down from the ceiling and appear to read over the shoulders of those who sip espresso and dream. It is clear that you are welcome for as long as you care to remain. On a day like this, who would want to leave the warmth of peach stuccoed walls, the perfume of fresh truffles grated over homemade pasta? We determine to settle in for the duration.

Are we here for the opera? Our waiter asks the question that is standard between July and early September, when fans arrive from around the world to be present for opera performed outdoors without microphones in the first-century Roman Arena. When we say that we are, he hands us the after-opera dinner menu and invites us back.

As the sky clears and we have had our fill of pasta, pastry, blackberries and wine, we walk back to the hotel via the Piazza delle Erbe, which adjoins the Piazza dei Signori. As cars are prohibited in both squares and the weather has discouraged pedestrians, the only sound is our own footsteps against stone. We pass beneath the large whale rib that gives the Costa archway its name. No one knows for sure why or how the rib got there, but we are learning to shrug off vexing facts, Veronese style.

Piazza delle Erbe, larger and brighter than its neighbor, was the forum when Verona was part of the Roman Empire. It is still circus-shaped and is probably the oldest continuous shopping center in the world. Its essential purpose remains unchanged, gossip and goods. Small statues and snow globes of, you guessed it, Romeo and Juliet, have replaced the herbs sold during the Middle Ages. My favorite is completely white but for the bright red lips of the kissing lovers. Romeo's aim is off.

I return to the piazza early the next morning to be here when Verona comes out to do its own business, rather than that of tourists. In the center, surrounded by red brick and ocher marble palazzos, and below a 14th-century clock tower (Verona's first), merchants create a ceiling of white canvas umbrellas above their stalls. Today they offer caged doves and goldfish as well as porcini, leeks, peppers, garlic, zucchini blossoms and eggplants. The air has taken on the woodsy scent of wild mushrooms and the sweetness of fennel. Sounds of commerce and cooing doves echo off the walls. The proprietor of a poultry stall holds a plucked chicken aloft for a woman who shakes her head and demands, "Plumper, plumper." She scolds him in a motherly you-can-do-better-than-that tone, and this being Italy, he responds with boyish obedience. They kiss on both cheeks once she is satisfied and she walks off, affectionately patting the bird's stiff feet sticking out of her wicker basket.

Patrons stop to wash their plums and pears in the 10th-century Fountain of Madonna Verona, named for the third-century Roman statue of a woman that stands above it. A dog leaps up and sits beneath one of the four angry heads that spew water thought to come from a Roman bath. A young man, after eating a particularly luscious peach, dunks his head in the great circular basin.

Verona's history is encompassed in this square. The Roman statue is a reminder of the prosperity the city enjoyed within the empire when it was strategically situated on the strada postumia, the major road from Rome to Germany. Behind the fountain a solid block of marble bears a winged lion and the memory of the time, in 1404, when Verona came under the control of Venice, where it remained until Napoleon's invasion in 1797. And everywhere here, as in the rest of the city, are reminders of the glory days of the medieval Scala dynasty.

The Lamberti tower in the corner of the square rises 273 feet, and an elevator ride to its top provides the best view of the city. From here you can see the rosiness of light reflected off red tiled roofs and peach marble facades, the full swing of the Adige River, the impressive might of the city walls and the fertile sweep of Lombardy plains stretching beyond them. Does it really matter that the guidebooks claim that the famous Lamberti family built the tower, even though there is no mention of such a family in the city archives? Remember, this is Verona. Suspension of disbelief is your passport to pleasure.

Bearing this in mind, I determine to venture to Juliet's house. I try not to be distracted by the glories of the Via Massini, a crowded and elegant pedestrian-only shopping street; Emporio Armani stands near Juliet's courtyard. I strive for the frame of mind that must have motivated the splash of graffiti on the red brick and peeling stucco walls of the 13th-century house with its Gothic door and charming balcony. "Daniela e Flavio," "Ila e Baby," "Laura is the Best." Near the rear of the crowded courtyard, Juliet stands demurely, forever nubile in bronze. Someone has left a note near the hem of her gown. It is written on a paper napkin stained with strawberry gelato. Shameless, I read it. "Dear Juliet, I was here but you were not." Indeed.

There seems to be an odd ritual involving this statue. Tourists, mostly young women in their 20's, line up to stand next to Juliet and have their photographs taken as they fondle her right breast. Because of the constant buffing it shines bright gold, while the rest of the statue has blackened with age. Later I ask about this practice when I meet Giulio Tamassia, director of the Club di Guilietta, which sponsors many Juliet-centered activities in the city and answers letters written to her by lovelorn from around the world. Yes, he is aware of the breast fondling. No, he has no explanations. I suppose it's no stranger than many other cult practices.

Ruskin referred to the tale of the two young lovers, a 16th-century novella by Luigi da Porto adapted by Shakespeare and moved to Verona from the countryside, as "sweet and pathetic." Standing here watching the throng enamored of teen suicide and vigorously rubbing Juliet's breast, I see only the latter and determine not to fight the crowds clamoring to get into the house and up the narrow staircase to stand on the balcony for another photo opportunity. I head for San Zeno Maggiore, one of Italy's loveliest Romanesque churches.

Where Juliet's house failed to move me, the bronze reliefs on the church's main door do not. Standing here alone and in silence, I stare at scenes of Noah building his ark, of Hell and Limbo, all full of movement and energy. There is a terrifying beheading of St. John and a sinuous Salome dancing for that head. Experts are at odds as to the exact dates of these archaic and powerful panels, suggesting anywhere from the 9th to the 12th century.

The warm blush of the facade gives way to a cool, gray interior lightened by a 13th century rose window. The somber setting is reinforced by Mantegna's painting of the Madonna and Child. Mary's mournful expression is reflected in that of her plump and naked child. No amount of singing or lute playing by the angels that surround them can ease their sorrow.

As I leave the church by the back door, I find myself in the garden of red-and-white-striped brick cloisters. Vines reach from tiled roofs to the deep green of the lawns. A magpie swoops down in pursuit of insects that have flown in on the evening air. There is no other movement or sound.

Back at the hotel I discover that we have had the good fortune to procure tickets for tonight's sold out production of "Aida." Unlike seasoned aficionados, we had not ordered our tickets a year in advance, and relied on the particular magic of Veronese concierges to pull the best seats out of a hat and at the last minute. We are presented with poltronissima numerata, tickets for numbered and, most important, cushioned seats in the first section directly behind the orchestra.

Our particular magician suggests pre-opera dinner at Bottega del Vino, a 10-minute walk from the Arena, and a favorite with local vintners, who come to stand at the bar and taste any of 820 wines from the cellar of the owner, Severino Barazan. We leave the enthusiastic crowds pressing against each other in the bar at the front of the restaurant, and work our way toward a quieter back dining room. The walls are lined with bottles of wine, above which are ornately lettered tributes to the vine from Aristotle, Galileo and Dante. It is here that Veronese can be assured of their traditional dishes. Perhaps, suggests Mr. Barazan, we'd like to try pastissada de caval, horse meat? Gnocchi for me, thank you.

I prefer my horses prancing, which they do as the triumphal march proceeds across the stage of the Arena. Burning torches and extras in military garb adorn the marble seats rising some 100 feet above sphinxes, obelisks and arches. Twenty thousand people are here, all are rapt, and many hold candles, traditionally lighted during the overture and held as they slowly burn out while the drama unfolds. Should you clap at the wrong time, or whisper, you will be scolded. The Veronese take their opera seriously. And how can you not, as Radames and Aida sing out their last breaths in an amphitheater where gladiators once fought? Against such a backdrop of tempestuous, exotic history, who is to say that love isn't worth dying for?

LETTERS FROM THE LOVELORN

In the following article, also from the *New York Times*, Alan Cowell tells about the peculiar business of answering letters from the lovelorn that Barbara Ascher mentions are addressed to Juliet Capulet, or Juliet Montague, in Verona. Cowell paints a somewhat sardonic portrait of northern Italian business acumen, but could one not equally condemn the economic motives of a number of sham tourist attractions in the United States?[3] Shakespeare might have been delighted with such operations. Besides, at least one could argue that the Veronese Club of Juliet has a scholarly side in producing accurate translation of a whole Mother Earth of romantic trouble.

FROM ALAN COWELL, "DEAR JULIET: LET ME TELL YOU ABOUT
MY PROBLEM"
(*New York Times*, "Verona Journal," Monday, March 15, 1993,
Section A, p. 4)

VERONA Italy—O Romeo Romeo. Wherefore art thou Romeo? Or Omer or Tony? Juliet's not the only person who'd like to know.

Last year, some 2,000 letters from the lovelorn across the globe arrived in this northern Italian city that Shakespeare endowed with fame beyond its Roman antiquities addressed either to Juliet Capulet or, since she was secretly wed by the time she died, to Juliet Montague.

And many of them ask the same question, albeit modified for different loves, that Juliet posed four centuries ago in Shakespeare's romantic tragedy set in this same town: Wherefore, or why, does love's faithful vow so often bind together couples whose families do not want them bound? Why is romance so tricky?

To scholarly purists the Club of Juliet—a private organization that receives, translates and answers Ms. Capulet's mail—may simply be perpetuating a myth that Verona has promoted since the late 19th century in the interest of drawing visitors to spend their money here.

Juliet's Recent Residence

First there is what the official city guidebook assures the visitor is Juliet's villa in Via Cappello: "Tradition has it that this was the house of the Capulets, the powerful Veronese family to which Juliet belonged."

But according to Giulio Tamassia, the president of the Club of Juliet, the 11th-century edifice was deemed to be Juliet's place only in the 1880's or the 1890's when a group of notables decided to purchase it.

"They wanted it to become the house of Juliet," said Mr. Tamassia, the retired head of a confectionery business, "because the myth of Juliet seemed threatened."

Even the street name seems to have been a bit of a guess. "Via Cappello is similar to Capuleti," Mr. Tamassia said, using the Italian name for the Capulets, Juliet's family, which was locked in a feud with Romeo's Montagues. Since the Italian word cappello means hat and since the building on Via Cappello is marked by a hatter's emblem, he reasoned, "It could be the house of the Capulets—they could have been a family of hat merchants."

The Balcony Question

Then came the vexing question of the balcony. "Romeo and Juliet" simply would not be "Romeo and Juliet" without the balcony even though Shakespeare's text refers only to "Juliet at the window above" after Romeo vaults over a wall into the Capulets' orchard.

The only problem was that the house on Via Cappello did not have a balcony until the 1920's, when, according to Mr. Tamassia, one was taken from another building of the same period and affixed to "Juliet's villa." Even Juliet's tomb is said by some to have been constructed from a horse trough.

But the municipal legerdemain seems to have worked. In 1937, the first of 10,000 letters sent over the years to "Juliet, Verona" arrived from an Englishman.

At first, various Veronese took it upon themselves to answer the mail. Then, a couple of years ago, Mr. Tamassia conceived the idea of the Club of Juliet, and enlisted students from the university here to help with translation and replies.

"The writers are often lonely people," said Laura Zanitti, one of two Italians who along with students from Mexico, Japan, China and Georgia read the heroine's mail and sign their replies as "Juliet's Secretary."

"We ask ourselves: What do they need?" Miss Zanitti said. "We try to give a personal answer and try to understand the sender." Sometimes they consult a local psychologist.

They also organized an annual competition for the best letter. The first prize was awarded in February to Chiara Cabassi, a 20-year-old Italian university student from Parma. Her letter described a more diffident Romeo than Shakespeare's who "does not know how to speak to me of love" and whose "dark eyes" leave her almost speechless.

Of the 2,000 letters the club received last year, 600 were from Italy and the rest from all around the world. Four-fifths are from women troubled by a Romeo they have already met. None, so far, have been vulgar and the nature of their ardor reflects cultural influences, Mr. Tamassia said.

"The Turks are very serious," Miss Zanitti said. "The Latin Americans are the most passionate. The letters from the Arab world are playful and superficial. They invite Juliet to big palaces where luxury solves every problem. They invite her to come and play their new Nintendo.''

Some letters recount stories reminiscent of the medieval Italian saga that scholars believe inspired Shakespeare.

"We seem to have something in common; we have fallen in love with men our fathers do not approve of us even to speak with," a 15-year-old high school student wrote from Chicago. Her tale was grim: she was two months pregnant, she said, and her boyfriend, Tony, "the leader of a big gang," is in jail.

"The reason he is in jail is stupid," she said. "One day when his head was full of thoughts of him and me, he sold some drugs to an undercover police officer."

A Pakistani Feud

A Pakistani woman living in Saudi Arabia wrote of her love for Omer, a man whose family had been locked in a feud with hers for two generations. "What should I do?" she asked.

The reply, Mr. Tamassia said, was simple: She and Omer should emigrate to the West, and be married.

Of all the letters, Mr. Tamassia said, only around 5 percent are addressed to Romeo, and they do not always have the silver-sweet sound of lovers' voices.

"Why are you going to kill yourself for a Capulet?" an 18-year-old university student from Amman, Jordan, wrote to Romeo from a region steeped in intractable divisions. "She is your enemy. Remember you are a Montague, and Montagues hate Capulets. So that even shows that you are a lot sillier than I thought."

RECENT ANALOGUES

Many articles referring to Romeo and Juliet describe the situation of lovers from two factions of a perpetual vendetta in the world's great hotspots, such as the Near East, Bosnia, Northern Ireland, Tibet, and the Tyrolian Alps. In these places racial and national differences seem to play a secondary role to religious hatred in producing what seem to be irreconcilable disputes. In the following article, Bob Herbert describes a movie documentary on a situation in Sarajevo that seems to argue for a common humanity that would transcend vendetta and hatred.

FROM BOB HERBERT, "ROMEO AND JULIET IN BOSNIA"
(*New York Times*, May 8, 1994, sect. 4, pg. 17)

If you watch "Frontline" Tuesday night on PBS you will see the story of two ordinary young people, Bosko Brkic, an Eastern Orthodox Serb, and Admira Ismic, a Muslim, who met at a New Year's Eve party in the mid-1980's, fell in love, tried to pursue the most conventional of dreams, and died together on a hellish bridge in Sarajevo.

The documentary, called "Romeo and Juliet in Sarajevo," achieves its power by focusing our attention on the thoroughly human individuals caught up in a horror that, from afar, can seem abstract and almost unimaginable. It's one thing to hear about the carnage caused by incessant sniper fire and the steady rain of mortar shells on a city; it's something quite different to actually witness a parent desperately groping for meaning while reminiscing about a lost daughter.

For viewers overwhelmed and desensitized by the relentless reports of mass killings and mass rapes, the shock of "Romeo and Juliet in Sarajevo" is that what we see is so real and utterly familiar. We become riveted by the mundane. Bosko and Admira could be a young couple from anywhere, from Queens, or Tokyo, or Barcelona.

We learn that they graduated from high school in June of 1986 and that both were crazy about movies and music. Admira had a cat named Yellow that she loved, and Bosko liked to play practical jokes.

Admira's father, Zijo, speaking amid clouds of cigarette smoke, says, "Well, I knew from the first day about that relationship and I didn't have anything against it. I thought it was good because her guy was so likable, and after a time I started to love him and didn't regard him any differently than Admira.''

Admira's grandmother, Sadika Ismic, was not so sanguine. "Yes, I did have something against it," she says. "I thought, 'He is a Serb, she is a Muslim, and how will it work?' ''

For Admira and Bosko, of course, love was the answer to everything. While Bosko was away on compulsory military service soon after high school, Admira wrote: "My dear love, Sarajevo at night is the most beautiful thing in the world. I guess I could live somewhere else but only if I must or if I am forced. Just a little beat of time is left until we are together. After that, absolutely nothing can separate us."

Sarajevo at the time was a cosmopolitan city coming off the triumph of the 1984 Winter Olympics. With a population of Serbs, Croats, Muslims, Jews and others, the city had become a symbol of ethnic and religious tolerance, a place where people were making a serious attempt to live together in peace.

But civilization is an exceedingly fragile enterprise, and it's especially vulnerable to the primal madness of ethnic and religious hatreds. Simple tolerance is nothing in the face of the relentless, pathetic and near-universal need to bolster the esteem of the individual and the group by eradicating the rights, and even the existence, of others.

When the madness descended on Sarajevo, Bosko Brkic faced a cruel dilemma. He could not kill Serbs. And he could not go up into the hills and fire back down on his girlfriend's people. Says his mother, Rada: "He was simply a kid who was not for the war."

Bosko and Admira decided to flee Sarajevo. To escape, they had to cross a bridge over the Miljacka River in a no-man's land between the Serb and Muslim lines. Snipers on both sides overlooked the bridge.

It has not been determined who shot the lovers. They were about two-thirds of the way across the bridge when the gunfire erupted. Both sides blame the other. Witnesses said Bosko died instantly. Admira crawled to him. She died a few minutes later. The area in which they were shot was so dangerous that the bodies remained on the bridge, entwined, for six days before being removed.

Only the times and places change, Bosnia today, Rwanda and Burundi tomorrow. Jews versus Arabs, Chinese versus Japanese, blacks versus whites. There are various ostensible reasons for the endless conflicts— ideological differences, border disputes, oil—but dig just a little and you will uncover the ruinous ethnic or religious origins of the clash.

The world stands helpless and sometimes depressed before the madness. Millions upon millions dead, millions more to die. It is not just the curse of our times. It seems to be the curse of all time.

THE SHAKESPEARE EXPLOSION IN WORLD CINEMA

In 1980, University of California at Berkeley Renaissance professor Stephen Jay Greenblatt published *Renaissance Self-Fashioning: From More to Shakespeare*. This work produced a marxian picture of a sequence of Tudor authors responding pro and con to an autocratic regime in England. Following publication of Greenblatt's book, in certain academic circles of English departments, and even among notable literati, a gradual debunking of Shakespeare as a great independent thinker and dramatic artist occurred. Sometimes this even culminated in Shakespeare courses being dropped from college or departmental requirements. By looking at Shakespeare in the context of current events of his own era, the New Historicists or New Historians (marxian critics) had called into question Shakespeare's supposed universality. And defenders of Shakespeare's genius were sometimes condemned as essentialists, believers in a bedrock and Shakespeare-inspired sense of an unchanging human nature that was supposedly an exploded theory (an idea contradicted by marxian theory).

Since marxians and Freudians always question the classical theory of an essential human nature, one might ask if it is possible to believe in a constant human nature, as Aristotle asserted in his *Nichomachean Ethics* (ca. 330 B.C.). He said that human nature is everywhere the same; one lights a fire in Greece exactly as one does in Persia, the perpetual enemy of Greece. But modern social scientists disagree. Under certain economic circumstances or certain parental training, could all people become better?

Every movement in culture seems to have an equal and opposite reaction. Just when some English departments began to flag in their defense of Shakespeare, some theater departments in the 1980s suddenly became intrigued by his dramatic genius. Then there was a worldwide explosion of Shakespearean performance with *Romeo and Juliet* at the leading edge. The following two articles (with addenda) from *Time* and the *Chicago Tribune* on the same subject—but with very different styles and aims—appeared the week Baz Luhrmann's 1996 film version of *Romeo and Juliet* opened in movie theaters.

SUCCESS AT THE BOX OFFICE

FROM RICHARD CORLISS, "SUDDENLY SHAKESPEARE: O.K., SO
HE ISN'T JOHN GRISHAM. BUT MORE AND MORE FILMS ARE
BETTING THE BARD CAN MAKE MONEY AT THE MULTIPLEX"
(*Time*, November 4, 1996, pp. 88–90)

Tabloid-TV anchors announce a bloody feud between two of Verona
Beach's most notorious clans—thug royalty, whose young princes have
the family name tattooed on their skulls. The streets of this resort town
sizzle with ethnic enmity, with nose thumbing on a nuclear scale, with
the attitude clash of drag queens and skinheads. When the hormonal
humidity is this high, only fools fall in love. So the daughter of one clan
has eyes only for the son of her dad's hated rival. She searches for him
in her dreams, by her swimming pool, beneath her balcony. "Wherefore
art thou Romeo?" she asks.

Oh, it's Shakespeare. Well, there goes the youth market, out like the
life in Claire Danes' and Leonardo DiCaprio's bodies at the end of the
turbo-glam teen weepie, *William Shakespeare's Romeo and Juliet*.

But soft, what light through mogul's closed mind breaks? It is the glim-
mer of belief that there might be an audience for movies based on the
plays of William Shakespeare. Since 1993, when Kenneth Branagh's
rompish *Much Ado about Nothing* earned $23 million at the domestic
box office on an $8 million budget, studios have begun to belly up to
the Bard. "*Much Ado* showed Hollywood how successful and enjoyable
a Shakespeare movie could be," says Lindsay Law, president of Fox
Searchlight Pictures.

Hollywood has flirted with the poet since its infancy; this week the
American Film Institute is showing the 1912 *The Life and Death of King
Richard III*, the oldest surviving U.S. feature film. For MGM in 1936, Leslie
Howard (then 43) and Norma Shearer (36) played Romeo and Juliet. The
movies have put Shakespeare in gangland (*Joe Macbeth*) and outer space
(*Forbidden Planet*, from *The Tempest*).

But now we're getting a plethora of iambic pentameter. Last Christmas
saw a stolid *Othello* (with Branagh and Laurence Fishburne) and the
brutal, enthralling *Richard III* (Ian McKellen). This week three Shakespeare films will be on view: *Romeo and Juliet*, Al Pacino's *Looking for
Richard* and the British *Twelfth Night, or What You Will*, directed by
Trevor Nunn, the former Royal Shakespeare Company artistic director
who has been named boss of the Royal National Theatre. Branagh has
his four-hour *Hamlet* ready for Christmas. Filmmakers are trying every

tactic—cultural intimidation, lavish spectacle, frenzied camerabatics and the casting of young stars—to put the masses in the seats.

The Pacino *Richard* places its director star front and center, performing scenes from the play, quizzing Brit theater luminaries and Manhattan street dwellers on the relevance of Shakespeare's poetry and the ability of American actors to speak it—trying to get a handle on the murderous Godfather of the House of York. In a way, the film is a high-minded remake of Pacino's *Heat*: he's the sleuth chasing down a charismatic killer. It's also naive, wildly self-indulgent and weirdly mesmerizing. While Pacino wrangles the text with such fellow seekers as Alec Baldwin and Winona Ryder, you get a clearer feel for the star than for the author. You come looking for *Richard* and find Al. "I don't like the word *teach* applied to this because I'm not a teacher," Pacino says. "But we hope to guide audiences into it without their even knowing how they got there." The quest took four years for Pacino: "I made four movies and did two plays during the time I was filming this." He hopes his celebrity will attract new audiences to Shakespeare. "He speaks to all of us about everything that's inside us," Pacino says. "*That*'s the thing."

The thing for studio bosses, who will never replace the NEA as arts benefactors, is to do good works and glean Oscar nods, who subsidize the projects by working for next to nothing. Branagh's sumptuous-looking *Hamlet* was shot for a mere $18 million. In its domestic release, the film need gross only about $12 million to break even. Why, Robin Williams, one of Hamlet's A-list co-stars, could earn that much on a single *Jumanji*-size movie.

And what of those British who weren't in Hamlet? Nunn corralled most of them—Ben Kingsley, Helena Bonham Carter, Nigel Hawthorne—for his *Twelfth Night*. A comedy of Eros about loving twins separated in a shipwreck and embroiled in a game of mistaken sexual identity, the piece now begins as an upmarket *Blue Lagoon*, veers into elaborate farce, then darkens till it seems a lost work of Chekhov's.

It's a handsome artifact, though, on its $5 million budget, and gives star treatment to Imogen Stubbs, who is Nunn's wife. "It's a welcome break from the American kind of film realism," she says of *Twelfth Night*. "When acting onscreen, you're often asked not to act; you're exploited for some quality the director sees in you. But in Shakespeare, you are forced to act—to tell the audience, 'This is a character. This is a *play*.'"

Twelfth Night is a play transferred to film. *Romeo and Juliet* is, defiantly, a movie—an assault on Hollywood's conservative film language that might have come from a more playful Oliver Stone; call it *Natural Born Lovers*. Director Baz Luhrmann envelops Romeo and his goodfellas in portentous slo-mo for the shoot-outs, giddy fast-mo for comedy scenes.

The camera literally runs circles around the lovers. When Romeo sees Juliet, his eye explodes in fireworks. The sound track pulses with rap and rock and sound effects that you'd expect in a Hong Kong melodrama; they shoot forth thunder. The style is studiously kicky, less RSC than MTV.

On its own terms (and for a thrifty $16 million or so), the ploy works: it's the societal psychosis from which the lovers flee and to which they ultimately succumb. Luhrmann, an Australian who pretty much let his camera go nuts in the egregiously overrated *Strictly Ballroom*, here makes reasonable, imaginative decisions that are, arguably, true to Shakespeare. "His stories are full of sex, violence, tragedy, comedy because he was, first of all, a great entertainer," Luhrmann says. "His audience was 3,000 drunken, fighting people, bear baiters and prostitutes." Sounds like a Friday-night crowd at a big-city 'plex.

R and J's style also allows the actors to speak the dialogue (all from the play) without worrying about whether they sound like John Gielgud. "We tried to bring the language to the actors," he says, "and not have the actors try to satisfy some spurious notion of the correct Shakespearean pronunciation."

Danes and DiCaprio speak most eloquently with their faces (hers strong, his soft) and with the hurt and ardor that make this a *Rebel without a Cause* for the '90s—1590s or 1990s. Sometimes it takes a radical like Luhrmann to get to the root of a natural-born screenwriter like Shakespeare.

—With reporting by Helen Gibson/London, Georgia Harbison/New York and Jeffrey Ressner/Los Angeles

ACTRESS CLAIRE DANES

The following brief article on Claire Danes, coupled with the above excerpts, raises some issues about her teen-age identification with Juliet. During the making of the film this straight-A student wrote three papers on *Romeo and Juliet*.

FROM BELINDA LUSCOMBE, "HER SO-CALLED BIG-DEAL FILM
CAREER"
(*Time*, November 4, 1996, p. 90.)

Try as she may, 17-year-old Claire Danes can't shake the angel image. She played an angel in one of her first paying gigs, a music video for Soul Asylum. She played the angelic sister, Beth, in *Little Women*, and in her

Photograph from the Australian director Baz Luhrmann's *William Shakespeare's Romeo + Juliet* (1996). The attractive seventeen-year-old Claire Danes with the charismatic twenty-two-year-old Leonardo DiCaprio, whose performance in this work and in *Titanic* electrified the world. Notice the costumes—an angel kissing a knight in shining armor. Reproduced by permission of Twentieth Century Fox.

most widely known role to date, on the TV show *My So-Called Life*, she was an angst-ridden teen called Angela. Now, amid the racy urban grime of Baz Luhrmann's *William Shakespeare's Romeo and Juliet*, she wears white, has a room full of china angels and dons wings for a party. But she insists, "I'm human. I think people see me as sweeter and softer than I do."

The innocent aura coexists, in person, with a more knowing and world-weary affect (after all, she was raised by artist parents in a loft in Manhattan's SoHo district and has been acting professionally since age 6). In one breath she confidently states a sophisticated opinion of Juliet ("more one-dimensional than people might expect") and in the next worries about how her looks are discussed in the press.

Hollywood, of course, just laps her up. Her mix of fragility and spine is perfect for that movie staple, the wise child. She has already made five feature films and won a Golden Globe for her television work. Currently she can be seen in the film *To Gillian on Her 37th Birthday*, in which she outshines far more experienced actors, including Michelle Pfeiffer. Next year she'll be working with Oliver Stone and Francis Ford Coppola. In fact, Danes is so hot she has a promotional deal with Prada's Miu Miu line, which ensures that she has as many free extra-groovy clothes as she wants. All this, and she just completed her SATs.

But life isn't perfect. She'd like to get more sleep and watch more TV. Plus she doesn't have a boyfriend. And even as she describes Juliet as "like a princess locked away in a tower, protected and isolated from the world," she admits it sounds like her life too. However, she notes an important difference: "My life has changed dramatically, but hers was always like that."

MARKETING SHAKESPEARE TO TEENS

The following is an article in the Tempo section of the *Chicago Tribune*, from the time Baz Luhrmann's film, *William Shakespeare's Romeo + Juliet*, opened in Chicago.

FROM LOU CARLOZO, "SHAKESPEARE ROCKS"
(*Chicago Tribune*, Monday, November 11, 1996, sect. 5
[*Tempo*]: 1, 7)

The box-office success of the sexy and violent new film version ([Elizabethan English intact] of 'Romeo and Juliet' stunned Hollywood. Will this turn on a new generation of teenagers to William Shakespeare? Or is this pox on the greatest playwright of all time? And what's next: Quentin Tarantino's version of 'King Lear'?)

After seeing "William Shakespeare's 'Romeo and Juliet,' " 17-year-old Kate Dell of Elmhurst issued this caveat: "I'd recommend it for teenagers, but not necessarily for adults."

To be sure, the latest big-screen Shakespeare was aiming for a young audience. Extensively advertised on MTV, "The X-Files" and "Friends," the new "Romeo and Juliet" relocated Verona to a modern beach resort (Verona Beach), replaced the swords with handguns, and gave the Montague-Capulet feud a decided street-gang slant. And the casting of heartthrobs 17-year-old Claire Danes and 22-year-old Leonardo DiCaprio didn't hurt its younger demographics.

What's more, the cutting-edge soundtrack has gotten heavy promotion from Capitol Records. No score for strings and flutes, it features The Wannadies, Butthole Surfers, Everclear and One Inch Punch; movie songs such as Garbage's "#1 Crush" and The Cardigans' "Lovefool" have been getting heavy modern rock airplay.

One element the movie didn't change was the play's challenging poetry and Elizabethan word play, a touch that has baffled some of the film's critics and even a few teenagers.

But if any Shakespeare purists are slamming director Baz Luhrmann's treatment, they may be, to borrow from the Bard, sick and pale with grief: "Romeo and Juliet" finished No. 1 at the box office last week, grossing $11.5 million its opening weekend—not bad for a film that cost $15 million to make. And true to the movie's marketing push, teenagers made up a majority of the ticket buyers.

If the success of "Romeo and Juliet" caught Hollywood executives by surprise, it has likewise captivated an entirely different audience.

At the University of Chicago's Lab School, where Darlene McCampbell teaches "Romeo and Juliet" to sophomores, the film has already begun to dominate class discussion. "I almost never use movies during teaching, but it's certainly going to have an impact," McCampbell said. "Kids who have seen it will have felt its power before they opened the book."

That's a good thing to McCampbell, who saw the movie Thursday night. "I just totally loved it," she said. "It's got this blend of an outrageous, in-your-face contemporary setting and characters who got the spirit of the play. It really brought alive that expression, 'Every generation needs its own version of a classic.' "

Most if not all high school Shakespeare teachers have yet to see the new film, but no matter—they spot in its appeal a topic for debate and discussion, a chance to use movie magic for making classroom Shakespeare more palatable.

Or is it the other way around? "I see the flurry here as not so much a tribute to Hollywood," said Carol Conway, a British literature teacher at Morgan Park High School in Chicago. "I see it as a tribute to what we [teachers] have done for Hollywood to get kids interested in Shakespeare."

Last week, Conway had 30 tickets to a "Hamlet" by Chicago's Shakespeare Repertory. It was no hard sell, she said: "Kids were begging me to go. I don't think that Shakespeare has the bad rap that people think he has."

That may not explain why high school students have bypassed the recent revival of Shakespeare on film. Kenneth Branagh's versions of "Henry V" and "Much Ado About Nothing" were no teenage hits, but Conway has an explanation. " 'Much Ado About Nothing' isn't in the curriculum, and the others that have been done are not," she said. " 'Romeo and Juliet' is. I give us credit because we teach it."

Cute stars don't hurt, either. "Getting Leonardo DiCaprio and Claire Danes, that's the draw," Conway acknowledged.

Beth O'Callaghan, 17, agrees. She considers herself a big DiCaprio fan, but that's not the only reason she saw "Romeo and Juliet." "I actually like Shakespeare," said O'Callaghan, who like Dell attends Fenwick High School in Oak Park. "This might actually get people into Shakespeare, if you liked the movie."

A few of O'Callaghan's friends found the 16th century dialogue a bit daunting. "Some people I know didn't understand it, but maybe they weren't trying," she said. "I thought it was easy to understand."

"I wouldn't worry so much about the students getting a grasp of the language," said Marilyn Halperin, the Shakespeare Repertory's education director. Halperin, who arranges Shakespeare performances for as many as 35,000 students a year, thinks "Romeo and Juliet" has exciting potential for drawing teens back to the Bard.

"With students, there's this whole mythology that he's boring, that they're not going to get it, that there's nothing in it for them," said Halperin, who saw the movie last week. "When they see a film they can relate to, it shatters the mythology. I like that very much."

That's not to say Luhrmann has created an ideal teaching tool on the order of, say, "Schindler's List." "For teachers in conservative schools, it may cause some problems,' Halperin said. "They were very careful where they went with the sexual strand, but with the violence strand, they went all the way. That may cause some concerns."

The new "Romeo and Juliet" draws inevitable comparisons to Italian director Franco Zeffirelli's 1968 version, which was controversially sexy in its day but has since lost its novelty with students. Teachers have used it in the classroom, over and over.

"I was excited when I heard the new film was coming out," said Eileen Brusek, an English teacher at Chicago's Whitney Young High School. "For so long, the only thing we've had to work with is Zeffirelli's film."

Brusek spots potential in comparing the Zeffirelli and Luhrmann films in class, "studying how directors approach certain scenes, and what they leave in or take out," she said.

"When I was 14, Zeffirelli made his 'Romeo and Juliet,' and it excited me to no end," said Robert Falls, director of the Goodman Theatre. "That was a 'Romeo and Juliet' for the 1960s; this is very much a 'Romeo and Juliet' for the '90s."

Falls has his own experience with risk-taking Shakespeare. In 1984, he cast a 24-year-old Aidan Quinn as Hamlet, with Talking Heads mood music and Quinn spray-painting the phrase "To be or not to be" on a wall.

"It's impossible to get too highbrow about Shakespeare; he's the greatest popular writer of all times," Falls said. "It's not going to be everyone's taste, but I really think it doesn't matter. It was geared to and created for young people, which I think is terrific."

If teachers, teens and theater scholars agree on one point, it's that youth lies at the heart of the matter. " 'Romeo and Juliet' is about kids," said Martin Mueller, an English professor at Northwestern University. "There's no other Shakespeare that's so much about young people, the things they do and the mistakes they make."

As the box office figures show, kids of the '90s are taking the new "Romeo and Juliet" to heart as their own. It has their music, their images of a fractured society, and their favorite stars. That may be good marketing, but apparently it's also good Shakespeare.

"Instead of looking at this thing as a sacred text, you can look at it as very open, very fluid, very full of possibilities," Halperin said. "Then Shakespeare becomes a creative playground. There's room for the student in there."

Or, as the teenage Dell put it, "A lot of people went there to see the actors, and found a story to it. I think they showed the story pretty well, and captured it well."

If adults insist on going to see the film, Dell thinks that's fine. But she did offer some advice she thought would help: "Listen carefully," she said. "It really moves fast. If you didn't know the story, you could catch on."

Romeos, Romeos

The 1996 film version of "Romeo and Juliet" is the fifth major movie about William Shakespeare's star-crossed lovers:

1936: Leslie Howard, 43, and Norma Shearer, 36, as the principals, were too old for the roles. Nonetheless, Shearer got an Oscar nomination, as did Basil Rathbone as Tybalt. The film was also nominated.

1954: This British version featured Laurence Harvey and Susan Shentall and was filmed in Italy.

1966: The filmed version of the Royal Ballet production. Margot Fonteyn and Rudolph Nureyev star.

1968: An Italian-British production, considered to be the best of the lot. Franco Zeffirelli directed; 17-year old Leonard Whiting was Romeo and 16-year-old Olivia Hussey played Juliet. Nominated for picture and director; won Oscars for cinematography and costume design.

NOTES

1. Had the world reached the point that for every "To be or not to be" or "Something is rotten in the state of Denmark," it would hear two "O Romeo, Romeo, wherefore art thou Romeo's?" or "Flaming youth's," or "Parting is such sweet sorrow's," or "Love's light wings's," or "Infant rind's," or "Tempt not a desperate man's," or "Star-crossed lovers's," or "Flower of courtesy's," or "A plague o' both your houses's," or "Be fickle, Fortune's," or "Death hath lain with thy wife's," or "Still-waking sleep's," or "Queen Mab hath been with you's," or, indeed, "The date is out of such prolixity's."

2. This happens in François Truffaut's film masterpiece, *Jules et Jim* (1961), where the heroine drives an unwilling Jules off a bridge.

3. One such example is Superman's town, Metropolis, Illinois, complete with a fifteen-foot, 4,000-pound statue of Superman and a host of trinket vendors and parades.

STUDY QUESTIONS

1. Read Goethe's short novel, *The Sorrows of Young Werther* (1774, see p. 185), and see if you think it could influence an unstable reader to commit suicide. Compare the effect to a likely response to the end of *Romeo and Juliet*.

2. Read or reread J. D. Salinger's *Catcher in the Rye* (1951), and see if you feel it beckons for imitation. Do you feel that Holden Caulfield is meant by the author to be writing from an insane asylum? Do a report.

3. To the best of your ability, analyze the style, the word choice, and the syntax of Steve Marshall's article on the double suicide of two eighth graders (p. 188). Do you find a lot of simple sentences and short paragraphs? What is the effect? Is the reader meant to have a specific attitude toward thirteen-year-olds? What might it be? Is the article selling fear and guilt? How?

4. Respond to the question posed on p. 190 concerning the reliability of sex and suicide surveys. If you think people may lie on such confidential surveys, who do you think are the most untruthful, boys or girls? Why? Is such lying suggested in *Romeo and Juliet*? Where?

5. Research the history of Verona in several encyclopedias, travelogues, and/or books. Does the town seem suitable as a setting for *Romeo and Juliet*? Verona is not a university town. Does that bear on the play or not? Present your findings to the class.

6. Listen to and study the opera *Aida*, and show how reference to it is appropriate in the article by Barbara Ascher (p. 195). What in *Aida* is similar or different from the story of *Romeo and Juliet*?

7. Analyze the article from the newspaper *USA Today* entitled "Romeo and Juliet and . . . Suicide" (p. 190). Would you ever choose to teach about suicide through the play? How would you do it? How do you evaluate the analysis with quotes by Ed Beckham, assistant professor of psychiatry and behavioral sciences at the University of Oklahoma Health Sciences Center? Would you adopt his method? Why or why not? 8. Look at the article by Bob Herbert, "Romeo and Juliet in Bosnia" (p. 204). The author seems to believe there is an essential human nature, as does Shakespeare. Do you agree with Shakespeare and the author of this article that human nature is always the same and always prone to strife?

9. Read the chapter on Shakespeare in Stephen Greenblatt's *Renaissance Self-Fashioning: From More to Shakespeare* (1980). Do you

agree that political regimes in a society could have such a certain effect on human behavior? Recall your own struggles with power. Develop a report on the subject.

TOPICS FOR WRITTEN OR ORAL EXPLORATION

1. Watch Martin Scorsese's *Taxi Driver*. Research John W. Hinckley Jr.'s attempted assassination of President Ronald Reagan, and read about Hinckley's trial. Give a report on your own conclusions as to whether Hinckley was insane. In the process, try to define insanity. Could *Romeo and Juliet* have the same effect on an unstable person as Scorsese's film apparently did?

2. Research Emile Durkheim's *Suicide: A Study in Sociology* (1951) on the question of anomie (severe antisocial depression or boredom). Deliver a report on whether you feel Romeo or Juliet or Mercutio shows signs of anomie.

3. What is the impact of the statistics in Steve Marshall's next-to-last-paragraph of the article about the eighth-grader drownings? Develop a thesis on how statistics are obtained, how they work, and how valuable they are. How would you set up an experiment to determine whether there was an increase in suicide rates after Baz Luhrmann's *William Shakespeare's Romeo and Juliet* was released in early November 1996?

4. Do you accept the suicide "cluster" theory implied in the article by Gould and Shaffer? How could it work with a performance of *Romeo and Juliet*? Do you agree that young teenage audiences are more likely to cluster? Recall that the Jonestown mass suicide of American settlers in a commune in Guyana of November 8, 1978, was mainly adults. Research that event, and develop a paper on these subjects. Take a position and defend it.

5. Is there any sign that Shakespeare in *Romeo and Juliet* suggests that young people indulge in copycat behavior? Or does everyone do so, child through adult? Take a position and defend it in argument form. Be specific.

6. Barbara Ascher, toward the end of her article "Trying to Avoid Romeo and Juliet," admits that she and her husband are romantics. Do you find that Shakespeare does the opposite? That is, does he appear to be a romantic until the end of the play, when we begin to suspect he is not? Develop a paper on this subject. Quote and show evidence.

7. In Alan Cowell's "Dear Juliet: Let Me Tell You About My Problem," the answers to various letters imply that one must escape parental

input in difficult love situations. How do the parents behave in *Romeo and Juliet*? Should they be escaped? Develop a paper on the case for elopement in the play. Be specific. Quote and show evidence.

8. Compare the two articles on the same subject, "Suddenly Shakespeare" by Richard Corliss and "Shakespeare Rocks" by Lou Carlozo. Develop a report on their stylistic difference and their difference in approach. What is the effect of Carlozo's dependence on interviews? Indicate which approach you prefer.

9. Watch Baz Luhrmann's movie, *William Shakespeare's Romeo + Juliet*. Also watch one other movie mentioned by the reviewers, perhaps Kenneth Branagh's *Much Ado about Nothing*. Which movie approach to Shakespeare do you prefer? Develop a thesis on the subject.

10. Our two reviewers, Corliss and Carlozo, insist that Luhrmann used Shakespeare's words, but neither seems to take into account how much has been cut. What would you cut? In reference to Luhrmann and Shakespeare's text, develop a thesis about cutting *Romeo + Juliet*. Be specific.

SUGGESTED READINGS

Burckhardt, Jacob. *The Civilization of the Renaissance in Italy*, 3rd ed. Oxford: Phaidon, 1995.

Dollimore, Jonathan. *Political Shakespeare: Essays in Cultural Materialism*, 2nd ed. Cambridge: Cambridge University Press, 1994.

———. *Radical Tragedy: Religion, Ideology, and Power in the Drama of Shakespeare and His Contemporaries*. Chicago: University of Chicago Press, 1984.

Durkheim, Emile. *Suicide: A Study in Sociology*, trans. John A. Spaulding and George Simpson. Glencoe, IL: Free Press, 1951.

Erikson, Erik H. *Childhood and Society*, 2nd ed. rev. New York: Norton, 1963; orig. 1950.

Ford A. B., and N. B. Rushford. *Suicide in the Young*. Boston: John Wright, 1984.

Freud, Sigmund. *Civilization and Its Discontents*, trans. James Strachey. New York: Norton, 1989.

———. *Totem and Taboo: Some Points of Agreement between the Mental Lives of Savages and Neurotics*. Norton Paperbacks on Psychiatry and Psychology. New York: Norton, 1962.

Goethe, Johann Wolfgang von. *Selections [incl. The Sorrows of Young Werther]*. New York: Suhrkamp Publishers, 1988.

Greenblatt, Stephen Jay. *Renaissance Self-Fashioning: From More to Shakespeare*. Chicago: University of Chicago Press, 1980.

Hager, Alan. *Shakespeare's Political Animal: Schema and Schemata in the Canon*. Newark, DE: University of Delaware Press, 1990.

Marx, Karl. *The Eighteenth Brumaire of Louis Bonaparte*. New York: International Publishers, 1963.

Phillips, D. P. "The Influence of Suggestion on Suicide: Substantive and Theoretical Implications of the Werther Effect." *American Journal of Sociology* 39 (1974): 340–354.

Rosenberg, Marvin. *The Masks of Hamlet*. Newark, DE: University of Delaware Press, 1992.

———. *The Masks of King Lear*. Newark, DE: University of Delaware Press, 1992; orig. 1972.

———. *The Masks of Macbeth*. Berkeley: University of California Press, 1978.

———. *The Masks of Othello*. Newark, DE: University of Delaware Press, 1992; orig. 1961.

Salinger, J. D. *The Catcher in the Rye*. Boston: Little Brown, 1951.

Glossary of Critical Terms and Names

Act. The major division of plays (*see also* Scene). Shakespeare's drama has five acts; most more modern drama has three, and some Eastern European, four.

Albigensian Crusade. A military excursion (1208–1333) internal to France called by Pope Innocent III in which troops from the north of France suppressed an ascetic sect called Albigenses in Provence but also the troubadours (*see* Troubadours) and Provençal language and culture. This atrocity occasioned the birth of the dreaded Inquisition (*see* Inquisition).

Alcibiades. Athenian statesman, general, and supposed traitor (450?–404 B.C.). Appears in Plato's *Symposium*.

Alexandrine. A line of poetry with six accents, often of twelve syllables; once standard in old French romances concerning the feats of Alexander the Great. (Brooke: "What if his subtle brain to feign have taught his tongue" 365.)

Alliteration. Repetition of consonant sounds, as in "Peter Piper picked a peck of pickled peppers," or Romeo: "Then love-devouring Death do what he dare"(2.6.7). *See* also Onomatopoeia

Anapestic. Involving a metrical foot with two unaccented syllables followed by an accented one. An anapestic substitution speeds up a line (and sometimes imitates the sound of horses's hooves at a gallop; as in Samuel Taylor Coleridge: "With a leap and a bound, the swift anapests throng"). Benvolio: "But every man betake him to his legs" (1.4.34). / věrў mán / is an anapestic substitution.

Aphorism. *See* Proverb

Aphrodite. Greek goddess of love and beauty; the Greek counterpart of the Roman goddess Venus and the Norse goddess Freya. Aphrodite's name means "made from the froth" of her father Uranus' (Sky's) severed genitals. In *The Symposium* Plato's man of taste, the conscious aristocrat Pausanias, says there is both a chaste Aphrodite and a lascivious one, a good and a bad.

Apollo. God of the Sun, both Roman and Greek; also the god of disease and cure, of stringed instruments and bows and arrows, and of poetry and prophecy. Twin brother of the Greek Artemis and the Roman Diana, goddess of the hunt and of the moon.

Apologue. A story with a point, a dominating moral, or other meaning, such as Aristophanes' myth of the halved double humans (which is also a cautionary tale, in this case indicating one should respect the gods).

Aristophanes (448?–385? B.C.). Leading comic dramatist in Athens in the fifth century B.C. Appears in and delivers a hilarious cautionary tale in Plato's *Symposium*.

Artemis. Goddess of the hunt and the moon. Twin sister of Apollo.

Aside. A short soliloquy directed at the audience usually not heard by the fellow characters (*see* Soliloquy).

Assonance. The use of similar vowel sounds for various effects including onomatopoeia (*see* Alliteration; Onomatopoeia). Lady Capulet's "The fish lives in the sea" (1.3.90). "Fish lives in" is assonance.

Athena. Goddess of wisdom; counterpart of the Roman goddess Minerva.

Aubade. Any song sung at dawn that contains a compliment. "Parting is such sweet sorrow" (2.2.185) is part of Juliet's aubade to Romeo in the first balcony scene.

Augustan. The style in literature and other arts contemporary with the reign of Caesar Augustus, the first emperor of Rome (27 B.C.–14 A.D.). Also the styles of the neoclassical (*see* Neoclassical) period in England from the Restoration of Stuart royalty in 1660 at least through the reign of Queen Anne in 1714.

Augustus, Caesar (63 B.C.–14 A.D.). Known as Octavian before he became the first Roman emperor in 27 B.C. reigning for forty-one years. Architect of the Pax Romana (the Roman Peace) in Europe and the Mediterranean world which provided the backdrop for the life of Christ.

Avant-garde. Experimental; novel; relating to artists or art that strains to be original.

Bard, the. A bard was originally a singing poet of heroic verse. It is a conventional term in capitals used by modern critics and theater people to indicate Shakespeare, the Bard. (*See also* Will.) Bardolatry is idolization of Shakespeare.

Bas-relief. Sculpture attached to a background, such as Lorenzo Ghiberti's fifteenth-century "Golden Door" to the cathedral (*duomo*) of Florence; or the Elgin Marbles (fifth century B.C.) from the Acropolis in Athens, now in the British Museum.

Blazon. A body catalogue comparing parts of the beloved's body to precious metals, gems, mythological figures, or special coloration ("your hair is gold," your teeth are pearls," etc.). Mercutio's "I conjure thee by Rosaline's bright eyes, / By her high forehead and her scarlet lip" (2.1.18).

Body catalogue. *See* Blazon

Caesura or Cesura. A pause within a line of poetry, usually at the point of a comma or period and indicated in scansion by a double line; Romeo's "Yet tell me not, / for I have heard it all" (1.1.174). *See also* Endstopped; Enjambment

Catharsis. "Purgation" or "laxative" in Greek. Aristotle uses the term to describe the purgation of pity and fear experienced by the audience of a tragedy.

Chaucer, Geoffrey. English poet (1340–1400), author of *The Canterbury Tales* and *Troilus and Criseyde*.

Chorus. Unlike in Greek tragedy where a group of several characters comment in unison and in elementary ways on the dramatic action throughout the drama, in *Romeo and Juliet*, the chorus is a single figure, probably elderly, who introduces the play and the second act with his simplification of the action of the play in sonnet form.

Chronographia. Telling time without using numbers. ("Dawn dances toward me in her pink negligee.") Friar: "The gray-eyed morn smiles on the frowning night" (2.3.1.).

Comedy. A play with a happy ending or with dominating comic activity; in ritual terms, a play that ends with one or more marriages planned or performed, as in Shakespeare's *A Midsummer Night's Dream*.

Conceit. An extended metaphor in lyric, such as the use of the body catalogue, chronographia, or love as a hunt. "Conceit" comes from the Italian *concetto*, or concept: *Romeo and Juliet*'s developed imagery of a lover "Death."

Conjuration. A magical calling on immortal spirits.

Context. The surroundings in life and art; a quote in context places it within the larger text.

Contrariety. The notion that to understand life, literature, and art one must understand simultaneous antinomies or yoked opposites. Contrariety in the narrowest sense lies behind Romeo's oxymoron "loving hate" (1.1.176) (*see* Oxymoron), and in the largest sense behind the notion of seeing Romeo, for example, simultaneously as a noble idealist in love and war yet a killer and self-killer bordering on genocide in Verona.

Convention. An accepted reality in fiction: for example, it is understood that duelists on a stage are not actually trying to hurt each other. See **Stock Character**.

Courtly love. A notion of love coming from the troubadour love poets where a male lover idealizes his beloved female who is normally married to someone else in an often complex and self-lacerating poetry born of his unrequited love. *See also* Troubadour

Cupid. *See* Eros

Dactylic. Involving a metrical foot with a strong beat and two weak beats, as in the jingle about the 1900s Chicago Cubs double-play team, "Tinker to Evers to Chance" (a line from "Casey at the Bat.").

Dante Alighieri. Italian poet (1265–1321), author of *The Divine Comedy*.

Deus ex machina. A theatrical move in which a god is lowered onto the stage to resolve some dispute in a drama.

Diana. *See* Artemis

Diatribe. An elaborate (sometimes bitter) rebuke, such as Friar Laurence's attack on Romeo and his love life (2.3.44ff.).

Dionysus. Greek and Roman god of wine, reed instruments, and all collective activities ranging from orgies to tragedy. His several names include Bacchus, Lyaeus, Bromios, and Liber.

Doggerel. Verse without true poetic quality. ("I before E except after C")

Doppelganger. A double figure who suggests a second side of one self, such as Jekyll and Hyde.

Dramatic irony. Also historic irony, or Sophoclean irony; occurs when a character in a drama accidentally predicts an actual outcome, as when Juliet thinks she sees Romeo "As one dead in the bottom of a tomb" (3.5.56) in the second balcony scene.

Dramatis personae. The list of characters of a drama after the title of the play.

Ekphrasis. Poetry about poetry and/or art, such as when Mercutio discusses Romeo's blazons to Rosaline's parts.

End-stopped. When a line of verse ends on a pause. Lady Capulet to Juliet, "But now I'll tell you joyful tidings, girl" (3.5.104).

Enjambment. Forcible one line running into the next without any pause. Juliet to Lady Capulet: "Or if you do not, make the bridal bed / In that dim monument where Tybalt lies" (3.5.202).

Epic simile. An extended explicit comparison (a comparison using "like" or "as" or "resembles") usually appearing in narrative poetry, such as the long similes about the sea in both Arthur Brooke's *Tragedy of Romeus and Juliet* and in Shakespeare's *Romeo and Juliet*. Brooke on Mercutio at the Capulet party: "Even as a lion would among the lambs be bold, / Such was among the bashful maids Mercutio to behold" (257).

Epitaph. A motto on one's real or imagined tombstone. ("Rest in Peace"; "A Shrew But Honest").

Eros. Olympian god of love; usually depicted as a blindfolded adolescent, shooting mortals and immortals with love-inducing golden arrows and loathing-inducing leaden arrows. His Roman counterpart is Cupid.

Eryximachus. Athenian doctor (c. 406 B.C.) who appears in Plato's *Symposium*.

Feet (in poetry). Often called a metrical unit, it is actually a unit of poetry's rhythm. There are five kinds of rhythmic unit: iamb, trochee, spondee, anapest, and dactyl. In scansion they are marked by a single line as in Mercutio's "That in/thy like/ness thou/appear/to us" (2.1.22). These feet are trochaic substitution followed by four iambs. *See also* Anapestic; Dactylic; Iambic; Spondaic; Trochaic

Foil. A dramatic character who serves as a contrast to another. Romeo's main foil is Tybalt, leading youth of the opposite house of Capulet and supposed protector of Juliet. Mercutio, supposedly immune to sexual attraction, and "young" Paris, suitor to Juliet, are also foils to passionate Romeo.

Folio. A Large and costly printed book normally bound in leather and folding a single large sheet for each pair of pages. The folio of thirty-six of Shakespeare's plays appeared in 1623. One of the two best texts of *Romeo and Juliet* appear in this edition. *See also* Quarto

Foreshadowing. A hint early in a work about the ending of the work, often by means of historical irony. For example, Romeo's misgivings before the Capulet party.

Frame narrative. A story within a story, such as Mercutio's Queen Mab speech. The structure of Plato's *Symposium* is a double frame narrative.

Gothic. Using images that suggest horror such as gargoyles.

Groundlings. Audience members who pay a mere penny to see a play from the yard of one of the open-air theaters (*see* Open-air theaters; Yard). Traditionally thought to be an uneducated audience, the groundlings might include the law-school dropouts who became the great lyric and dramatic poets of the next century.

Hera. Greek goddess of marriage and of domestic jealousy and strife; sister and wife of Zeus. Counterpart of the Roman goddess Juno.

Hermes. Olympian messenger God, patron god of thieves and of the underworld and of secrets. Counterpart of the Roman god Mercury and the Norse god Woden.

Heroic couplet. A rhymed pair of iambic pentameter lines. ("And yet, by Heaven, I think my love as rare / As any she belied with false compare" Shakespeare sonnet 130.13–14.)

Heroic sarcasm. The taunting overfamiliarity of antagonists. ("Sister, did you know this was a one-way street?") Mercutio in response to Tybalt's "what would thou have with me?": "Good king of cats, nothing but one of your nine lives" (3.1.75).

Hexameter. A line of poetry with six feet. *See also* Alexandrine

High fiction. Stories not meant to be actual or realistic, ones that have all the elements of folklore, coincidence, ring-plots, magic, giants, symbolic characters and landscapes and huge moral content. The Friar's magic death-counterfeiting sleep potion comes from high fiction, as does much of the coincidence and compressed action of the play.

High romance. Originally "romance" meant all stories written in the vernacular versions of Latin, the Romance languages, with their popular scenes of good and evil (*see* High fiction), and their ballad or fairy tale-like emphasis on love and the nobility of the common man.

Historical irony. *See* Dramatic irony

Homonym. A word that sounds identical to another. ("sale/sail"; "carol/carrel")

Homophone. A syllable that sounds identical to another. ("sale/sail")

Hyperbole. Rhetorical exaggeration, often through the use of metaphor ("I've told you a million times") Benvolio on Romeo: "and swifter than his tongue / His agile arm beats down their fatal points" (3.1.164).

Iambic. Involving feet that have an unaccented syllable followed by an accented one. ("Because, because")

Iconography. The inscribing of traditional images in painting, statuary, or fiction. Often mistakenly used for iconology (*see* Iconology).

Iconology. The study of traditional images in painting, statuary, or fiction and their meaning. One could do an iconological study of the repeating image of the galloping horse, the stormy seascape, or any recurring mythic figure such as Apollo, in *Romeo and Juliet*.

Identical rhyme. Rhyming with the same word. ("Look death in the face; / I meet your face")

Impresa. A symbolic image often used in heraldry, such as the dolphin wrapped around the anchor.

Internal evidence. Evidence inferred from the text of a work of fiction; for example, the inference that Shakespeare saw himself as an old man with a young daughter. Thus we have Egeus and Hermia in *A Midsummer Night's Dream*, Polonius and Ophelia in *Hamlet*, Prospero and Miranda in *The Tempest*, and so forth.

Inquisition. The Papal courts in France, Spain, and Italy designed to root out heresy and enforce religious orthodoxy by any means up to and including burning "heretics" at the stake. The Inquisition came about during the Albigensian Crusade (1208–1333) in the south of France (*see* Albigensian Crusade).

Irony. In the largest sense, that which makes one smile or laugh in literature (*see* Pathos). Irony can also be that which is cutting, such as sarcasm (*see* Heroic sarcasm), or reversals in action (*see* Dramatic irony).

Jeremiad. A prophetic rebuke and/or lamentation.

Journalistic paragraph. A curtailed one or two-sentence paragraph akin to a headline.

Juno. *See* Hera

Jupiter. *See* Zeus

Langue d'oc. *See* Provençal

Litotes. A "double negative," understated comment that often explodes into a strong positive. ("Leonardo DiCaprio is not unattractive.")

Loki. Norse god of play and practical jokes, fellow of the god Woden.

Lycanthropy. Wolfmanism.

Melancholy. Sadness (even depressive madness) brought on traditionally by an excess of a fictive fluid in the body, black bile. Shakespeare often portrays love melancholy, career melancholy, and cosmic or religious melancholy. Romeo's state at the opening of the play is melancholic (for love of Rosaline).

Mercury. *See* Hermes

Metaphor. An implicit comparison. Lady Capulet to Juliet on Paris: "Read o'er the volume of young Paris' face" (1.3.82).

Metatheater. Theater about theater or drama about drama, such as the play within a play of *A Midsummer Night's Dream*.

Meter. A regular pattern of rhythm against which the actual rhythm plays, like a metronome against a musical piece.

Minerva. *See* Athena

Minnesingers. Medieval German love poets and singers. From Minne (love) and Singer (singer). Counterparts of the troubadours in Southern France (*see* Troubadours). Heavy influences on Gottfried von Strassburg's *Tristan* (1215).

Motto. A pithy phrase to sum up an issue. ("Where's the beef?") *Festina Lente* (Hasten slowly).

Move (poetic or dramatic). A term indicating a rhetorical strategy such as arousing sadness or laughter (*see* Irony; Pathos) or an authorial fictional strategy to catch up or involve a reader or viewer in a story or drama.

Neoclassical. Any age's or person's predilection to revive classical culture in the present. Often connected with the Augustan Period in England (*see* Augustan), but the whole Renaissance and Shakespeare are to some extent neoclassical.

Neoplatonism. The school of philosophy that presents versions and extensions of Plato's idealism (founded on religious argument) from Plotinus to the present.

Nom de plume. French for "name of the pen," an author's adopted name, pen name, or pseudonym. For example Samuel Clemens wrote under the *nom de plume* Mark Twain.

Onomatapoeia. A sound imitation in language. ("Bang"). Often effected by alliteration or assonance ("His skis hissed on the crystalline snow.")

Open-air theaters. Unroofed public theaters just outside London, such as the Globe, the Rose, or the Theatre.

Ovid. Augustan love-poet (43 B.C.–A.D. 17?), author of *The Metamorphoses*.

Ovidian mode. Based on understanding of the *Metamorphoses* of the Augustan poet, Ovid (*see* Ovid). It is a poetic manner or mood that pictures a world of unthinking satisfaction of desires for violence, love, and fame in a largely country world controlled by interested Olympian Gods. *See* also Pastoral mode; Petrarchan mode

Oxymoron. A two-word paradox, often in the form of a substantive denied by its modifier. ("Jumbo shrimp") Juliet's "A damnèd saint, an honorable villain" (3.2.79).

Palmer. A medieval pilgrim, often carrying a palm leaf in token of having visited the Holy Land.

Paradox. An apparent logical contradiction that contains an inner meaning. *See* Oxymoron

Pastoral mode. A traditional (and largely unchanging) poetic manner or mood that pictures shepherds' songs (often complaints) in an Edenic or paradisial green world or blond world (the world of beaches and wetland shores). It descends from readings of the Sicilian Greek poet, Theocritus (c. 270 B.C.). and the Mantuan Augustan poet, Virgil (70–19 B.C.).

Pathetic fallacy. Personification of nature to indicate its grief (but also often its love). ("The buttercups are crying.") The Prince, in the final speech of the play, says: "The sun, for sorrow, will not show his head" (5.3.306).

Pathos   that which makes one sad in literature or art. See **Irony**.

Pentameter. A five-foot verse form.

Persona. An authorial mask; a character through which a poet chooses to represent himself in a work (perhaps like Shakespeare's Chorus, but certainly Sir Philip Sidney's Astrophil).

Personification. Spiritualizing an element of nature. ("Oh, Wall, tell me . . .") Romeo's "Death is amorous" (5.3.103).

Petrarchan mode. The elementary mode of the sonnet. Based on readings of the Italian Francis Petrarch (Francesco Petrarca) (1304–1374) who developed in his sonnets of *Rime* (1351?) the manner and mood of the self-lacerating unrequited lover related to Romeo and also sometimes the mood of nostalgia for the "pre-national" Rome of the Roman Empire.

Phaeton. The first-born son of Apollo, killed when he lost control of the reins to the chariot of the sun.

Plato. Ancient Greek philosopher (ca. 428–348 B.C.) whose dialogues often have Socrates as his hero.

Plotinus. (205–270), classical founder of neoplatonism.

Primary source. The original text or artifact. *See also* Secondary source

Provençal. The Romance language of southern France used by the troubadours (*see* Troubadours). Synonymous with langue d'oc.

Proverb. Like aphorism, a pithy quasi-poetic statement of a truth about human nature. ("He who hesitates is lost." "Fools rush in where angels fear to tread." "A rolling stone gathers no moss.") Romeo's "in such a case as mine a man may strain courtesy" (2.4.50).

Pun. A verbal joke based on a homonym. ("White sale/sail." Mercutio's "dreamers often lie" (1.4.51)—i.e., lie in bed and tell lies.

Pythagoras. Pre-Socratic philosopher (ca. 580–500 B.C.) famous for the Pythagorian formula, studies of harmony, and belief in transmigration of souls.

Quarto. A pocketbook-size hardback book made by folding a single page in four and printing on all surfaces. *Romeo and Juliet* appeared in a bad quarto (Q1) and a good quarto (Q2) in 1597 and 1599. *See also* Folio

Refrain. A repeated line or word in poetry. The name "Romeo" becomes a refrain in *Romeo and Juliet*.

Repartee. Dialogue made up of witty retorts usually employing bantering opponents' words against them. A comic form of stichomythia (*see* Stichomythia). Romeo and Mercutio outside the Capulet palace just before Mercutio's Queen Mab speech (1.4.53–95):

ROMEO:	I dreamt a dream tonight.
MERCUTIO:	And so did I.
ROMEO:	Well, what was yours?
MERCUTIO:	That dreamers often lie.
ROMEO:	In bed asleep, while they do dream things true. (1.4.50)

Rhyme. Two words ending with similar sound.

Rhythm. The patterns and counterpatterns of emphasis in language.

Romance. *See* High fiction; High romance.

Scene. The smaller subdivision of a play (*see also* Act). Sometimes there are many scenes in an act, sometimes only one. Scenes are the units of continuous action in a play. Unlike in some Greek tragedy where the action all takes place in one locale, a new scene in *Romeo and Juliet*— with the exception 2.2—also calls for a change in location.

In fiction or drama, the term "scene" can also indicate a mere unified episode. Therefore the comic Musicians' Scene in *Romeo and Juliet* is only part of its "scene" in the sense of a dramatic subdivision. This scene runs from 4.5.96 through 4.5.145.

Secondary Source. A later reaction to a text or artifact.

Sight Rhyme. A second word that looks like the first but often does not sound like it. ("I love clove.")

Simile. *See* Epic simile

Slant Rhyme. Imperfect rhyme, such as "rhinocerous"/"preposterous" or "form"/"charm." Sometimes used for comic effect.

Socrates. Athenian philosopher (470?–399 B.C.). He appears as a character in most of Plato's dialogues, including *The Symposium*.

Sonnet. A fourteen-line poetic form developed in the Middle Ages. The continental sonnet usually has a stanza of eight lines followed by a stanza of six. The Elizabethan, or Shakespearean, stanza has three quatrains (four-line stanzas) followed by a heroic couplet.

Sophoclean irony. *See* Dramatic irony

Spondaic. Involving feet that have two accented syllables; designed to slow down a line. In Coleridge's "Slow spondee stalks . . ." the "Slow spon" is spondaic.

Stage directions. Announcements in the text of entrances, exits, and actions such as drinking, kissing, or dueling in a play. Often incomplete, wrongly placed, or non-existent in the texts of *Romeo and Juliet*.

Stanza. A grouping of lines in poetry with a rhyme scheme. A sonnet can be used as a fourteen-line stanza.

Stichomythia. Use of the same word or words in the end of one stanza and the beginning of the next. In dialogue, short competitive speech using one's opponent's words. *See also* Heroic sarcasm; Repartee.

Stock character. A conventional figure, usually in comedy; for example, the forgetful old man, or the bright young idealist (*adulescens*) like Romeo, or the jester or clown like Peter.

Sublime. That which causes delicious panic, like a raging sea on the other side of a window pane.

Symbol. A metaphor that has enduring significance in a work; the universal as represented by the particular. (Salt water as the liquid of life in *Romeo and Juliet*)

Tetrameter. A four-foot line of poetry. ("Others because you did not keep.")

Topical reference. Specific reference to contemporary news in a work of fiction, such as an earthquake mentioned in *Romeo and Juliet* (1.3.24).

Tragedy. A play that ends unhappily with catastrophe and/or death. In ritual terms, a play that ends with an actual or planned funeral.

Trimeter. A three-foot line of poetry. ("One had a lovely face.")

Trochaic. Involving two-beat feet, with an accented syllable followed by unaccented. ("Once upon a midnight dreary.") Often suggests a heartbeat.

Troubadours. Itinerant medieval lyric poets—commoner, aristocrat, even royal—in Southern France, who glorified female love objects and all aspects of courtly love (*see* Courtly love) in lyric poetry in the Romance language Provençal or langue d'oc (*see* Provençal). The poetry of the troubadours might be light (*leou*) with refrains (*see* Refrain) and other repetitions, or complex (*clus*) with complicated verse forms (such as the double sestina or sonnet) developing arcane conceits (extended metaphors in lyric). *See also* Conceit

Understatement. Apparently saying less than one means, but actually saying a lot. ("Not bad.") *See* Litotes.

Virgil. Augustan epic poet (70–19 B.C.), author of *The Aeneid* (*See* Augustan).

Werther Syndrome. Supposed copycat suicide, learned from fiction.

Will. Shakespeare's nickname in his own life, the source of many of his puns, such as "Whoever hath her wish, thou hast thy Will," the first line of the playful and bawdy sonnet 135. *See also* Bard

Woden. *See* Hermes

Yard. The half-moon rounded space in front and to the sides of the lip stage of the open-air theaters in which the groundlings stood (and stand in the new Globe Theater in London) to enjoy the play. *See also* Groundlings; Open-air theaters

Zeus. King of the Olympian gods; counterpart of the Roman god Jupiter and the Norse god Odin.

Index

About the Author

ALAN HAGER is Professor of English at the State University of New York at Cortland and author of *Major Tudor Authors: A Biocritical Sourcebook* (Greenwood, 1997).